Men Who Fought...
Boys Who Prayed

Blessings to the Haleys

W Carter Tucker

WALTER CARTER TUCKER

Men Who Fought...
Boys Who Prayed

A Combat Chaplain's Story: Vietnam

TATE PUBLISHING
AND ENTERPRISES, LLC

Published by Tate Publishing & Enterprises, LLC
127 E. Trade Center Terrace | Mustang, Oklahoma 73064 USA
1.888.361.9473 | www.tatepublishing.com

Tate Publishing is committed to excellence in the publishing industry. The company reflects the philosophy established by the founders, based on Psalm 68:11,
"The Lord gave the word and great was the company of those who published it."

Book design copyright © 2013 by Tate Publishing, LLC. All rights reserved.
Cover design by Jeffrey Doblados
Interior design by Mary Jean Archival

Published in the United States of America

ISBN: 978-1-62902-100-3
1. Biography & Autobiography / Personal Memoirs
2. Biography & Autobiography / General
13.10.14

To my wife, Pauline, and our
Children, Paul, Lesley and Amy,
who faithfully waited and prayed for my
safe return,
I dedicate this book.

And
To my grandchildren: Carter, Meredith, John,
Nathan, Aaron, David, Rachel, Taylor and Philip,
who pried stories out of me as no one else could.
May they see an end to war.

Finally
It is dedicated to the thousands of
Americans, that gave their lives in defense of freedom.
Their names are engraved in granite and marble
all over the world, and forever in the hearts
and memories of
loved ones.

Contents

Foreword

"Sir, my name is Matt Spencer. I am a private in the U.S. Army. I am AWOL!"

Those were the first words he had spoken since getting into my car a few miles back. We were both on our way to Fort Polk, Louisiana. I was on the way to report for my first day of active duty as an army chaplain. He was getting ready to report to his basic training company to "face the music." I was really excited. He was really scared.

January 17, 1966 had begun early for me back at the Old Union Baptist Church parsonage, near El Dorado, Arkansas. For the nervous soldier, it had begun a hundred miles northwest with wake-up words from his father, "Son, you can't keep this up. You better get going. Your leave papers say you were supposed to be back long before now. Fifteen days past what the papers say, is what you are. It is not about to get any easier, but it is bound to get a lot harder. You need to hit the road, and you need to do it today. They'll come looking for you. Go now!"

January 2 was significant for both Private Spencer and me. That was the day he was due to return to BCT from his Christmas leave and it was the day I was alerted for active duty with the military. Long before email and cellular phones began to play such an integral part in people's lives, a telegram brought the message. When a friend brought the Western Union message, my thoughts reverted to childhood days and similar deliveries. During World War II the sheriff would drive slowly by our house in the country on his way to deliver a telegram to some mother who would soon be grieving over a son who was missing in action or worse. My telegram on that cold winter day contained no such message. Instead it said this: "Your request for active duty is approved. You are to report to the Personnel Officer, Fort Polk, Louisiana, NLT 2359 Hours, 17 January 1966. Call the number below to verify this message."

Surprise! One filled with glad anticipation, but still a surprise. Thoughts rushed in almost faster than I could deal with them: Vietnam is getting hotter by the day; three children, ages 3, 6 and 8; my wife of eleven years is not aware of the changes we are about to face; I'm already a veteran, four years in the U S Navy, Submarine Service; there won't be much time to give notice and resign as pastor of the church I'm now serving; I have no idea what the pay scale is for a first lieutenant with four years longevity; a simple phone call to the number listed and I can turn this down, no question asked. Lots of thoughts, but they faded fast.

With the yellow telegram in hand I approached my wife with a question, "If I were to get called to active duty as a chaplain, how much lead time would you like to have?" To that she responded, "Couple of weeks, I guess!" "Good," I said. "We've got it with a day to spare" As an old saying goes, it was time to get in high gear.

So 15 days later, I'm on my way. In the small village of Hodge, Louisiana, a short distance from Ruston, I spotted a soldier, looking weary, thumb out, in a rumpled, slick sleeved, Class A uniform. It was Private Spencer. Had there been a poster boy for "Seventeen going on 50," he would have been it. After a quick stop in Winnfield for some food, I headed the 1964 Chevelle toward Leesville and Fort Polk. The soldier, a look of dread clouding his face, directed me to his company in the training brigade at North Fort, also known as The North Forty. "I'll go in with you," I said. He seemed grateful. The first sergeant heard my explanation about how I met Spencer and accompanied him back, and he took it from there. On the way to the young man's basic training unit I had warned him, "You will probably get yelled at a lot and called some names you don't normally hear in Sunday School. So be prepared, Matt. Don't let it throw you." It quickly became obvious that if he expected to hear yelling he would not be disappointed. As I got in my car for the drive to South Fort, the decibel level in that part of the North Forty was in the high range.

I never saw the young GI from northwest Louisiana again, or the Top either. It seems somewhat ironic that the first soldier I had the privilege of counseling was absent without leave and only two weeks from being a deserter. Though he was my first counselee, there would be many more. Hundreds. From that first eventful day I was certain that a power even higher than the Chaplaincy Endorsing Agency or Department of the Army had called me into this. That thought never changed or wavered.

It surfaced many years later as I gathered informally with a group of contemporaries- all retired, or as some liked to say, "for sure *tired* but not quite *retired*." As so often happens with retirees, talk about the past crept in. With that subject as a springboard a minister, who served in his chosen profession almost 60 years, asked a question, "Have you ever thought about and put in words the most memorable and rewarding year of your life's work, or as in my case and with some of you, the greatest year of ministry?"

"Good question," several responded, and began some serious recall. A retired banker remarked that it would almost have to be the year when, out of all the loans made, not one resulted in default. A respected businessman said, "Well, some of you will be hearing this for the first time. That year for me would be the one during which I finally defeated the bottle and convinced my family that I was serious about it and they could trust me at last. Talk about the year that was, men, now that was it. Prime time. Bumper crop!"

Long retired pastors reminisced about the great revivals they had been privileged to experience. Two spoke of successful building programs. All nodded agreement when one spoke of getting a raise to the almost mythical "hundred-a-week". Being involved in the lives of young men who "answered the call" and went on to become leaders of renown, several recalled with gratitude. We heard wonderful memories and testimonials of loyal service. Decades condensed to a single year.

My most memorable year? The one year that was more rewarding than all others? That was easy for me, though I had known many that featured superb highlights. My wife and I could never forget the mission trips we took to numerous countries over many years. The first Bible Lands pilgrimage stands, even after two dozen similar trips, like the bright beacon of a lighthouse. Unforgettable experiences among special people in many lands. We learned some important cultural truths that classrooms can't provide.

The question I was to address though was this: What is the single most memorable year of your life's work? It has to be almost the entire calendar year of 1967, as a chaplain to the 2/27 Battalion, 25th Infantry Division, Cu Chi, Republic of Vietnam. The 2/27 is best known as the "Second Wolfhounds." People who know what was going on that year and the kind of unit the 2nd of the 27th Infantry Battalion was might look askance at my answer to the "best year" question.

Even I sometimes wonder why I would choose those 365 days. It was, after all, a long 12 months away from my loving family. A year sleeping (napping?) in a foxhole a fourth of the nights and in sand-bagged bunkers another fourth; hitching rides on anything that would get me to my scattered "congregation" in order to offer and lead 3-5 field services a week; conducting on average almost two funerals a week; counseling, befriending and working hard to console hundreds of 18-21 year-olds in bomb craters, fighting positions and burn wards; kneeling over casualty bags at GRO (Graves Registration); writing sad letters to parents, wives and children and dealing with fear all the while but trying not to show it.

Very few amenities were available and most would have been superfluous anyway. No organ, or piano, or pews, or building to house them. No printed orders of service. No altar or prie dieu. No choir or orchestra. The congregants—sometimes three or four and sometimes a hundred—sat on the ground with M-16s or other weapons across their legs, bandoleers over their shoulders. Most had fragmentation and smoke grenades hanging on their web gear. All had varying degrees of apprehension stamped on their faces.

Why would one identify that as the most memorable and rewarding year of his life? With the absence of so many things we have come to take for granted and the presence of so many things most would gladly do without, why indeed? I have pondered that question for many years and can answer only for me: There comes a time when "stuff" simply does not matter very much; a time when it is just you, the person next to you...and God! To find that those are enough was (and is) a rewarding discovery.

That was the year. Unique and unforgettable. Twelve activity-filled months that, in the presence of energetic young American soldiers, taught some valuable lessons and left some indelible images. It is mainly on those images that the following pages are based. For a number of reasons, some of the names in this story, I invented. Many more are real. The events recorded here are real.

Introduction

Some things slip out of mind. Others stick like they were held there by super glue. Memories of my tour as chaplain to the 2nd of the 27th Wolfhounds stuck. In writing this book I had the advantage of consulting a day-by-day journal I kept during the year. With all the moves my family and I subsequently made with the military, it is a near miracle that the journal survived. It did survive and is now a treasured document written on smudged pages of two stenographic notebooks. It was not until 6 December 1996 that I began reading, one entry a day, words that had been written 30 years earlier. Even after all those years, some of the entries awakened thoughts that were hard to deal with.

All of the events in this book took place as written. Some of the names are fictitious, either because I did not enter a name to match the event back in 1967 or because I was unable to get permission to use a person's name. Nor did I always list in my journal what company a soldier was in, so there are times when a particular company may get credit for a deed that should belong to another. For instance, the episode of the soldiers chasing after the sniper in their boxer shorts, my journal did not identify the company they were from. Those who were involved in that and other memorable events will know.

It has been my privilege to attend a few Wolfhound reunions over the past few years as well as do some remembering at the Vietnam Wall in Washington, DC. I know of no greater camaraderie than that which existed (and exists) among those soldiers. It was a profound honor to be close by them when they fought…and even closer when they prayed. May God's grace shine on those great Americans, wherever they (you) are. And may God bless those who waited. Especially those who waited. And waited!

CHAPTER 1

Arriving

How can we sing His songs in a foreign land?

—Psalm 137:4

Journal entry, 7 December, 1966—"Spent my first night in Vietnam in the VIP tent—two army cots and an aluminum wash pan."

Darkness. Literal and emotional! Darkness of night. Darkness of spirit. That seemed to define the invisible emanation that shrouded the chartered jet as it touched down on the runway of Tan Son Nhut airport near Saigon, Republic of Vietnam. It was only 8:00 p.m., but for passengers on board, who had just completed a trip across 12 time zones, it could have been midnight. Or the wee hours of yesterday. Or tomorrow.

It had been a good flight with friendly and supportive flight attendants. The announcement that we'd land in Honolulu to drop off some passengers and pick up some others was met with cheers and impromptu hula dancing. Soldiers whooped as some of their buddies offered to trade places with the Honolulu-bound passengers, who might rather go to Vietnam. (There were no takers.) The adventuresome spirit continued, especially for those of us who had a deep interest in the Pacific campaigns of World War II, as the plane landed on a tiny piece of land known as Wake Island. I spent a while exploring and thinking about the dozens of marines, sailors and civilians who died defending this little island 26 years earlier.

Passengers were much more subdued during the refueling stop in Okinawa. By then, loss of sleep and fatigue were twin torments. But there was something else. Something was stamped on faces that stared straight ahead. Next stop, Vietnam…and the war.

The hilarity that had begun to wane on take-off from Honolulu had now ended. No more macho statements. Just silence, except for the constant roar of jet engines, reminding all on board that the journey to war was continuing. Then there was a change in pitch and altitude. Distant flashes that resembled lightning began to appear on the horizon. Not lightning, but artillery batteries responding to a fire mission, so said those who had set foot on this land in former times. Other lights, bright and constant, slowly descended. "Flares," said the vets. "There is probably some activity near the perimeter and Spooky is shedding some light on the subject."

Even the quietest conversation ceased with the squeal of tires on the runway. No more words. Stewardesses, congenial from the start, became mute as the plane rolled on. Low wattage light bulbs spaced about every 100 feet on the buildings to our left appeared no brighter than the old coal oil lamps that once lighted country homes. The dim lights did little to dispel the silent gloom.

At last the silence was broken: "This is the captain speaking. Welcome to Vietnam! When the plane comes to a full stop, please exit quickly. Just as soon as your luggage is unloaded and this big bird is refueled, we'll take on another load of passengers and head to the U.S. I wish you were going with us. But we'll see you again in a year. Okay? All the crew joins me in saying, 'Thank you! Thank you for serving our country in this land.' And guys… God bless you!" Thirty seconds later the exit doors opened and a collective sigh said it all, "This is it!"

Departing the plane was somewhat like severing the last tie with America and home.

The entire crew of the big 707 stood at the doors to say goodbye. One of the mom-type attendants, her eyes glistening, gripped the hand of an exceptionally young looking GI for an extra few seconds. Her quivering lip and countenance sent a mute message: "Oh, you are just a little boy. I can't believe you are old enough to be a soldier."

The military is well known for its unwritten "hurry up and wait" policy, but at this point things moved along at a fast and efficient pace. There was already a beehive of activity around the plane as new arrivals were directed to the air force buses that were waiting nearby. The drivers were poised and ready. It was obvious they had gone through this drill many times.

Lieutenant Thomas and I wound up sharing a bus seat which was not unlike the one I sat on between my home in Coleman, Arkansas and Drew Central High School, years before. Thomas and I had met back at Okinawa and, though we were both tired and sleepy, conversed about home and family. We were later assigned to the same battalion in the 25th Infantry Division.

Back in OCS, ROTC and maybe other places where 2nd lieutenants were produced, there was a saying that the average life span for an infantry combat platoon leader in war was three months. Maybe few believed it. Certainly no one wanted to, least of all the future platoon leaders. But it was more than a simple saying for Thomas. Little did we know that in 102 days I would sadly kneel and pray over his lifeless, poncho-covered body in a place known as The Horseshoe.

No one asked why our bus had heavy wire mesh over the windows. Word had already circulated that the mesh was to repel hand grenades that might by thrown by the countless bicycle and moped riders that filled the streets. An APC with a mounted .50 caliber machine gun led the convoy. At the rear were two jeeps with mounted M-60s. Our driver said that normally only jeeps accompanied the bus convoys to Camp Alpha, but that a recent ambush attempt had prompted the transportation officer to add the APC for a while. He said he preferred jeeps because they traveled faster than the APCs.

The wire mesh might keep out explosives, but not the heat or the odor. Heat hit like a steam room. It had infiltrated everything as soon as the plane doors had opened. Stifling. Oppressive. High temperature. Extremely high humidity. The smell hit next. The source of the odor remained a mystery, but it made the olfactory portion of the uninitiated sit up and take notice. How might one describe it? The odor from a big 1940s-era tomato canning factory in my hometown comes close. Rotten tomatoes mingled with an open pit filled with raw sewage. We soon became accustomed to it.

Next stop, Camp Alpha, a place hundreds of thousands came to know well. Here the old timers, still young, but now seasoned combat vets, waited for their ride back to The World. They watched the new ones arrive. The "Newbies" had to run something closely akin to a gauntlet, with those who were about to leave on one side of the wide hall and those just entering on the other. There was a low partition between the two groups. Some of those bound for home shouted unsolicited messages to the incoming guys: "You'll be sorreee!" "Cannon fodder!" "Charlie's target!" "Hey, GI better makey head keepy down!" New arrivals in country had been warned about the razzing they might face but it still caused hearts to beat a little faster and instill thoughts of what the year might hold.

I couldn't help but notice that the more haggard looking vets didn't participate in the trash talk. Those with the proverbial thousand-yard stare looked straight ahead, making not a sound. Forty-five years later a combat vet described these guys as the ones who left the USA at age 20 and returned a year later at age 40. I wondered what those young men had encountered up to that point. (I would soon find out. Not from them, but from others like them.) The soldiers with scars and those who walked with a limp did not speak a word either. A captain, who would soon be a company CO, said, "Chaplain, it's not hard to identify the front line grunts and the rear echelons in that group, is it?" The captain's one-sentence observation made me recall the words of an Iwo Jima invader: "Those who have gone through the most, talk about it the least."

Though it looked chaotic, at least it was organized chaos. All military personnel, both the entering and the leaving types, were systematically herded in the right direction. Being the only incoming chaplain on the flight, I did not have to wait long before being escorted to a cubicle for a session with a MACV administrative chaplain.

"Okay," he began, "again, welcome to Vietnam. It is late and I know you are about dead on your feet, so we'll get through this as quickly as possible. Tell me a little about yourself. Your family. Your motivation to become a military chaplain."

"This time, last year, I was pastor to a good congregation in South Arkansas. Though I really wanted to be a military chaplain, I had begun to wonder if I'd ever be offered the chance, or if maybe I was pursuing something that was not in God's big plan. I had completed the chaplain basic course by correspondence and submitted all the required paperwork. I don't discourage easily, but that word began to dog my tracks. Then came January 2 and a telegram that got the ball rolling. My wife, Pauline, and our three young children are now in a tiny house, the only one I could find to rent, in Okmulgee, Oklahoma. I saw them last as they stood looking at my plane's departure through a fogged over window at Tulsa International Airport. That was what, about 24 hours ago? A no more supportive quartet could a husband and father ever have than those four."

"I see in your record that back in the summer you came down on orders for duty in USAREUR (Germany). Is that correct? You were on orders?"

"It is correct. I was taking the basic course in residence at Fort Hamilton. At about midpoint I received orders for Germany. I know it may seem crazy, but those orders were disappointing to me. I had volunteered for active duty with concurrent duty in Vietnam. So I went to the school commandant and requested assistance with getting the orders changed. I got the impression he didn't fully understand my motive in wanting to go to Vietnam. New orders were issued. They arrived at Fort Polk a week after I did."

"Interesting! Well, you must know this already, but there is no spot of land on the planet where you are more needed than right here. So getting right to it, there are two places where we need chaplains immediately. One is with a missile outfit over near the coast. I have never seen that place, but reports are that duty there is like being on R and R fulltime. Swimming pool. Tennis and handball courts. Believe that? That is one option. The other present and pressing need is in the Second Brigade, 25th Infantry Division. You would be assigned to the 2/27 Infantry Battalion, an outfit known as the Wolfhounds. I feel obligated to tell you that the 2/27th is always in a 'kicking contest' of some kind. It is made up of straight-leg, hard charging, CIB-wearing soldiers. A proud outfit is what I hear. Now, does that little speech give you any lead as to what you'd prefer?"

"Yes sir, it certainly does. Something tells me I will always regret volunteering this far if I don't ask for the 25th Infantry outfit. I've never heard of the 2nd of the 27th or the Wolfhounds, but it just sounds right."

"Then it will happen," said the interviewer. "Thank you, Chaplain. I wish you the best in your new assignment. One of our guys will take you to the BOQ hut. Try to get some sleep. Someone from the 25th will pick you up tomorrow about mid-morning. Soon thereafter, you'll be on your way to your new assignment at Cu Chi."

Cu Chi? I had never heard of that place either. But then, Saigon and Hanoi were about the only cities that had a familiar ring to them. Before the next day ended, I had learned that Cu Chi was a village near the 25th Division Base Camp, the place to buy cheap souvenirs and where GIs were either "Numma One" or "Numma Ten" to the kids.

"As the crow flies" it wasn't all that far from Camp Alpha to Cu Chi—perhaps 35-40 miles. If the crow had to walk, or latch onto a military convoy, travel time was vastly increased. It was by the latter means that Chaplain Paxson, 25th ID chaplain, traveled my way. Thankfully, sleep had come easily and the breakfast I found in a nearby mess hall was welcome. When Chaplain Paxson showed up, I was sitting on my old US Navy seabag writing my first letter home. He quickly set me at ease with his naturally friendly nature, the kind of new friend you like to meet in an unfamiliar setting.

"I am so pleased to see you, Chaplain Tucker. I hope your first day in country has gone well so far. My intent was to take you back to Division by helicopter but when I checked at the flight line not a single one was available. Just about everything flyable is committed or on standby to support an operation in the Ho Bo Woods. The convoy is not bad though, just takes longer, and it will be an experience worth remembering."

"Thank you for coming. This is one of those times when it is unbelievably rewarding to link up with someone who knows where we're going and how to get there," I said.

"What do you say we slip over to the O Club for a snack then make a quick stop at the PX. If you need something it would be wise to get it here because this PX carries some things that are difficult to get up our way. By the time we make those two stops, the afternoon convoy should be formed up and ready to go. Normally, it gets rolling around 1400 or a few minutes after. Help me keep an eye on the clock."

The convoy consisted of all kinds of vehicles, including fuel tankers, two and a half-ton trucks, tanks, tank retrievers, jeeps, wreckers and flat-bed 18-wheelers loaded with canvas covered cargo, including artillery rounds. A heavily armed duster (tank-like vehicle) took the lead. Armored Personnel Carriers and jeeps were scattered throughout. In every truck and jeep soldiers rode shotgun. Chaplains are non-combatants, so neither Chaplain Paxson nor I had a weapon. His jeep driver carried the old standard issue .45 in a shoulder holster. Another young soldier, who sat in the back seat with me, carried an M-16. He did not have the "tough guy" appearance, but I had to assume he could aim and fire the rifle.

Once rolling, it was full speed, or as fast as the slowest vehicle could go. We were near the front and could see that the convoy commander was constantly on his radio attempting to keep the formation tight. The road was narrow and dusty. Any person standing less than a meter off the narrow shoulder was in danger of getting clipped. The drivers had one goal and that was to keep up with the vehicle ahead of them.

Jaywalking was not recommended when the convoy was rolling. One Vietnamese woman, carrying large baskets of pineapples on each end of a pole across her shoulders, got too close to the speeding traffic. A two and a half-ton truck mirror grazed one of her baskets, which got crushed under the five-ton that followed. The woman fell into a trash-lined ditch, screaming, shaking her fist and, no doubt, saying uncomplimentary things about the American fighting men. Other pedestrians paid no attention to the woman.

Speed discouraged ambushes and sapper squads, I was told. So the convoy went all out like a sprinter with his eye on the tape. The thought crossed my mind that if I could survive this ride, the rest of the year should be a snap. But the drivers, those 19-20 year olds whipping noisy, smoking vehicles down narrow roads, through country villages and around sharp curves, loved it. You could sense it in the way they changed gears, gripped the steering wheels and in the looks on their faces. Looks that said, "Don't mess with me today, Charlie. I've got to get somewhere." These were the types of youngsters that volunteered to be door gunners, tunnel rats and Long Range Recon Patrol team members.

After about 90 minutes of travel at 30-35 miles per hour, which road conditions and closeness of onlookers made it seem more like 60 MPH, we began to slow. The lead vehicle had entered the Vietnamese village of Cu Chi, Hai Hgnai province. The kids here knew many of the soldiers, some of whom began tossing food and gum in the general direction of outstretched hands. The "convoy and kids" thing had become a tradition, our driver said.

Once all the vehicles had cleared the village, we slowed even more and finally stopped. Tropic Lightning Division—the 25th— base camp lay straight ahead. It was a huge area enclosed by heavy chain link fence topped by endless coils of razor wire. Beyond the main gate were rows and rows of tents erected behind mountains of sandbags—a city of thick canvas, Quonset huts and millions of green 12x16 inch nylon sandbags.

While we waited for the military police and the convoy commander to get everything cleared for our entry into that gigantic complex, a sergeant in the three-quarter ton truck behind us strolled up to greet two of the "most dust covered chaplains" he had ever seen. It was a proper description. He also wanted to point out something in the area that we might not know. The division chaplain said, "Sure, Sarge, give us the quick tour."

"Look to your right at the little clump of rubber trees about 150 meters out. Do you see a black object in the tallest tree?" We did. It was about one-third down from the top.

"Do you know what that is? That black thing in the tree?" We didn't.

The sergeant explained, "Those are the black pajamas of a VC. Last summer, the morning convoys kept getting sniper fire right about here. He'd fire off two or three quick rounds then stop. The guy came to be known as No-Hit Charlie. His only hit was a round through the canvas cover of a troop vehicle. The bullet barely missed a soldier heading for the airport and home. No one had ever been able to spot him from the road. One morning before daylight, a sniper team was inserted about 50 meters from where we are right now. As the morning convoy was moving out on the way toward Saigon, No-Hit fired his usual few rounds. Sharp eyes picked up his movement this time, though. Eyes with high-powered binoculars and a sniper scope. The VC had tied himself in that tallest tree over there. The black object you see is No-Hit, the Viet Cong sniper, still in his black pajamas. He got zapped almost six months ago and his body is still there. Strange!"

The mysterious black object in the rubber tree was clearly visible. We could see it, but the sergeant's explanation about how it came to be there sounded a little suspect. Still it was a good story, the kind that has a tendency to grow with each telling. (Almost a year later, on my way to Bein Hoa on the same road, I looked to the left as we passed that spot. The black pajamas, now faded almost gray, were still there.)

Once inside the gate, the convoy broke up and vehicles scattered to deliver their loads of replacement personnel, ammunition, aviation fuel, field and garrison rations and tons of other supplies. Our driver took the first right, speeding toward Headquarters Company, our destination, passing the 12th Evacuation Hospital on the way. I would get to know that place well.

A scene that would become all too familiar was unfolding on the chopper pads near the hospital. Two helicopters, one with red crosses painted on each side, the other with no markings, were discharging two walking wounded and three wounded on litters. Medics from 12th Evac were working hurriedly to get their patients into the emergency room. Physicians and RNs ran alongside the litters, evidently taking vital signs and doing everything possible to ward off shock. Only minutes inside Cu Chi base camp and already I had over-the-top respect for medical personnel and for those who flew into some hot landing zones to evacuate the wounded. That respect never lessened. Rather, it grew as I became more and more involved with the dustoff missions and the highly motivated medical professionals at the hospital. They saved many lives.

Dusk found us at the division chaplain's office. He suggested that we join the Headquarters Company, Second Brigade mess hall for supper on the outside chance the brigade commander might be taking his evening meal there. He was, and we talked for a few minutes. The brief conversation was the only one we ever had. I considered it a fortunate stroke of fate that I would not be on the brigade staff, but a member of the 2/27 Battalion staff, Lieutenant Colonel Sheldon, commander. During my year with that unit there would be three commanders, all of them prime examples of outstanding leadership, genuineness, selflessness and respect for subordinates. They even possessed a trait that may sound out of place for military leaders—humility.

"I checked with the Division S-3 and learned that all your line companies and battalion staff are in the field but are on track to return by noon tomorrow," Chaplain Paxson said. "Specialist Curtis will take you to our fabulous guest house where you can bunk for tonight. We'll help you with in-processing tomorrow and get you linked up with the 2nd Wolfhounds. Sound like something you can deal with?"

"A good plan if I ever heard one," I replied.

So, off we went. A half-mile away, Division artillery was conducting a fire mission. A noisy battery of 8-inchers was sending rounds on their way. A short drive got us to the guesthouse, where SP4 Curtis dropped me off. There were two cots, but I was the only guest for the evening. There was more than enough company though with the artillery, helicopters, the flares on the perimeter, the heat…and the firm assurance that this was where I was supposed to be.

Sleep did not come easily, but an earnest prayer did. "Lord, make me equal to the task that lies ahead. Keep me faithful to your Word and your call. Let me serve bravely and set a godly example before the officers and men whom I have yet to meet." I then reclaimed some verses from the Book of Psalms that I shared with my congregation the last Sunday before going on active duty: *He shall call upon me, and I will answer him: I will be with him in trouble; I will deliver and honor him.*

Tomorrow would be special, I thought. And it was. When the Second Wolfhounds returned from their week-long operation they found a new guy in the 144 square-foot thatch-roof hut which I later named the "Ye Holy Hootch". It was located just ten feet from a chapel under construction. After in-processing, I had an official meeting with Trojan 6 (Battalion Commander) and the XO (Executive officer). They extended a cordial welcome that really set me at ease.

Between noon and 2000 hours (8:00 PM) I made courtesy calls on three company commanders and first sergeants. Alpha's CO invited me to have lunch in their mess tent. A few hours later, it was to Bravo Company for supper. Between noon and dark, I spoke with at least 50 soldiers, visited four WIA (wounded in action) patients in 12th Evac and enjoyed a warm soft drink with Lieutenant Chuck Glasscock and his Recon Platoon. After listening to my first radio transmissions in the Battalion TOC (Tactical Operations Center), I retired to my little grass-roof hut about 11:00 p.m. to think of home and make tentative plans for the immediate future.

There would be even busier days, a great many of them. The Wolfhounds were all over the AO (Area of Operation) and into a lot of stuff. The officer back at Camp Alpha told me they were forever in some kind of "kicking contest". He was right. Keeping up with them was not a job for the lazy, fearful or out of shape.

CHAPTER 2

Long Way From Home

The Lord will keep you from harm. He will watch over
your life.

—Psalm 121:7a

*Journal entry, 10 December 1966—"Sapper squads were expected
during the night."*

"There are a lot of ways to die!" That fact had long been
fixed in my mind, having been present at the aftermath of
automobile accidents, suicides, homicides, drownings and death
from natural causes. The Boi Loi Woods served as the stage
for a new chapter on that gruesome subject: Land mines and
"friendly fire."

In-processing required a minimum of time. Supply was issuing
my field gear (poncho and liner, mosquito net, steel pot, flak vest,
jungle fatigues and boots) when Captain Kimery, Battalion S-1
reached me with news about a staff meeting. "You need to be
there," he said.

The Battalion Commander opened the meeting, introduced me
as the new battalion chaplain, made a few comments then turned
the meeting over to the S-3, who gave a briefing on an operation
that was due to kick off early the next day. He began, "Boi Loi
it is, guys. Most of us have been there. Those who have know it

is not a nice place. Booby traps will be a real threat. Emphasize those dangers to your troops. There is good intelligence that at least one company of NVA (North Vietnamese Army) is in the area, so contact is almost assured. Brigade is screaming for BC (body count) from this one. You know what that means. Now, the commander and I will meet with company commanders and our aviation support leaders to fine tune insertion plans. The rest of you are dismissed to go about other duties if you wish. Prepare well. This may be big.

About three hours later, Major Lawson, the S-3, saw me at work in the dimly lighted Chapel. He dropped in to say hello and chat a couple of minutes. I learned in those two minutes that he was a dedicated man of God. He was near the end of his tour and had the look of someone who needed a long break. Every step he took and every word he spoke mirrored fatigue. "I want to welcome you to the Second Battalion. You are about to rub shoulders with some great American citizens and fighting men. I sense that you are the spiritual leader and role model they need, that we all need," he said.

"Well, that most certainly is my desire and prayer. I plan to meet more soldiers and conduct my first field service tomorrow, if possible, in the Boi Loi Woods," I replied.

"And, Chaplain, in addition to extending a welcome, I also want to apologize to you," Major Lawson said.

That statement came out of left field and I had no idea what it meant. Apologize? Why?

But he continued, "I very much dislike those two words, 'body count', that you heard me use in the staff meeting. It sounds so heartless and cold, like killing is something you keep score on. I know it must be something a clergyman has trouble with because I sure do. Unfortunately, that is what war is though—a violent game in which people die. If we don't take them out, they are only too pleased to take us out. That's an awful way to put it, but that's the way it is."

As he left the open-sided chapel, which would eventually be screened, I thought about those solemn words he had spoken. They reminded me of a quote I had heard or read somewhere. It goes something like this: "Among those who long for peace and the end of war, it is the military leader who longs for it the most."

The lead company went into CA (Combat Assault) mode. The landing zone was cold (no firing from below), something pilots and grunts pray for. They quickly set up a perimeter. I got out on the fifth lift, which was composed of eight Hueys flying staggered trail. It was my first flight in a chopper with no doors. I sat on the deck next to the door gunner.

As we approached the LZ, the gunner began swinging his .30 caliber M-60 back and forth like he was writing on an invisible poster board. The skids didn't touch down. All passengers jumped the last two feet to the ground. I high-fived the door gunner on my way out and he shouted, "Good luck, Padre." I thought, *Here I am at last*!

Specialist Mah, Battalion Medic, waved me over to his position. "You can dig in with us if you like, Chaplain," he said, and we shook hands like friends who had known each other for a lifetime instead of, at most, three minutes.

A few steps away I spotted a dark green poncho, and could not take my eyes off it. I was quite sure it covered bodies lying side by side. Jungle boots, toes pointed skyward and still, left uncovered. My look at the medic must have had a question mark at the end. "Just got it. Minutes ago, not more than 20," he said. "They were setting up a tent over near that biggest tree and detonated a land mine." Over the bodies of PFC Robert Twing and PFC Bobby Hudson, soldiers I had not even met, I read the 23rd Psalm and silently voiced my first prayer in the field. At the same time I experienced my first combat zone lump-in-the-throat, the first of many.

The next flight to land was a dustoff. Somber faces, dusty and sweaty, watched as fellow soldiers were loaded and whisked away.

The war was over for them. Eleven days later, I conducted my first memorial service in Vietnam for those two young men and wrote letters of condolence to their next of kin in Florida and Illinois.

"When it is night you long for the light of day!" I had read those or similar words in many books about combat. High noon is usually more desirable than midnight. It is small consolation to be told, "If you can't see the bad guy, the bad guy can't see you." The three or four soldiers at LPs (listening posts) and OPs (observation posts) breathe easier when the sun begins to peek over the horizon. By the time the last company had arrived and set up night positions, all the sunny spots had become shadows. The word was passed: Be on high alert for sappers.

I put my entrenching tool to work on a little deeper hole. Specialist Mah was busy with the same activity about 10 feet away. We shoveled dirt in silence. A few meters toward the center of the perimeter, I heard a command that had not yet become part of my military vocabulary: "Hang it! Fire!" Immediately following those words was a sound—Thoomp! The mortar platoon was tossing out some rounds that were supposed to warn the guys on the other side that they should not come calling tonight.

On it went, the mortar platoon leader's subdued voice calling out the command: "Hang it! Fire! Thoomp! Hang it! Fire! Thoomp!" Each Thoomp sound was followed by an explosion about 200 meters out. Flares began appearing 50 to 100 meters outside the wire forming eerie shadows as they drifted down. Over in the Bravo section, a machine gun chattered several times between midnight and 0130. Somewhere in the distance a sniper kept pinging away at us, though his fire was high and ineffective. Artillery, from some distant firebase, began delivering support rounds. I watched with admiration as the FO (forward observer) walked high explosive rounds up and down the wood lines where most of the fire seemed to be originating.

There would be much scarier nights than the first one in the Boi Loi. But not yet having anything to compare it with, a nagging thought that this could be my last night on earth kept rising to the surface. Amazingly though, a feeling of tranquil calmness also surfaced. I came to terms with the thought and hid it away in an area of the brain, heart and soul that had a label: Faith. With mental pictures of my wife and three precious children vividly before me, I prayed. It could have been aloud or silent. These many years later, I honestly do not know. "Lord, this is in your hands. Should one of these mortar or sniper rounds take me out, I earnestly request that you stand by those I now picture. Give them the strength to handle it bravely and well. Assure them, beyond any doubt, that my last thoughts were of them. Cover them with your love and grace. Direct their steps, especially those of my wife, if she is presented with the task of raising our children alone. Let peace reign there with them as it does here with me."

Any fear I had of death and an uncertain future fled away. It never returned.

Combat troops rarely know what day it is. Sunday is the same as Tuesday, Saturday or Thursday. Later, when the luxury of being back in the rear for a day or two came, they may fill in the blanks of their short-timers' calendars, but the actual day of the week escaped all except those of us who needed to know. So, when a field altar, consisting of my cross-emblazoned steel helmet on a C-rations case, was displayed, soldiers began to ask, "Chaplain, is it Sunday?"

This time it was. But most weeks the same scene played out Monday through Saturday more than on Sunday. After meeting a few soldiers and conducting a quick service with Alpha Company, I took a chopper to the 1/5 Mechanized location for another field service. Having gotten word that the 1/5 Mech chaplain was on R and R, I offered to conduct a religious service for his unit which was operating a few kilometers from the 2/27. Chaplain Downes, a priest, called on me often to minister to his non-Catholic troops and I invited him to assist with my soldiers who desired to attend mass and receive communion from a priest. Mutual cooperation became an indispensible way of life that I came to appreciate greatly and missed when it was no longer available.

The pilot, with no other mission on his schedule, shut down the engine and waited for me. His was the last ride out that night. Had he not waited, I would have been stranded. Profound words of gratitude were heaped on that young WO1. I was even more grateful for the late evening flight back to Cu Chi when I visited our TOC (tactical operations center) early the next morning and learned that the 1/5 had been hit hard at 0300 with small arms, mortars and Rocket Propelled Grenades. The attackers were repelled, but several of the guys I had dealt with just hours before were wounded.

That night attack on the Mech battalion and many later attacks on the Wolfhounds taught me a valuable lesson. Admittedly, it took some time to fully register but the lesson did come: Don't waste time or effort attempting to figure out the more dangerous or safer locations and travel accordingly. Sometimes, word would come that base camp was likely to get a rocket attack "tonight." Or, word from the field might be that the bad guys are everywhere and will undoubtedly attack with grenades and satchel charges following a mortar barrage. Access to such intelligence could have caused one to think, "It looks like the field is in for a hairy night, so I'd better stay in base camp. Or, forward may be safer tonight because the spooks think base camp will get rockets."

As chaplain, I was free to go here and yonder if transportation was available. I saw right away that attempts to avoid danger made no sense. With no defined front lines as there had been in past wars, rear echelon took on a different meaning. Only later in my tour did I discover that there were a few who tried to play the second-guessing game. I found it best to let rumors about enemy troop movement affect the schedule as little as possible, which worked out well. Even in a "bad" place, I considered it the right place.

Unless my enlisted assistant really wanted to go to the field, he would stay back to keep the chapel shaped up, take care of clerical matters, maintain our jeep, and set up my counseling schedule. On Sunday morning, there were three services to oversee in garrison: the battalion chapel, Ambush Academy and the Dog Platoon. Often there were two services in the chapel. On Sunday afternoon, as soon as possible, I'd grab a resupply or chow run to one of the companies, where a field service was announced and usually well attended when the tactical situation permitted. Then I'd check in with Trojan Six or the S-3 to let them know I was in the area before going to a second company for another field service and an overnight. Company Commanders Brewer, Pitts, Springer, Wikan and others were always welcoming and cordial. Usually they would say, "How about having chow and digging in with Alpha (or Bravo or Charlie)!" The invitation was accepted dozens of times.

Those nights were extreme in one of two ways: Hot and dry, with mosquitoes for company, or torrential monsoon rain, with mosquitoes for company. During the monsoon rains you could never get dry. During the dry season you could never get cool.

It was on to the next unit shortly after daybreak and a C-Rations breakfast. Hopefully, Wednesday night or Thursday by noon would find me back at base camp writing letters, studying, counseling, welcoming new arrivals and visiting with wounded soldiers in the hospital. And arranging for memorial services. Always memorial services.

From the first week as a combat chaplain, I noticed that soldiers who attended field services or sought counseling rarely said anything about their friends who had been killed in action. They just didn't want to bring it up. Rarely did they mention their names again or talk about how they died. What they wanted most was to erase the scene from their minds, do their time, stay alive and get back home in one piece if possible. But didn't do it without a twinge of guilt. Their take on the subject quite often was, "Chaplain, I'm just glad it wasn't me. My buddy caught one with his name on it and I deeply regret that he will no longer be sleeping in the bunk next to mine. But I'm still trucking." That was how most of the guys thought of it and about the only way they knew how to face it.

It was at that time I began to see the old saying, "there are no atheists in foxholes," could be more half-truth than fact. I saw it then, and later among prison inmates on death row, that the "atheists in foxholes" saying didn't tell the whole story. Sad to say, some facing the bullet, electric chair or lethal injection table go out shaking a fist and cursing whatever "gods there may be," at least symbolically. Only a very few, but in something so fraught with eternal consequences, few is much. During many years of association with military and prison chaplaincy, I witnessed only three who made a point to let the world know they fell into that category. Even with those, who could know what was really going on between the created and the Creator in those last seconds of earthly existence? Something good, I have long hoped.

A couple of days back in base camp was enough to convince me that my real duty at that time was out where I could become more acquainted with those under fire. So after half a Sunday and most of a Monday, it was back to the Boi Loi and my hole near the Headquarters Company aid station. At the time, I was still getting oriented and learning who was who and what was what. A slick, flying a basic load of ammunition and water to Bravo Company, gave me a ride. I was the only passenger and had a good "first class" seat on a five gallon water can. Darkness had barely finished exerting its full presence when danger and death's reality struck again. Friendly fire's potential is just as lethal as that of the enemy machine gunners who make it their mission to kill.

The night was unusually quiet, almost like the eye of a tornado. No cracks of sniper fire. No movement detected outside the wire. The mortar platoon, sending greetings in the form of sporadic rounds, was the main sound of the near serene evening.

I even considered taking off my boots and socks to better enjoy a peaceful sleep. Suddenly, an ear-splitting sound broke the secure feeling. It was close by. "Inside the perimeter, in or very near Bravo's sector," the medics reported as they grabbed their aid bags and ran toward a voice calling out, "Medic!" This was one of the many times I saw their dedication in action. Even without knowing when and where the next one might fall, they ran on.

Then came the dreaded report: Short round! Death dealing stuff from a tube that is our own. It may have been a defective round, but that did not diminish the feelings of remorse the mortar team felt. They had fired a projectile that took the lives of SP4 Ray and SSG Hoopii. Sergeant Hoopii, from Hawaii, was an old-timer in Bravo, a specially loved and respected NCO.

I had been the recipient of a salute (seldom rendered in the field except when the "birds and stars" showed up) and a fast handshake from Sergeant Hoopii just hours before his untimely death. He helped unload the ammo and water from the chopper that provided my most recent flight from Cu Chi. Our mutual greeting lasted no more than 10 seconds, but in that short time I spotted his friendly nature and pleasing personality.

Peaceful sleep was not to be after all because I spent most of the remaining night hours visiting with Bravo Company leaders to obtain memorial service type information about Specialist Ray and Sergeant Hoopii. They, along with two others—one a Specialist Four and the other a First Sergeant—killed by a land mine the day before, would be remembered in a special service when their respective companies had their next stand down. The First Sergeant already had a port call and was due to leave for the States in two days. He had gone to the field to see his guys "one more time" and remain only long enough to have supper with them and say "so long." He and SP4 Detamble were helping carry hot food to an area cleared for the serving line when they triggered the mine.

This thought lingered for a while: Close (the Top Sergeant was) but still a long way from home. I came to look forward to the times when my journal entries would read, "Things much better, today. No casualties."

For several reasons, memorial services were seldom held in the field. One was attendance. Barely a third of the company soldiers could attend such official remembrances while on an operation. There were too many other duties to perform. Also, holding them in garrison allowed the GIs to get their minds off the environment in which their fellow soldiers died. But on a spring Thursday afternoon, at the invitation of Lieutenant Berg, I met his platoon. "If ever they needed a word from on high," he said, "it is now." I knelt in the center of a circle of about two dozen grim-faced soldiers. The last two days had been rough. They had lost some good friends, two killed and several wounded. What we did in the circle was have a pre-memorial service, something I had never done before. I said a few words, read from Psalms, prayed briefly and invited them to share what might be on their minds. Most remained silent, but two responded with some good words.

About halfway through our 20-minute session, another person quietly approached and sat down on the periphery of the circle. He wore a dark green uniform but he obviously was not a second battalion soldier. As the platoon returned to their positions, I met Morley Safer. Mr. Safer, a war correspondent, was spending time with 25th Division units. On this operation he was embedded with the 2/27. I offered him a choice between my pound cake and fruit cocktail. He chose one and I took the other.

"How did you come to be in Vietnam?" he wanted to know.

"Chaplains are volunteers. There is not a chaplain in the military who did not request active duty, or who was not assigned to the duty by their endorsing agencies," I said.

"You probably know this, but people in the U.S. are already becoming impatient with this war," Mr. Safer said.

I did know, although in early 1967 the American military was still held in fairly high esteem, not as high as in World War II, but not in outright scorn either. Things would get worse in the future. Then he asked, "Is it all that difficult for you, as a Christian minister to be assigned to a combat unit such as the 25th Division? And is it difficult to justify being in a place where a shooting war is going on? Where people kill and get killed?"

"Is it difficult? To a degree, yes, it is difficult. To be separated from my family and to watch these young people deal with fear and death is truly a tough deal. But the difficulty for me, personally, does not begin to approach that which the officers and men here in the boonies deal with. As to being able to justify it, I don't see that as my task. Those soldiers you see out there filling sandbags, pulling razor wire, and cleaning weapons to better encounter what could happen tonight or in the next minute are enough justification for me. If things go the next few months as they have for the last few, some of those youngsters will never again see their hometowns or participate in a family reunion. My sole motive is to be here to help them walk through it and, if possible, assist them in being prepared to face what tomorrow might bring. Justify? I don't suppose that fully addresses the question, but it is about as close to it as I can get."

We both went silent, stared across a rice field, and finished our "box lunches." That done, we stood and exchanged handshakes. Morley Safer was one of two journalists/reporters I met and spoke with at some length during my first year in Southeast Asia. The other was Ike Pappas. Both of them were personable, professional, all-round quality men. With a final wave of his hand, Mr. Safer moved on to other things. So did I, to encourage, be a friend and intently listen to soldiers talk about fears, dreams, girl friends, wives, children, mortality, disappointments, faith and home. Home was the major topic with most. Home, the address so far away and which, so thought some, they would never see again. For too many it was true.

The other side is always called the enemy. Even in athletic events, the team that opposes your team is the enemy. In war, enemies are those who shoot at you, erect booby traps and punji stakes designed to maim, cause infection or death. The bad guy, the one who counts cadence to a different drumbeat, is pleased to see those on the other side give their lives for their country. He is the enemy. The enemy! Friend of stealth and darkness. Expert in multi-level tunneling. Uniform—immaterial. Age—immaterial. Maybe it's the village barber that grooms GIs. The enemy, existing on rice. Making do with little. Humping it, missing loved ones. Waiting for his one shot from a spider hole.

That last word took on a new meaning one day in a small settlement. On a sweep in the village of Phu Hoa Dong, Bravo took fire from a clump of underbrush and returned fire with force. A platoon closed in on the clump but found no sign of the shooters. A dog handler and his alert dog were with the company that day and were called forward. The dog alerted on a small square of vegetation which turned out to be camouflage over a trap door. The point man volunteered to open the hinged door. As he cracked it open a few inches, the platoon sergeant rolled in a grenade and yelled, "Fire in the hole!"

The door, thought at first to cover a tunnel entrance, had instead covered the entrance to an oversized spider hole, about four feet square and six feet deep. From it were pulled three slight-built men and two Chinese Communist (ChiCom) rifles. The grenade had done its gruesome work. Looking at the bodies of those three VC, the enemy, who had no doubt meant to kill but failed, I wondered if the trap door was in their front yard. Were they cousins? Brothers? Classmates? Would their mothers ever know what happened to them?

At first light not many days later, I accompanied Charlie Company across a field where a firefight had taken place during the night. NVA soldiers had attacked in force. They were beaten back, suffered heavy losses, and retreated into the darkness.

Grim reminders of battle were scattered all about. We almost stumbled over a cheap mandolin in a plastic bag, not a scratch on it. Lieutenant Steward picked it up and said, "Here, Chaplain, you need this!" Inside the mandolin was a sticker: Made in Saigon. I positioned it across my chest like a bandoleer and hiked several kilometers with the battalion to the next bivouac point. For years, I would look at that little mandolin and think about the owner. Did he drop it while trying to escape to safety? Was he injured? Killed? How did he come by it? Did he bring it from home? Would he be pleased to know that in 2011, forty-four years after it was taken from the battle site, I presented it to the Wolfhound Regimental museum at Schofield Barracks in Hawaii? War prompts more questions than answers.

Something similar occurred in connection with a hammock that no doubt was once the property of an enemy soldier. The hammock was found in a tunnel complex near Bao Trai. SP4 Bill Lowry, one of our "tunnel rats," brought it out and presented it to me as a souvenir. After several days of carting it around, I decided one night to lash it between two trees in War Zone C and try sleeping in it. The hammock became part of an unusual episode, which will be related in a later chapter.

Events surrounding the spider hole, the musical instrument and the hammock led to thoughts, then and now, about those on the other side. Were fond dreams shattered as much for them as they were for those on our side? Did they miss home and family as much as American soldiers did? Did they feel far away, even in their home country?

CHAPTER 3

Close Calls

...I have escaped by the skin of my teeth.

—Job 19:20

Journal entry, 28 February 1967—My hammock took two rounds. I had rolled out of it no more than 10 seconds before.

"Dear Mama, Well, I have now been in Uncle Sam's army a month. There is not much to say. Oh yes, yesterday, I got run over by a tank." Your GI son, Roy Gene Little.

Roy Gene was in basic training when he sent that newsy note home. The tank episode came close to sending his mother into orbit. Frantic calls like the one she made often reach the unit chaplain. This one did. She was barely able to relate the "run over by a tank" part before breaking into sobs. After learning Basic Trainee Little's exact address I assured his mother that she would get a call back just as soon as I learned what had happened.

His company was on the rifle range, and his drill sergeant got me in touch with him:

"Little! Front and center. The chaplain needs to see you," the sergeant yelled.

In the shade of a scraggly live oak I heard more about the story that upset his mother. What the short note didn't say was that he and his squad were in a concrete pit when the tank rolled over them. The tank added battlefield reality to a soldier's training. Seeing and hearing that huge track vehicle roll across their "foxhole" was high drama for a soldier in basic. His mother, who had visualized her son in a full body cast or traction, cried again upon hearing what really happened. Joyful tears this time, and words from a happy mom, "I'm going to kill that 17-year-old kid for frightening ten years off my life!"

Though this was not one, there were more than enough close calls and narrow escapes. SP4 Frailey, whose first name and hometown I never learned, was badly wounded when Delta Company, on a sweep near base camp, received machine gun fire from a cleverly concealed bunker. Several casualties resulted, including PFC Burns, who lost an arm. Frailey, a compress bandage on his neck and awaiting dustoff, told an interesting story about how things had gone during the nine months he had been in country.

He spoke quietly as gunships continued their strafing mission close by. "Chaplain, I've always heard that the law of averages eventually catches up. I guess this was catch-up day for me. I'm not superstitious, but number 13 keeps running through my mind. I have kept count of my near misses. There were twelve before today."

He pointed to twelve black grease-pencil marks on his helmet cover. He spoke about how some of them came to be there: Shrapnel grazed a smoke grenade on his web gear. The heel of his left boot had been blown away. The faded green sock, in which he carried his Cs, had been torn to shreds by grenade fragments. A non-swimmer, he almost drowned during a canal crossing. A friendly "butterfly bomb" sent deadly pellets into the earth just inches from his head. "Twelve shots at cheating death," he said. Actually number 13 turned out to be a close call as well. He had recovered in two weeks and rejoined his unit.

Once all the casualties had been evacuated, Delta Company began moving back into base camp, entering a locally famous but secondary gate named Ann Margaret. I joined Delta for supper in their mess tent. Specialist Woods and I ate together and talked about the recent past. Of the two that were KIA near Cu Chi that October day, one was his best friend, a fine young man by the name of Gary Hawkins. The loss of Gary hit Woods extremely hard, but as is the case with most combat veterans facing similar situations, he didn't show it outwardly.

While we talked and worked at swallowing "pre-fab" roast beef and rice, another soldier sitting across the table told me something I had already heard, but listened to with intense interest. His close friend in another 2/27 company, had taken a round an inch from the top of his helmet. The bullet penetrated his steel pot and helmet liner, left a bruise on the back of his head and plopped out on the opposite side. "Hot lead on his shoulder! A power stronger than the bad guy's bullet was present that day, Chaplain," the soldier exclaimed joyfully. I couldn't have agreed more.

Everyone who knew the lucky soldier wanted to see and take a picture of the miracle helmet. The owner had told his buddy, "I don't ever plan to be far from it, but now it ain't no good for shaving or bathing. The water keeps running out. I can't keep from smiling when I look at it."

Living to talk about close calls should authorize one to laugh right out loud.

The first time I had anything like a lengthy conversation with Lieutenant Steve Ehart, it was about close calls he and his soldiers had been involved with. Steve would eventually be a company executive officer and then a company commander, but at that time he was a platoon leader, the assignment about which it was said that if one could make it a full three months he might actually make it. If there is such a thing as a happy-to-still-be-here laugh, then he exhibited one that late evening in front of my little house, which by then was known by all in the Second Battalion as Ye Holy Hootch.

Most of that conversation I still could recall with clarity. Such things have a way of sticking like super glue. But nearly a half-century is bound to cause some blurring, so forty-five years after our late evening conversation at Cu Chi base camp, I contacted Steve with a greeting and a question, "Do you remember the very first talk we had when you expressed a renewed religious faith and gratitude that you and your platoon were spared?" I asked.

He answered, "No way could I forget even the smallest detail." So he reviewed it for me through an informative email message.

"We were doing a search and destroy along a stream down by the Oriental River," he began.

"I was walking number two in the column behind PFC Battles, a soldier from Rome, Georgia, who was on point. He tripped a booby trap, which, we found out later, was an intricate device made with two hand grenades. Clear fishing line, almost invisible in the undergrowth, was attached to the pins. The grenades were securely taped to shrubs and were well hidden among the brush and leaves. Whoever rigged that booby trap knew what he was doing. The blast was huge. The point man was seriously injured. Thank God for Ranger School, where it was hammered into our heads to keep six to eight paces between you and the man ahead of you, thus preventing multiple casualties from one explosion.

"After putting out security, four of us moved PFC Battles to a small clearing and waited for the dustoff to come in. Just as the helicopter was making the final approach there was another explosion about 20 yards to my rear, in the same area we had just walked over carrying our wounded man. One of my platoon soldiers, bringing Battles' helmet and weapon to the small clearing where the chopper was going to set down, had tripped another booby trap. Now, instead of one evacuee, we had two. My adrenaline was maxed out. Heart pounding hard.

"What kept running through my mind was this: 'Two booby traps in less than 15 minutes and I don't have a scratch. God is in this. Mom and Dad's prayers for their son have been answered.

"That day I vowed to turn everything over to Supreme Six. He has never let me down."

Two days later, Steve hopped a flight to visit PFC Battles with the 3rd Field Hospital in Saigon. One of his legs had been amputated at the knee. They talked about his inability to complete the tour, and his life with only one leg. He would be evacuated to Japan and eventually to a hospital in the States.

"That brief visit in the hospital was the last time I ever saw him," Lieutenant Ehart, who retired as a colonel years after we served together with the Wolfhounds, wrote, "but to this day I have wondered what happened to him and what he did after Vietnam." That thought stays firmly on the minds of many who went through fire and pain together. "I wonder what happened to...?"

The question takes on even deeper meaning if they experienced near misses together and walked away.

Less than a week later, Specialist Wolfe, a member of the Tracker Dog Team, faced something that would remain forever vivid to him. A few minutes after a wooded area in the Long An Province was surrounded by two Alpha Company platoons, three handlers went in with their dogs. A Viet Cong, clad in black pajamas and carrying a weapon, had been observed entering the woods. The tracker dogs, with their keen sense of smell, would sniff him out.

Wolfe's dog quickly alerted, much the same way a good bird dog comes to point on a covey of quail. "When my dog alerted I knew it had to be the enemy soldier we were looking for," SP4 Wolfe volunteered.

"Were the other handlers close by?" I asked him.

"No. They were somewhere on the other side of the woods and not in sight."

"So you attempted to get out of there, I guess, knowing the VC had a weapon?"

"Yes sir, I eased my dog back the way we had entered the thick brush. I knew the thing to do was pull back and let the 'grunts' know what they were facing. But as I backed around the end of a head-high hedge row, I almost stumbled over a guy squatting in the grass. A whole lot faster than I can tell it, he stuck the end of his carbine in my stomach and pulled the trigger. The gun snapped. It snapped, sir! His gun snapped! I beat him to the ground with my hands. He was scrawny as could be, a hundred and ten pounds at the most, and shaking like a leaf in a strong wind. He was deathly afraid of my dog. The little guy seemed relieved when the lieutenant came and took him away. I tell you though, I'm the one who was relieved!"

With watery eyes, he stared in the distance at something, or nothing. I pretty much knew his thoughts as he walked away: *I am standing upright and walking around.*

Wolfe's encounter was close and personal, with a carbine pressed hard against his mid-section. Ehart did not see the person or persons who fashioned the booby traps, even though they could have been close by. The near-misses for both came from fighters who had pledged allegiance to the other side. The soldier standing beside Sergeant Hoopii when he was killed experienced a close call from friendly fire—a short round.

Sergeant Herb Beeson and I learned that one can experience a close call from an unknown source. Whether friendly or unfriendly, we would never know.

During Operation Junction City, Sergeant Beeson and I were walking back to our night positions after having chow together. The evening was uncharacteristically quiet, almost too pleasant for a war zone. Taking more of a stroll than a hike, we were in no particular hurry to cover the 150 or so yards.

There were no thoughts of rank or protocol in the field, so I was walking on his left. Suddenly, with no "excuse me" or "hold up a second," I knelt down to tie a dangling boot string. Beeson continued at the leisurely pace we had been walking. The boot string incident took only seconds. When I looked up, Beeson was on the ground about 10 feet ahead. He was making no sounds at all, but was writhing and jerking, evidently having a seizure. Medics were by his side in less than a minute. They could find no reason for the immediate change that was taking place with him.

The Battalion Commander's helicopter was quickly put in service as an evacuation chopper for a flight to the 12th Evac hospital.

The doctors and nurses were stymied at first, but their thorough examination finally revealed a tiny flesh wound on his left shoulder.

"That must be the culprit," they said.

A couple of X-rays revealed the problem. A small caliber bullet or projectile of some kind had entered the front part of his left shoulder, gone between two ribs and lodged in his heart. The trauma had somehow caused him to suffer a seizure. Dr. Alexander (Captain, USA) attempted to explain it to me, but my ministerial mind didn't catch it the way a medically trained mind would have. All I knew for sure was that Beeson was injured.

A hop on a resupply bird got me to the hospital early the next day. When I saw Beeson, who was by then stabilized and free of pain, he told me the story as the doctor had explained it. The "left shoulder" part, the entry point for the projectile, caught my attention. For it was on his left, with perhaps 10 inches separating us, I was walking before dropping down to take care of the untied boot.

Maybe he didn't catch the irony but it was not lost on me: Did he take a round from an unknown origin that could/should have been mine? Once in a while, to this day, I think about that episode. A person has to be pleased to learn that he could have gotten hit but didn't. I am reluctant to think that it was Providence that made me stop suddenly to take care of the boot lace rather than wait until arriving at my destination. Would it have been my left shoulder instead of his? Close calls rarely have a clear answer.

But they do prompt prayers of gratitude. There would be other occasions and other prayers of thanks.

The hammock, taken as a souvenir from a tunnel complex, has already been mentioned. It was in my chaplain kit during the first days of a battalion search and destroy mission in an area designated War Zone C. On February 28, the day after my 35th birthday, I decided to give the hammock a try. We were in a triple-canopy jungle. Trees were plentiful. Two, just the right distance apart, worked well. I secured the little green nylon cloth between the small trees, placed a poncho liner inside it and reclined the only way a person can in a hammock—U shaped. A minute after lying down, I remembered that PFC Smalls had requested to speak with me when we had some time. "I've got time now," I thought, and rolled out of the uncomfortable little bed and got ready to head toward the sector where Smalls' company was set up. It was dusk, but the thick jungle canopy made it darker than it would have been in a more open area. I grabbed my red-lens flashlight and took off. Ten or 15 steps into my journey a pistol shot sounded out in the area I had just left. Like everyone else close by, I hit the ground. Within seconds someone called out, "Friendly. No one hit," and I continued my night visit, thinking no more about the shot. After visiting with Smalls, who told me that he had "given his life to Jesus" and wanted to be baptized when we got back to Cu Chi, I headed back to my VC hammock, being grateful for the young soldier's decision as I went. A surprise was waiting to greet me.

It became apparent that white residue of some kind was sprinkled on the poncho liner and the sagging part of the hammock. It was foot powder, the kind that soldiers are encouraged to carry and use to help prevent immersion foot.

"Hey guys", I said to my closest temporary neighbors, "you know where people go who sabotage the chaplain's fancy bunk," waving the powder can as I made my little speech and as they laughed.

But something was wrong, something that became obvious under the flashlight's dim glow. The foot powder can I had left in the hammock had a hole through it. So did the hammock and liner. Bullet hole. Colt .45. Three soldiers, now more serious, helped me do a thorough inspection. The poncho liner which was wadded inside the hammock had been perforated in six places. The .45 slug hit right about where a person's rib cage would be, where mine would have been had I not jumped up suddenly to make a call on PFC Smalls.

The GIs who helped me sort it all out wanted to go after the careless shooter. "Ain't no need to have that kind of stuff," one of them said. I urged them to let it go. Hopefully it would serve as a wake-up call for the one who could have created all kinds of havoc, but fortunately didn't.

I learned what happened. About 60 feet away a soldier was cleaning one of the old faithful army .45s, or more likely playing with it, and accidently fired it. I don't think he ever knew how close he came to being the first GI to take out the battalion chaplain. My wife and children were glad he didn't attain that notoriety, though they didn't know anything about it until many years later when my son asked about the holes in the hammock. As for me, I was glad the soldier was denied that dubious claim to fame. I expressed that bit of gladness to the "One of the throne" many times.

Soldiers involved in combat sometimes experience close calls and don't know that they did until later. It may be the next day before the soldier walking point learns that he missed a feces-smeared punji stake by only inches or that a loaded and cocked Light Antitank Weapon (LAW) was lying on the deck of a helicopter beside a seriously wounded soldier. An errant boot against the firing mechanism could have produced terrible consequences, maybe could have even brought the aircraft down. Instead, upon landing at the hospital, the door gunner spotted the ready-to-fire weapon and, with shaking hands, disarmed it.

He glanced over at me and, with a nervous laugh said, "Chaplain, this is serious stuff. Somebody was watching over us today." I nodded in thankful agreement.

Maybe there is no such thing as a close call if one is not present when the event in question takes place. Still, it kicks the mind in gear and leaves you wondering what "might" have been. Why weren't you there at that particular time when for weeks and weeks before you had been there? I pondered that question for years following an event during my second tour in Southeast Asia.

After spending 21 months in the States at Ft. Sill, Oklahoma, I was alerted for a second tour. The 212th Combat Aviation Battalion at Danang was my duty assignment. I became chaplain to a large battalion of pilots and maintenance personnel at Marble Mountain, Chu Lai, Hue/Phu Bai, Vietnam and Udorn, Thailand. The headquarters and Wings of Freedom chapel were at Marble Mountain. My normal schedule took me to Hue/Phu Bai on Tuesday and Chu Lai on Thursday, hitching rides on spotter planes (Bird Dogs), Hueys, Mohawks, Beavers and Otters and anything else that could make it over the Hai Van Pass.

Only one time the entire year was a flight to Phu Bai not available to support that long established schedule. That one week only I went to Chu Lai on Tuesday and notified the guys at Phu Bai unit that I'd be up to see them on Thursday. It worked out well and on Wednesday morning, Major Ken Kimes flew me back to Marble Mountain. The next day it was to Phu Bai, 48 hours later than usual. Not long after landing at the Phu Bai airport, another "close call" was revealed. The company commander, a major, could hardly wait to be my escort, something he had never done before.

Each Tuesday evening after a meal in the company mess hall, I'd offer a chapel service in a large bunker, maybe attend a movie (usually a Western), after which I'd find my way to a green plastic-covered couch in the company day room. That was where I slept. Nearly every Tuesday night found me there. When I showed up on Thursday, the major's first words to me were, "Padre, I want to show you something!"

The green couch was what he wanted me to see, and see it I did with an increased pulse rate. There was a hole in the metal roof, now covered temporarily with a heavy tarp. During a rocket attack on Tuesday night, a projectile had come through the roof and exploded in the day room. One can only imagine the decibel level it generated. The green couch had taken a 12-inch by 3-inch jagged piece of shrapnel through the back, at about seat level. The wicked looking piece of steel was embedded in the lower wall on the other side of the room.

The major and I viewed the scene in silence. He understood why I stood with lowered head and closed eyes for a few seconds. I wanted to jump and yell "Hooray," but didn't.

Who knows the answer to such things? Some would undoubtedly call it luck, coincidence or just a normal, garden variety stroke of fate that the aircraft could not fly north the previous Tuesday. I could only look to the next day with profound gratitude and call it God! Lieutenant Colonel Hickerson, 212th Battalion CO, suggested that henceforth I might consider sleeping in the bunker. His wise suggestion made sense and was happily followed, at least for a while.

Because of the presence of so many aircraft and the threat they posed on the NVA and Viet Cong, Phu Bai airfield was hit often, but not one rocket exploded in or near the company day room during the remainder of my tour. The battered green couch was placed outside the gate and quickly claimed by two diminutive Vietnamese men. They somehow succeeded in loading it on an ancient bicycle and disappeared down a narrow street in the direction of Hue, pushing the bike and balancing the couch.

Soldiers, even the seriously wounded, consider it a close call if they live to talk about it. They got hit, but it was still only a close call if the heart is still beating. I learned this within days after I joined the 2nd Wolfhounds. Two days before Christmas, Charlie

Company's Lieutenant Howard was leading a platoon-size patrol not far outside the Division perimeter where enemy movement had been reported by a listening point (LP). About 900 meters out, Howard, moving through thick brush, snagged a trip wire that was attached to a grenade. Booby trap! The lieutenant and his RTO—Specialist Dickson—received shrapnel wounds in their lower extremities. The grenade explosion was instantly followed by rifle fire from hidden positions, probably spider holes. Under intense return fire from the Charlie Company platoon, the Viet Cong quickly broke contact and disappeared.

Later in the day, I saw Howard and Dickson in the hospital. Neither had the magical million- dollar wound. When I arrived at Specialist Dickson's bedside he asked if the lieutenant had said much about what had happened that morning and I told him he hadn't, not to me anyway. He said the platoon leader would never say anything that made himself appear heroic, but would downplay the encounter instead.

"Chaplain," the RTO said, "in two or three minutes we went through some stuff I won't be able to explain or understand if I live to be a hundred. The Lieutenant won't either, even if he'll talk about it."

"Is that right? What made it so mysterious?" I asked.

"We both got hit by the booby trapped grenade and went to the ground. Small arms fire started coming in. A few seconds later our platoon started throwing out some lead. M-60s were chattering away. Grenades from our M-79s were exploding close to where the bad guys seemed to be hiding. With all that going on, the Lieutenant and I were still taking fire and couldn't tell where it was coming from."

"You were in thick terrain out there, but somehow they had you in sight?" I asked.

"We must have stumbled across a narrow firing lane and hit the ground right in the middle of it. After a few seconds, we inched into some thicker brush, but even there the rounds continued to hit close by. Those shooters must have been intent on taking out the antennae and the men standing close to it.

"When we got to the hospital chopper pad, one of the medics said to me, 'That canteen is not going to be much good to you now.' A bullet had gone through the cover, cup and canteen. The poncho rolled up and tied on the back of Lieutenant Howell's belt was punched through with several holes, probably by one round, but it was torn to shreds. Another round nicked my web belt, but didn't leave a burn mark anywhere on my skin.

"When we hit the ground, I yanked the radio off my back and set it between the lieutenant and me. While he was giving a situation report, the radio took a round through the battery pack and instantly went dead. The noise of battle had started from silence. It ended the same way. Suddenly there was no gunfire. I guess the ambushers dropped back into their spider holes and disappeared into the famous Cu Chi tunnels.

"But, you know something, Chaplain, having those bullets come so close and never so much as graze either one of us seems like a miracle to me!"

"Specialist Dickson, do you know anyone who could think otherwise? A man of faith knows what happened, doesn't he?" I could think of no better comment.

"You are looking at a Razorback fan whose faith has been reawakened and renewed. From now on I'll think of every day as a gift from above," Dickson said.

Lieutenant Howard later told pretty much the same story as his RTO. He was placed on light duty for a few weeks while his leg wounds healed. During that time I learned that he was a trained vocal soloist, a talent he shared often during the Wolfhound Chapel worship services. Before he was cleared to go back on line, he had formed a chapel choir. What great guys they were. They tried hard, those "Howling Hounds."

One day, after Howard was no longer on a profile and back with his platoon, we were enduring a monsoon downpour under my poncho, eating whatever the mess sergeant had given us. He summed up that late December close call in an unusual but profound way: "Maybe you have read Charles Darwin's Origin of the Species?" I told him I had once struggled through it. "I recall," he said, "that the book used the phrase 'Survival of the Fittest.' It has nothing to do with Darwin, but I now know that there is such a thing as 'Survival of the Fortunate.'"

Pretty good insight, I thought.

CHAPTER 4

Reality

...so take courage and do it."

—Ezra 10:4

Journal entry, 18 January 1967—"Ten KIAs...gray day for the 2nd 'Hounds"

Reality sets in. Quite often it is followed by or accompanied by fear. But no soldier facing the trial of battle wants to admit to such an emotion as fear. He just faces reality and hopes for the best. His thought: "If the person next to me can deal with it, so can I."

In his book, *A Hundred Miles of Bad Road*, Dwight Birdwell got to the heart of reality quickly. As he awaited assignment, the old-timers and even more, the rear echelon guys, were full of less than consoling words.

"What's your MOS? Armor? O man! Let me tell you, there was an armor track out there on the perimeter the other night that got hit by a rocket propelled grenade. It burned 'em alive. Burned 'em to a crisp!"

Tom Brewer, in his book, *Searching for the Good*, got a full dose of reality when his assignment officer said, "You are being offered a choice of In Country assignments and you tell me you want the Wolfhounds? They have a high casualty rate and are always dropping into a hot LZ. Always in the boonies! No one ever sees them but Charlie. They just completed an operation up near Tay Ninh. They kicked some and got kicked a lot, too." Mothers and wives don't take well to introductions like that. They create anxiety for the strongest.

Reality explodes with certainty when you discover that adversaries use real bullets and that dead men don't rise again in this world. It splashed all around me at the sight of two young men who were killed the first hours of my first field operation. The people on the other side wanting to kill us, will be pleased to do it any way they can and they do not know that I am one of the "good guys." Two men, sleeping the eternal sleep, quiet and still, lay before me. Sadly, such became a common sight.

My education in reality progressed with my first staff meeting. Intelligence was that the place where we would be operating was crawling with NVA soldiers, a battalion or more, and that they were battled-tested troops. Even the name of the area of operation (AO) sounded sinister—Iron Triangle.

"We're going in with a double basic load of ammunition," the brigade CO informed us. "Tell your soldiers to load up with all the grenades and bandoleers they can carry. The first hours will be crucial," he continued. "Now men, we probably face a high casualty rate on this operation. I sincerely hope they won't be needed, but an extra supply of casualty bags will be in place for our use. Doc (Battalion surgeon), make sure your company medics have more supplies than they might normally take to the field." After questions had been addressed, the commander dismissed the meeting with, "Let's take it to 'em!"

That being my first of many similar pre-operation staff briefings, I came out of it with head spinning and heart thumping. We're talking about American youth getting killed and next of kin receiving dreaded notifications. How did the chaplain fit into all this? That was my next decision.

The last part of my reality trilogy came on a day while flying with Trojan Six through two refuelings of his C and C

Huey. I never did that again, but I used the occasion this once to get to know the CO better and learn how best to get to my "congregation" fast. When he'd land to confer with company COs, I'd use the time to hold a brief field service or visit with soldiers in their defensive positions or work stations. About an hour into the second refueling, we were circling over a small wooded area. In the woods a limited firefight was taking place. Trojan Six was in radio contact with the commander on the ground.

From the edge of the wooded area a figure in the familiar black pajamas appeared. He stopped to fire a couple of rounds in our direction, and began running along a narrow trail. His ChiCom rifle looked almost as long as he was tall. Trojan Six, speaking calmly, almost conversationally, said to the captain below, "We've spotted a man with a weapon running toward that little village north of your location. I'm going to drop lower and shoot him! Will be back on station in one zero (One Minute). And it happened just as he reported.

When we were low enough to be effective, the right door gunner took out the shooter just as he took aim at the approaching helicopter. I had seen people die, mostly in hospitals, but never at the business end of a .30 caliber machine gun. It was nothing like the cowboy movies, where there would be a lot of staggering, falling, rising, gasping, getting off another shot or two and finally lying in silence. The little man in black just crumpled and lay perfectly still. The pilot hovered at two feet while the crew chief jumped out and policed up the weapon. We were back on Command and Control station in one minute. I had just undergone more continuing education in reality...of war.

The 25th Division's Second Brigade had three combat battalions—the 1st of the 5th Mechanized, the 1st of the 27th Infantry and my bunch, the 2nd of the 27th Infantry (Wolfhounds). On occasion, I was asked to provide chaplain coverage for the 1/5 and the 1/27 if their chaplains were away for some reason. As was stated earlier, the 1/5 Mech chaplain, a Roman Catholic priest, invited me to conduct field services for his Protestant troops during the Boi Loi Woods operation. I came to have high respect for those Mechanized soldiers. Like any proud outfit, they wore their unit crest with pride. I would have the honor of setting up a field altar on the back of their personnel carriers again. It was an honor made possible by something one would never requisition.

The Second Wolfhounds had spent two weeks on an operation near Tay Ninh, and were tired and scroungy when they returned to Cu Chi. I had managed to change jungle fatigues about every three days but most of the soldiers were wearing the clothes they had on when the operation started. Same socks, too, making their feet prime targets for jungle rot, also known as immersion foot. They were ready for some hot chow and the relative comfort of an army cot. After a cold but welcome shower I took to my little sandbagged hut by the chapel like it was the grand suite in a grand hotel and planned the next few hours: Read some letters from home; write two; outline three Sunday services; nap. Halfway through the first letter, a runner from Battalion appeared at the screen door, "Hey, Chaplain, you in there?" he called out.

"Yeah, Lou. What's up?"

"The Colonel wants to see you. He's at the TOC. Can you come now?"

"Give me a couple of minutes to get into my boots and I'm on the way."

"Yes sir, I'll tell him you will be right over. Sorry to bother you."

Three minutes later I entered the Tactical Operations Center, a small steel structure with five layers of sandbags on its sides and roof. Lieutenant Colonel Sheldon was on the radio with Brigade. They were talking about 1/5 Mech, which had been ambushed as they were forming up to convoy back to base camp. The only casualties so far were three wounded, including the chaplain. Chaplain Tom Downes had been hit. How bad was not reported. My Battalion Commander wanted to know if I could work in a trip to the 1/5 on Sunday. He felt that news about their chaplain being WIA would take a toll on morale. Of course I agreed.

An APC from 1/5 picked me up at 1300 (1:00 PM) the next day and we sped to the first of three mess tents for chapel services. At the third one, Tom Downes was in attendance. Wounds he received the previous day were minor. A few small pieces of shrapnel had caused some small shoulder wounds for which he was treated at the battalion aid station and released. After the brief service and communion we had a chance to converse a few minutes.

He began, "I tell you, Chap, it happened so fast and unexpectedly. One second I'm riding merrily along on atop an armored vehicle and the next there is a tremendous explosion and I've got this stinging sensation in my shoulder. In a flash, the reality of danger and death settles in on you." There was that word "reality" again. It kept appearing and would for many months to come.

It was dark when the same vehicle, accompanied on the return trip by two jeeps mounted with M-60s, dropped me off at the Holy Hootch. It had been an activity-filled first day of the week: six chapel services, two communion services, seven counseling cases and one opportunity to rejoice with a grateful chaplain. I stood a minute between my house and the chapel and watched a slowly descending flare near the Ann Margaret and listened to a 175 battery send huge projectiles to some distant grid square.

On a crudely printed sign just outside Dau Tieng were these words: "Things Need! Here Buy. Good Qualy. Good Prize." Another entrepreneur hawking souvenirs. But none of the army vehicles had time to stop that day. Nearby, an element of the 1/27 was pinned down along a rice field berm by machine gun and sniper fire. Stingers (gunships) were hosing down the woodline a hundred meters away, but the firing continued. Only one enemy bullet found its mark and that was on an American who neither carried nor fired a weapon. Battalion Chaplain John Durham was hit in the back, supposedly by a sniper.

His injury was the news that greeted me upon returning from R and R in Taiwan. It had been a relaxing five days away, visiting with missionaries Barker and Graham in Taipei and Taichung. I do, by all means, think it is true that bad times don't last. But in this case, neither do the best of times, at least not for more than five days. Then it was back to reality and war, where people shoot at one another.

It was more personal and in bold letters this time: Another chaplain is WIA. Seriously wounded was the word. He was still in surgery at 0430 (4:30 AM) when I checked at 12th Evac Hospital. Though still a little groggy, he was able to speak when I saw him at noon. The surgeon was confident that John would recover, but his time with the 1/27 in Vietnam was over. I assured him that his soldiers would receive chaplaincy coverage. Tom McGinnes, Brigade Chaplain, would help see to that.

So for two weeks, until Chaplain Durham's replacement arrived, I had the privilege of ministering to all the Wolfhounds in the U S Army. During that time, any initial apprehension I may have had about "being next" evaporated. I recalled and quoted some words from the 23rd Psalm that I had learned as a child in the card class of Pleasant Springs Baptist Church near Monticello, Arkansas: *Yea, though I walk through the valley of the shadow of death, I will fear no evil: for thou art with me...*

How people in the local villages learned what was supposed to be highly confidential information came to be a thing of amazement to me. They seemed to know things before the American soldiers knew them. This was evident after my first Tay Ninh pre-operation briefing. Everything in that sinister sounding staff meeting was, Trojan Six said with emphasis, FYI (for your information) only. He reminded all personnel at the meeting that they should treat everything they had heard as top secret.

In midafternoon, Specialist Franks and I drove into Cu Chi village to pick up some laundry that belonged to several of the battalion staff officers, check on some orphan children, for whom we had been providing clothing, and regrettably to get some previously ordered engraved name plates.

"Big Cap," the little shoe shine boy I had met on my first trip into the "Ville," spotted our jeep and was right there by the passenger side when it stopped. He had already put the "Numma One, Dai Wei" tab on me because the first time he shined my boots I gave him 10 dong instead of the asking price of eight.

"Dai Wei chappin, numma one. VC numma ten!" he exclaimed. "You for me shine boot?"

I told him yes, even though a shine in the dust and grime of that land lasted only until the first step was taken. He got busy. That seven-year old knew his business. While brushing, daubing, shining and looking intently at the good results of his labor, he made a statement that sent me reeling: "Tomorrow you go Tay Ninh. Yes. You come back Tay Ninh you give me polish. Okay."

It was not a question, but more of a statement that one might make on Tuesday: Tomorrow will be Wednesday. He didn't pursue it, for to him it was a fact that tomorrow we'd be going to the place he named.

"Maybe next time I will bring you polish, Big Cap." I said and gave him 10 dong. (The price later doubled.) Where, I wondered, did that little guy learn classified information?

When the battalion arrived at the pre-arranged forward base camp, strung concertina around the perimeter and generally got set up for the night, the kids started arriving. Some were begging, others were selling tiny green bananas, pineapple and pastries that looked sort of like donut holes.

Among the dozen or so children was a little girl I had seen in Cu Chi village. She was a pretty child who looked about 10. Her specialty was chunks of fresh pineapple which she carried the way a waiter carries a tray of food. She was known to many of the soldiers as No Can Do. That name stuck because when someone tried to get pineapple for less than her asking price she would say, "No can do!"

I waved to her, paid her set price for a little plastic bag of pineapple, and silently asked myself, "How did this little girl know the exact place to go? How did she get here? She had to walk, and yet she arrived almost as soon as those who had made the trip in a fast moving military convoy. Evidently, she had gone up the day before, knowing that the battalion was on orders to move north. Big Cap had it right, "Tomorrow you go Tay Ninh?" If troop deployments were well known to the kids on the street, then the enemy would know as well, I thought. And wouldn't the ammunition carriers coming down the Ho Chi Minh trail know right where to drop off their mortar rounds?

Late that evening, Captain Royal, the battalion S-4, and I talked about how secrets come to be common knowledge to the wrong people. His thoughts on the subject made sense.

"Think about it," he began, "barbers on base hear soldiers talk. They may pretend to understand only words that relate to their work, like Hot Toc or close cut, but most of them understand a lot more. If a soldier getting a haircut asks his buddy to loan him a pair of socks for the operation in the Horseshoe or Michelin Rubber Plantation, the barber is quite capable of catching the meaning.

"Or, how about those little Mama Sans you see cutting grass with machetes? They observe soldiers packing rucksacks and loading trucks with supplies that are not used in garrison. They may even see you loading your field kit with Gideon New Testaments and extra pairs of socks and underwear. Like the barbers and other civilian laborers, they hear Duc Hahn B and Phu Hoa Dong and quickly put two and two together. And before you can say "sappers in the wire," the word gets passed on and maybe to the wrong citizens."

I told Royal that I, as a child during World War II, remembered a poster of Uncle Sam, finger pressed to his lips and the words, "Shhh. Loose lips sink ships." We agreed that talk in the wrong places was a serious breach. But a shoe shine boy? Knowing tomorrow we go Tay Ninh? Huhh!

It has long been known that American soldiers are soft touches for children. In all wars, at least in my memory, soldiers tossed candy and extra rations to kids along their line of march, made them unit mascots, obtained clothing and medical care for them and donated large portions of their monthly pay to support orphanages. Generally speaking, the GI trusts children and may tell them innocent sounding things that should not be revealed. Because of that trust, in Vietnam it was almost impossible for him to fathom that among the hordes of children surrounding his vehicle there might be one capable of removing the gas cap and dropping a thermite grenade in the tank. That children could be intelligence gatherers was almost incomprehensible. "This cute kid can't be a threat!" So, saying to children, wearing steel pots and boonie hats and flashing smiles for cameras, "I show pictures later, will be away, maybe 10 days, tomorrow I am going to Duc To, or Trang Bang, or Tua Hoa," was ill advised and may have compromised the mission.

The same respect holds true for women. Beyond the most obvious ways, American soldiers in general view women differently. A special respect for the female gender still lingers in the psyche of young men. Why is that? Maybe it is because they have mothers or sisters, or it could be from thoughts of a grandmother who raised them and gave sound advice. Such respect was quite clear in a story SSG Pinkston related. He told me the story as I stood by his hospital bed to which he would be confined for three more days.

Staff Sergeant Pinkston and his under-strength platoon were walking a narrow trail, one that was bordered on each side by thick underbrush. The area was laced with criss-crossing, maze-like pathways. He and an enemy soldier arrived at an intersection at the same time. Pinkston said he was carrying his M-16 at the ready position, the way he had been taught in numerous training exercises— finger on trigger, on automatic, ready, pointed chest level at a guy in a khaki uniform.

"But, Chaplain, it was not a guy. It was a girl," he said. "I saw and hesitated a split second. I must have hesitated because I remember thinking, 'this is a female!' She looked as surprised as I was, but she got off the first shot. It hit me in the right side. Clean through. In front, out back. The Doc says no vital organs were hit. Time stood still about then, but I must have shot her in less than a half second. She fell backward like a Mack truck had hit her and I don't think she ever moved. And you know something, Chaplain, even though she tried to kill me, I don't feel very good about wasting her. It just seems like a man ought not to shoot a woman!"

That story was still vivid on my mind when, several weeks later, something similar took place. The entry in my personal journal on 24 October 1967 began like this: "This was an unbelievably strange day. I'm sure I will never be able to explain it. About 0600 an ambush patrol from Bravo Company received automatic weapons fire…"

These many years later, those three sentences are enough to make me recall it as if it had taken place last week or yesterday. Though the fire on the AP was heavy and from several weapons, no one was hit. They immediately returned fire with M-16s, burning through at least two magazines each. While the rifles were firing, the M-79 man began lobbing in some grenades. A minute or so later, all was quiet. Bravo Company swept the area and discovered four bodies with automatic weapons lying behind them.

SP4 Sanders was recounting the episode and said, "Riflemen are supposed to be pleased when they win battles the way we won that one, yesterday. But we saw something when we swept the area that we had never seen before. I don't mind telling you that I came close to throwing up." There was a grimace on his face as his mouth formed the punch line: "The four soldiers lying dead beside their rifles were women." (It was later revealed that all four of the young Vietnamese women were nurses from Cu Chi district).

Specialist Sanders said he went behind a bullet-riddled hovel, dropped to his knees and prayed for a short time. "Chaplain Tucker," he stated in a whisper, "I don't ever get down like that to pray. Mostly, I just utter silent words before going to sleep or when we are humping it through the bush, but for some reason I found myself this time with both knees on the ground and head bent low. In a few seconds behind that little house, I thought about my little sister back home and I wondered if any of those four lying dead a few feet away had a child, or a brother or sister, or dreams for the future. I hoped they had at some serious moment in the past said, 'Lord, I believe.' Some of my buddies wouldn't understand, but I prayed for those who attempted to take us out."

His words left me searching for something to say. What could one think except that he had given renewed meaning to some words from the Gospel of Matthew: *But I tell you: love your enemies and pray for those who persecute you.* It shouldn't have been a surprise that the young soldier would express such empathy for four persons on the other side of the conflict. It was his God-given nature to be concerned about others. Military duties permitting, he attended chapel services in garrison and field services in bomb craters, in small jungle clearings or in mortar pits surrounded by sandbags.

With his touching words still on my mind, Sanders and I shook hands and he walked the short distance between the Wolfhound Memorial Chapel and Bravo Company. Back to work at getting ready for the next operation. His genuine concern for those women who had given their lives stayed vividly on my mind for hours. Little did anyone know that in less than three weeks—19 days—three dreaded capital letters, which I came to dislike almost more than anything, would refer to him. SP4 Sanders, E., age 20: KIA.

In late spring and early summer, Brigade began giving the 2/27 one assignment after another, with almost no down time. Maybe those orders were coming from Division, MACV, or even Washington. I had no way of knowing. Though a non-combatant whose knowledge of tactics and combined arms was limited, I could see that our soldiers were dragging their tracks out. Tired. Morale had spiraled downward. Many of the officers were physically and emotionally fatigued. Sleep deprived, too. One, a close friend and loyal to the chain of command, shared his concerns with me as someone who would listen and not betray his confidence. "Hey, Chap, if we keep this up some people are going to start making dumb mistakes and get hurt. And for what?" I understood what he was talking about and had experienced the reality of his concern in the past 72 hours.

Three days before our late night conversation, I had walked all day on a battalion search and rescue mission, moving with different units during the day. Sometimes I assisted medics with their litters. Sometimes I lugged a base plate for the mortar guys and at other times carried a metal container of .30 caliber ammunition for the machine gun crew. We fought mosquitoes and waded through the shin-deep water of rice fields. On three occasions, we forded murky canals and paused after each crossing only long enough to burn off leeches.

Three companies of weary soldiers and the Headquarters staff closed in on our night location at 1600 hours. A short time later, word came from somewhere that the battalion would not dig in for the night. At a hurried staff meeting we learned that in one hour we were to begin a night move to a grid coordinate six klicks (kilometers) away. A company commander, with whom I was sharing a canteen of lukewarm coffee, stated with frustration, "Somebody up at the head shed must be seeing stars, either on his chest or epaulet, or both…Okay, guys. Saddle up!"

The march began on time as ordered but with no small amount of grumbling and hurry-up-and-wait complaints. It was supposed to be silent. Everything that rattled was to be tied down. No talking. No lights. Don't bunch up. Keep the man ahead of you in sight. Painful, water soaked feet stumbled a lot. Weapons fell to the ground from hands that were finding it difficult to take tight grip. Finally at 0500, we closed on our second night location with barely enough strength left to dig shallow holes. The field first sergeants and platoon sergeants were forced to exert firm leadership to get their exhausted troops to set up a proper perimeter. I never learned, nor did I try to learn, what the night move was designed to accomplish, if anything. Like all those not on guard, I slept on the ground for a couple of hours, my combat chaplain's kit for a pillow.

The officer who confided in me was right. People started getting hurt needlessly. They started doing Charlie's work for him. Skin began coming off soles of feet. A "suspicious" toe wound, probably self-inflicted. Heat exhaustion. One death and several injuries from careless handling of hand grenades. The medics began asking, "What is going on?"

I got back to base camp two days before the battalion finally extracted and went directly to 12th EVAC. As I walked by one of the operating rooms, a hand reached out and grabbed a handful of my fatigue blouse and yanked. It was Doctor Bob Alexander, army surgeon, whom I had met and spoken with at length a few days before. As he pulled me inside the OR, a nurse held a pan of antiseptic water, indicating that I should wash my hands. At the same time, a medic was placing a mask over my nose and mouth. Washed hands were then pushed into rubber gloves and a light green surgical gown was pushed over my out-stretched arms.

All that took place in seconds. Captain Alexander motioned me to his side, saying as he did so, "I need another pair of hands. Hold this," and I grasped a small electric floodlight. "Keep the light directed so that it shines on both my hands," he instructed. "Hold this above your head." And one of the nurses gave me a bottle of intravenous fluid with tubes attached. I had no idea what was in the bottle. Maybe it was plasma or whole blood. As the surgeon's skilled hands worked in a soldier's mid-section, he mumbled something about the non-combat injuries from the Second Brigade. "What is happening out there these days?" He was not looking for an answer, which was good, because I definitely did not have one for him. But I kept thinking about what the officer had said several days before.

Growing up, especially in my early teen years, I aspired to be a medical doctor, one who made house calls and cured people with things taken from a little black bag. Doctor Robert Hyatt, a highly respected and much loved small town physician, used to carry a black bag on his rounds. Out of it he performed all kinds of miracles. Or so I thought, anyway. But the closest I ever came to medical school was the day Bob Alexander, from Okmulgee, Oklahoma, pressed me into service at the 12th Evacuation Hospital, Republic of Vietnam. My job must have been performed well. I held the bottle high with one hand and the light steady with the other. The soldier with a sucking chest wound made it. And reality, both of war and life in general, and struck again, and stuck.

CHAPTER 5

Night Sounds And Sights

You will not fear the terror of night.

—Psalm 91:5

Journal entry, 26 March 1967—Captain Royal whispered, "Hey, Chap, the bad guys are all round the perimeter. Go back to sleep!"

Easter came on the 25th of March that year. Scriptures and resurrection songs began with the Ambush Academy at 0730. After a brief devotional about the empty tomb, the ten soldiers in attendance wanted to sing an Easter favorite, "Were You There?" On the last verse, a teen GI who had a baritone voice that mimicked Johnny Cash, sang an acappella solo: "Were you there when He rose up from the dead? Were you there when He rose up; from the dead? Sometimes, I feel like shouting glory, glory, glory! Were you there when He rose up from the dead?" When he finished the other 18-19 year old GIs broke into grateful applause and I joined them. No stiffness in that Resurrection Sunday service, no coats and ties or Easter bonnets, no written liturgy, just sounds that still resonate.

Wolfhound Chapel was next at 0830. Lieutenant Howard led the recently formed choir of nine soldiers, seven of whom were recovering from minor wounds, in "He is Lord." We got a special treat when the lieutenant sang a down home gospel version of

"Wounded for Me," a beautiful hymn I had never heard. By 1100, Howard and I had completed a service with1/5 Mech, our third on that 1967 Easter morning. The day had so far been filled with quiet reminders of better times in a homeland far away. Things would become much noisier before the next day dawned.

At 1330, I hitched a ride with a convoy to Duc Hoa, conducted a field service and distributed several boxes of clothing to children who had assembled nearby. I was amazed at how orderly they lined up and patiently waited to receive items of clothing that had been sent by the WMU (Women's Missionary Union) of my former church in Weinert, Texas. Soldiers not then needed for security detail had a grand time handing out gifts and playing with the children, who loved rubbing the Americans' hairy arms.

At 1700, a half-loaded slick gave me a 20-minute ride from Duc Hoa to battalion forward. With darkness fast approaching, there was time for only one more field service, which was advertised in the chow line as an Easter Sunset service. It was held on the burned out remains of a building in a cane field and was broken up by snipers as the 50 plus GIs were saying "Amen" to the Lord's Prayer. That ending proved to be a harbinger of what the night would be like.

I dug a foot-deep trench on a canal levee near the Battalion CP. It was my lodging spot for the night. It was wide and long enough to hold an air mattress, over which I constructed a crude bamboo frame for a mosquito net. By then it was dark. Former calmness soon gave way to night noises, heightened anxiety and profound gratitude for the American soldiers dug in nearby.

Seated on the ground close to Major Loffert, the Battalion S-3, I learned that a resupply Chinook was in-bound with a basic load of ammunition. Since very little had been expended the last two days, some heavy contact must be expected, I surmised. Our mortar platoons began dropping rounds on the outer fringes of the landing zone, but lifted when the huge helicopter approached. Guided by S-4 personnel with strobe lights, the Chinook hovered progressively lower until its sling load of ammo made contact with the ground. Then it cut loose and flew away while the cargo was swarmed upon and carried to its respective destinations. I soon learned why the night resupply was more than a precautionary measure.

An inflated air mattress added a little comfort to the shallow hole in the ground. The green net kept some, but not all, the mosquitoes at bay. Large field rats sped by on occasion, sometimes colliding with the net. Fortunately none gnawed their way inside; not that night, anyway. Occasionally, a rifle shot could be heard in the distance, but our guys were not making a sound. A great Easter day had turned grim with the dark of night. I was on the verge of falling asleep when Captain Royal came by with his announcement: "We are surrounded. Go back to sleep!"

"Surrounded! What do you mean surrounded?" I asked. Still whispering, he said that LPs were detecting movement all along the perimeter, and that on the side opposite the canal it was quite heavy. He continued with another bit of information.

"In exactly four minutes from now a mad minute will commence. Be ready for a lot of noise and sounds of battle you may never have heard before. Most of the shooting should be our guys."

A mad minute? Sixty seconds of sustained fire would break the silence and create tremendous shock effect for those on the business end of 2/27 weapons. Every M-16 and every M-60 and .50 caliber would be firing into their assigned targets. Every mortar tube would be systematically pumping out rounds. For this show of power, no hand grenades would be thrown but the M-79 grenade launchers would be part of it.

Timing could not have been better. Thirty seconds before the mad minute's kickoff, we took some sniper fire. I could see tracer rounds zipping across the levee thirty or forty feet from my too-shallow foxhole. I reached up and pulled the plug on my air mattress. That act lowered me only about an inch but as the air escaped it felt like a foot or more.

A glance at my watch told me it was time. And was it ever? The firing did not begin sporadically, with one shot here and another there, but all at once. Every watch must have been perfectly synchronized because everything went off with one huge bang and continued, without any noticeable let up, for almost a full minute. It seemed more like ten or fifteen. I could only imagine the terror of being on the receiving end of all that. Surely nothing for 300 yards, four feet and below could survive a fusillade like that. And as suddenly as it started, it stopped. For a few seconds, the entire area was shrouded in deadly silence. Quiet, as in the eye of a storm.

Sleep was impossible after that display. Nor was sleep advised, because a half-hour later Charlie company and the Recon platoon's sector detected heavy movement again. More night sounds on the way. First, Spooky appeared and lit up the area with flares. He was soon ordered to vacate in favor of another type of aircraft—Puff the Magic Dragon. In the distance, Puff's tracers looked like colored liquid spewing slowly and harmlessly from a nozzle, spraying back and forth across some distant garden. The sound from it was similar to that of a baseball card being struck by the spokes of a fast pedaled bicycle.

"Pete," I inquired of Captain Elson, "do you know the volume of ordnance that baby is pumping out?" He said Gatling-type rotating machine guns, mounted in a C-47 cargo plane were capable of firing 6,000 rounds per minute.

It was a long night. At about 0300 Charlie Company's sector came under attack by what was later identified as an element of the 269th NVA Regiment. Their early morning move proved to be ill fated. The open field, across which they attacked, was pre-set in our artillery's computers. The forward observer only had to give the word: "Fire mission. Fire for effect." The rounds were headed our way in seconds.

The close-in fire support and .30 caliber machine guns resulted in a lot of casualties outside the perimeter. The only things remaining at first light when Recon swept the battle site were a few articles of clothing and some personal items that the NVA soldiers had dropped during their hasty retreat. It was here that the Recon platoon leader discovered the mandolin that eventually became a welcome addition to the Wolfhound Regimental museum at Schofield Barracks.

With all the probing, sniping and attempts to break through the perimeter, not a single American soldier was injured during that unusual Easter and the morning after. Sgt. Burton, who had a close call helping with the Chinook's sling load of ammunition, commented that it was almost like he had gone into the depths and out again like Jesus did.

At first, it is difficult to tell the difference between "incoming" and "outgoing" when the subject is rocket or mortar fire. To the uninitiated the sound is about the same until one actually experiences an "incoming" up close. I had been with the 2/27 almost three months before going through a mortar attack at Cu Chi base camp. Never again was there any problem distinguishing between the sounds after hearing the first one splash and send its hot steel every direction.

I was in my hut attempting to compose a sympathy letter to Lieutenant Ray Steward's wife, when a tremendous explosion occurred near the Officer's Club about 75 yards away. For the first time ever, but not the last, I jumped into the two feet by three feet hole that had been dug and sand bagged for the chaplain's use. I didn't stop to check for spiders, but I knew they were there. Several more mortar rounds fell in the battalion area but they seemed to be "walking" toward the huge ammunition yard where thousands of artillery rounds were stored.

After a minute or two, I grabbed my helmet and ran toward the TOC near which I thought one of the first rounds had hit. It was darker than any midnight I'd ever known, with no moon and no artificial light of any kind. On the way, I bumped into someone and identified myself as the chaplain, hoping that the person I had encountered was a friend, not a stranger wearing black pajamas and carrying a satchel charge. He wasn't. It was the maintenance warrant officer who recognized my voice.

"Do you know what happened?" I asked him.

"The first round hit our 100 kilowatt generator and the second one hit on the path between here and the TOC. At least that's the word I've gotten so far."

"Do you know if anyone has been hit?" I wanted to know.

"I heard two new guys in temporary quarters may have gotten it. Hope that's wrong."

I knew that would be Lieutenant Neptune, our recently arrived Medical Service Corps officer and Tom Brewer, an infantry captain, who would probably be commanding a line company soon. I had seen them both earlier in the evening at the O Club, which was just a large tent anchored to a wood floor. I rushed down to the aid station, hoping to learn something and dreading what it might be.

They were both there. Neptune was severely wounded in his upper back and the back of his head. He appeared to be very seriously injured. The medics were not optimistic about the young officer who had recently come on board to be their boss. Captain Brewer, who had literally dragged and carried Neptune to the aid station, had received some shrapnel wounds also. The battalion surgeon removed the small pieces of steel and bandaged the wounds they had caused. The doctor saw no reason to admit Tom to the hospital. A few months later, Tom would begin seeing the inside of numerous operating and hospital rooms.

Every time I recall and relive the events of that evening, I become more convinced that Tom Brewer saved the life of Lieutenant Neptune. It was Brewer's foresight and fortitude that got the badly wounded young man to the right place in a hurry. The next day his condition was still uncertain. From that day until the spring of 2011, I didn't know if he was dead or alive. But at a Wolfhound reunion in Branson, Missouri, we met again for the first time in 44 years. Knowing how near he had come to having his name engraved on the black marble memorial wall in Washington, D.C., I was thrilled beyond words. Some stories do have a good ending.

By 2200 (10:00 p.m.), the splat of incoming rounds had stopped. There were flares over an area where the firing was thought to have originated. A battery of 105s was saturating the area with high explosive rounds. Otherwise, things were relatively calm. Though it was late, I decided to make a trip to the hospital to see if there had been other casualties. As I parked the Wolfhound Watcher (my jeep) near triage, an all too familiar sound caught my attention. Dustoffs! UHI helicopters (Hueys) had been pressed into service.

Maybe it was psychological or my imagination, but I had come to think that I had the ability to tell if a Huey was transporting KIAs just by the sound they made on approach to the hospital. It seemed that if KIAs were aboard the blades beat the air with a sound that was different from that of a supply helicopter or a commander's C and C ship. Even in my hootch, a mile away from the hospital, I would sometimes be awakened to that blade-against-air-beat and think, "O Lord, how many are on board?" More often than not, it would prove to be true that casualties had come in at that very hour.

The KIA-sound was especially distinguishable when two or more choppers came in together. It was like one was saying to the others, "let me in first to unload my precious cargo," or "you go first, while I clear the tears away." Those "different" sounds of identical aircraft surely must have been my imagination, but once you hear so many and, standing in the prop wash, observe so many combat boots with feet perfectly vertical and still, maybe a sixth sense comes temporarily into play. Miraculously, there were no other casualties from the mortar attack. The dustoffs I heard had transported multiple WIA from the 1/27, the Second 'Hounds' sister battalion.

All chaplains in Vietnam were encouraged to attend semi-annual conferences hosted by the senior chaplain's office. The meetings were designed to provide training updates. But they also gave chaplains an opportunity for fellowship with professional contemporaries, eat a meal or two at a real table and sleep in a guest house or hotel for a couple of nights. The latter served as a uniquely welcome respite for those who served in combat units such as the 25th or 101st Divisions.

As for me, I could take or leave such conferences and didn't find them all that helpful. Chaplain Branscum and I reconnected at the only one I attended. Our paths had crossed briefly at Fort Polk a few months earlier, and I had even dropped in at his Vietnam location for a few hours. What a place that was, with a swimming pool and magnificent view of the South China Sea. "Is this Vietnam, too?" I wondered. I also met Edward Willis, chaplain for the R and R center at Vung Tau. Both of them knew something of the 2/27 Wolfhounds, mostly from the numerous news stories in the *Pacific Stars and Stripes*. They both expressed interest in visiting my unit in the future. Their words, though spoken at different times, were almost identical, "I'd like to see how it is out there!" That was understandable for they rarely heard a gunshot.

Chaplain Branscum came first. Three companies had just returned from a three-day operation the day he arrived. Several had been injured by a command-detonated mine as they came near their pick up zone (PZ) so two of the eight ships that flew in staggered trail to pick up grunts had to do dustoff duty first. Six men who expected to be having a hot meal at their company mess tent were hospitalized instead.

"Jim," I said to Chaplain Branscum, "I really need to see some wounded guys in the hospital. You are welcome to go with me if you like." He wanted to go, saying that he'd like the opportunity to visit the hospital with me. We went to triage first, where there was a frenzy of activity. I located two of my guys right away. One was missing his left foot and half of his left hand. Though sedated, he was in intense pain and calling for his mom. The other had a vicious wound in the right rib cage. Shrapnel of some kind, a large piece, had hit him in the side and ripped out a softball-sized chunk of tissue and bone. He was conscious but his eyes appeared to be unseeing. I wet a piece of gauze with water from my canteen and placed it on his forehead. His lips moved slightly but made no sound.

From triage we went to the burn ward where patients were being stabilized for a move to bigger hospitals, first to Japan or Okinawa and then to the USA. I quickly located my soldier and bent low to speak with him. His ears had been burned off. His head was a solid scab. The only parts of his face that looked remotely like what he had been born with were his lower lip and chin. Had he been able to smile he probably would have, as he did almost constantly before his injury.

"Don't forget, we love you and pray for you every day," I said. "Things are going to get better, you just watch. It will take a while, but you are going to come back from this and have a good life." He whispered a labored "thank you" and three words that deeply touched Jim and me: "Jesus...my...Lord."

When we got back in the little army jeep, Chaplain Branscum was drained, almost void of color. He could barely walk, or talk either, and it took him a minute to get composed enough so that he could utter a word. "Tuck," he finally was able to get out, "Do you deal with things like this a lot?"

"Unfortunately, Jim. Yes! Burn injuries are unusual for the leg infantry, but the Mech guys and Tankers know such injuries are a reality, especially if they face a enemy that has RPGs. I'm constantly amazed at these kids. They fight hard, support each other, perform unbelievable tasks, get very little recognition, suffer horrible injuries...and die."

"I don't see how you do it! I really don't see how you do it! I know we are in war, but those are sights that, for some reason, I never expected to see. Those three guys we saw almost sent me into a doubled-over state of sickness. Man, how do you do it?"

"Admittedly," I said, "it takes some doing with a lot of deep breaths. What I don't see is how *they* do it, how those teenage boys and twenty-something leaders do it. To me, that is the real mystery."

My good friend hitched a ride with a pilot who agreed to drop him off at Long Binh. He entered the 25th Base Camp at 1500 and left at 1630. Ninety-minute education!

In mid-July, Ed Willis, the Vung Tau chaplain I had met earlier, came up for a visit. He wanted to see how the infantry lived and I had offered to show him. While we were having a cup of coffee with the battalion S-3, I asked him if he'd like to accompany me to the Horseshoe where I needed to do some follow-up counseling and have a field service with Alpha Company. "You'll definitely see how the grunts live," I told him. "They are presently in an AO that sometimes gets pretty hot. We've taken a lot of casualties in that little strip of land." He said he'd like to do it so I obtained some field gear for him and we were on our way with the first available resupply chopper.

A 1300 field service was publicized at noon chow. Chaplain Willis and I talked with soldiers who were waiting to receive their first hot meal in four days. As always, the young men were pleased to chat informally and share concerns as well. A dozen or so formed a semi-circle on the ground for our scheduled service. We were still on verse one of "O Beautiful for Spacious Skies," when an AK-47 began throwing lead our direction from about 200 meters away. That broke up church in a hurry. Chaplain Willis and I rolled into the waist-deep water of a nearby canal. The soldiers, weapons at ready, ran back to their respective platoons and fighting positions.

The sniper had fired only 10-12 shots our way before friendly 105 artillery rounds, on course for the shooter's location, began whistling overhead. The high explosive rounds would land and the rifle shots would stop momentarily. The 105 battery would stop and the AK47 would start again. It became like a game I once played as a child—"I Dare You-You Dare Me!" That went on for several minutes. None of the sniper rounds came close to our hiding place in the canal or to any of the Alpha Company soldiers. Still, the shooter was a nuisance and had to be silenced.

I could hear the Forward Observer's instructions to the artillery guys at a firebase a few kilometers away. "Right, five zero. Down, two five. Left, six zero." He was walking the HE (High Explosive) rounds along a wood line that served as the shooter's cover. During the exchange between the sniper and U S Artillery, more than a hundred 105mm rounds fell on that small strip of woods. I later learned the exact number was 106. The FO's radio operator summed it up well: "Man, that guy with the rifle was a costly little dude!"

In only a few hours of field duty in a combat zone, Chaplain Willis got a small taste of what infantry soldiers go through. It was a most unusual experience for him. I got the impression that he didn't like it very much. I understood why he wouldn't. The first time under fire, even if minor and relatively harmless, raises the anxiety to levels not known before. Sights and sounds out there were vastly different from ones most had ever seen or heard. You never get completely used to them and you are pleased when they are no longer there.

CHAPTER 6

Finding A Way

There is hope…you will look about you and take your rest in safety.

—Job 11:18

Journal entry, 30 January 1967—"War does strange things to people."

Miserable! Combat troops were rarely comfortable or much above the miserable stage. The monsoon season made things even worse. One of the vivid memories WWII veterans have of the winter of 1944-45, especially during the Battle of the Bulge, is temperature. They were always cold and could never get warm. Those who served in South Vietnam have a similar memory, especially during the rainy season. They were always wet and could never get dry. Many problems accompanied the heavy rainfall. Transportation, both land and air, was difficult at best and often impossible. Rust on weapons. Upsurge of mosquitoes. Suddenly swollen streams that had to be crossed. Men drowned. Inability to use a pinch of C-4 to heat a cup of coffee. Water soaked jungle fatigues, boots and socks. Skin turning rubbery and peeling off the soles of feet.

It was the latter—soldier's foot problems—that Trojan Six spoke about in the midst of a downpour. We stood face to face a foot apart and could barely discern what the other was saying.

He was yelling. I was straining to hear. Then the rain stopped as quickly as it had started. During one of the lulls, we pulled the poncho hoods from our helmets to better converse. He shared a deep concern that was on his mind.

"Chaplain, do you think you'll be going back to base camp, tonight?" he asked.

"Yes sir, I need to make some hospital calls. If a bird drops in I'll try to get on it."

"Good, that ought to work out. I'd like you to do something for me. I guess you know our doctor (Battalion Surgeon)?" the Battalion Commander said. I did know him. "He needs to come out and take care of some ailing soldiers. Some of these guys have such bad feet they can hardly walk. Immersion foot is causing us more problems than the Viet Cong right now. Last Wednesday, I learned that Doc was due back from R and R the next day. What is this, Monday? And we still have not seen him. You don't have to tell him this, but if he doesn't get out here and apply some of his medical skills to these feet and sniffles, he is not going to be pleased with my next recommendation."

I took a resupply chopper out just before dark. It landed at Division Headquarters in a heavy rain. We could barely see the landing pad from a hundred feet altitude. But, as always, I was amazed at the skill of those young pilots. I hitched a ride to the hospital and from there to the 2/27 battalion area and the Holy Hootch. A dry set of fatigues and socks made things feel better as I made my way to the battalion surgeon's quarters.

"Doc," I said to him, "the commander needs your help in the field. There are a lot of bad feet and, according to one of the company medics, some possible upper respiratory cases as well. We can't get back out tonight but what do you say we take an early flight tomorrow? All the mess halls will be taking hot breakfast to their units. My chaplain assistant will drive us to the chopper pad. I'll give you the take-off time when I learn it."

The doctor had never been to battalion forward during his few months in country although he had participated in a couple of Med Caps in nearby villages. At 0600 the next morning, he was at the agreed on meeting place and in five minutes we were at the chopper pad. Three-quarter ton trucks hauling steaming cans of chow and coffee were right behind us. We climbed aboard the Slick and sat on the steel deck. The pilot yelled, "Clear," and hit the button.

The battalion surgeon and I were the only passengers on that flight. The look on the doctor's face reflected anxiety and fear. Then I saw something else. He had a .45 pistol in his right hand. He was waving it back and forth the way a briefer would point to numbers on a chart. I glanced up at the door gunner who had also seen the waving side arm. He gave a slight shrug and facial twist that carried a non-verbal message: "What's with this guy flying at 1800 feet with an unholstered .45?" Was there a round in the chamber? We did not know. Had the physician gone through any training on the use of that weapon? No way of knowing that either, but I thought the answer was probably "no."

We came straight into a cold LZ, but the gunners were alert, swinging their M-60s in the direction their eyes were looking. I jumped out as the company KPs ran out to unload the containers. Doc hesitated, reluctant to jump off the chopper that needed to get airborne again. I reached to assist with some of his supplies and yelled above the engine noise, "We're here, Doc. Let's go!" He finally jumped off, a medical bag in his left hand, the pistol still in his right.

One of his company medics escorted him to the field aid station where, I was told, sick call was due to begin almost immediately. After a breakfast of pancakes and bacon with Alpha Company, I began visiting among soldiers and distributing the ten pairs of new (and dry) socks I'd been able to scrounge from the Headquarters Company supply sergeant. Except for the intermittent hard rain, things were pretty quiet. Once in a while, a gunshot could be heard 500 meters or so out. There seemed to be no concern that it might come from a weapon pointed our way.

After about four hours and two field services, I began my way back to the aid station to see if the doctor would like to share in a delicious C-Ration lunch. I was also prepared to assist him in getting set up for his first night in the field, although I assumed he'd want to stay with his medics. They had a nice little bunker with overhead cover.

"Hey, Sarge," I said to the NCO sitting at a small table near the bunker entrance, "has the doctor seen a lot of foot cases? He did let the battalion commander know he was out here, didn't he?"

"I took him to see the colonel right after the chopper dropped him off," he told me. "I set up for sick call while they were talking. He came back here to the aid station, looked at some feet and gave out some medicated foot powder and a few cold packs. The sound of that rifle in the distance made him nervous, I could tell. A few minutes later, he told me that he was going to see someone he knew near the LZ. When he hadn't returned a half-hour later, I set out to see if I could find him. The sick call line was long. I asked some guys at the LZ if they had seen him. They told me he jumped on a Huey that had brought out water and Cs. And that was it. Mysterious as all get out!"

"You mean he left without telling anyone? He has gone back to base camp?"

"Evidently, Chaplain. That's what the guys told me. Trojan Six is not going to be pleased with that exit, is he?"

"My guess is 'not pleased' would be putting it mildly."

When I returned to Cu Chi two days later, the battalion surgeon had departed the premises. No one I spoke with seemed to know where he went or when he left, although I was confident he left with official orders. I never broached the subject with Trojan 6 and he didn't volunteer anything. The personnel officer would have told me the story, I suppose, but knowing wouldn't have changed anything. The doctor was just transferred to another duty station. That's all I ever knew or needed to know. His replacement, a younger physician who appeared to thrive on living in the boonies with the 11Bs (riflemen), arrived two weeks later. He found his way. Hopefully the other one did too.

"Tomorrow? You are leaving for The World, tomorrow?" I responded to Specialist Manuel's report. He had caught me in my hootch late at night and dropped in to say goodbye. Bruce was a full-blood Native American. We had seen one another often over the past few months, both in base camp and in the field.

"Bruce, time does go on, doesn't it? I remember when we first met, not long after I joined the Wolfhounds. You were an old-timer and I was a newbie."

"I remember it, too. You talked to me in the mess hall one day and a couple of times in the Hound House (Enlisted Men's club)," he said. "But on Christmas day—December 25, 1966—I came by your cabin and we talked a long time. I had been drinking nearly all day, sir. I was half drunk. You didn't get on my case about smelling of alcohol and you didn't call me 'Chief' either. Chaplain, I remember that. You called me by my name and not Geronimo or Crazy Horse or Chief. Why does a man remember stuff like that?"

All that came back to me. When we were in base camp, he made it a point to drop in almost every day, usually in the early evening. He was taciturn, but during our times together he would often open up and talk up a storm. Fellow soldiers, except for his own rifle team, hardly knew him at all except as Pima 'Chief,' an epithet that was not offensive to him, but he was pleased when someone called him Bruce. I was the recipient of a special accolade from him that Christmas Day, the cost of which was little but meant much, hopefully, to both of us. He avowed that I was his best friend.

Now it was May 8, 1967, half a tour from the prior Christmas. It was the day that Lieutenant Doug Collander, A 1-6, and PFC Jones received booby trap wounds. Manuel was going home. I thanked him for coming by and asked if he had any wishes for the future in addition to returning home in one piece? He said he would like to have a job that would support the wife he hoped to have one day and that he could stop drinking—not just cut back but stop altogether.

"Every time I think about it, I will pray that your wishes will become realities," I promised him. Thirty years after returning from Vietnam, I read my journal for the first time and have gone through it annually ever since. When the May 8 entry is read, I think about Bruce, utter a prayer, and wonder how things turned out for him. I often wonder if he became a total abstainer. Maybe he did. I hope so, for he badly wanted to.

Ironically, the next day, SP5 Kennelly came by before daylight with an almost identical wish. His words, "Chaplain, I want to stop 'boozing it up' because I'm starting to do things I don't remember."

Kennelly was truly a clean-cut young man, a really strike 18 year-old soldier and field medic. (To be a Specialist Five, the same rank as a three-striper sergeant was phenomenal for one who had been in the army such a short time.) He had joined two days after his 17th birthday. Were my words and friendship any help at all? I wonder still and well remember thinking, "This teenager, whose high school class graduates this month, has too many problems to be concerned about memory loss due to alcohol consumption." Something tells me he defeated the demons and traveled on a good path, one on which he is still walking to this day.

One of my sisters lived in East Point, Georgia. A letter from her revealed that a family with whom she and her family attended church had a son in Vietnam. His name was Gary Jones, the executive officer for one of our Wolfhound companies. I knew Gary well. We had talked many times but had not made the connection between our family members in Georgia.

Busy leaders don't have much time for anything but taking care of their soldiers, staying adequately trained and doing all the things necessary to make an operation successful. But in the rare stand-downs and during slack times in the field, Gary and I found some moments to talk about home and the future. Later, our conversations turned more in depth, reaching to a counselor/counselee level.

That was after he had met Ann Cunningham, a delightful young nurse at the 12ᵗʰ Evac hospital. The Second Wolfhounds claimed Ann as "their nurse" and she claimed them as her soldiers. Of course, as an ER and an OR nurse, she saw injuries of the worst kind and they all hurt her deeply. Though she couldn't show it, her hurt was greater when a member of the 2/27 lay seriously wounded on a gurney or table in front of her. Most of the single officers, and maybe the non-singles as well, "fell in love" with Lieutenant Cunningham. But she fell in love with Gary Jones only.

With the hectic schedules they had, their rendezvous times were few and very brief. When the battalion was in base camp on Sunday and when things were slow at 12ᵗʰ Evac, Ann would attend chapel with Gary. That something special was going on between them became obvious to close friends. Something electric, as when a young man and woman fall in love. Potential suitors saw it too. They continued to flirt with Ann but it was no longer serious. Among those who knew, competition ceased.

One Sunday after chapel, Gary and Ann asked if I had a few minutes for them. Of course, I said yes. When the chapel was emptied except for the three of us, they sat on the front pew and I pulled up a plastic chair in front of them. They were holding hands and Ann, tough combat nurse that she was, appeared a little nervous.

"Chap," Gary said, "Annie and I plan to get married one of these days. It will have to be when things settle down and when we get back to the States." Ann squeezed his hand tighter and gave him a look that only a person in love can give. Then she spoke.

"Would you be willing to perform our wedding ceremony if we don't wind up at duty stations too widely separated?"

I told them that I was on orders for Ft. Sill, Oklahoma, and assured them that distance would not be a factor. "I am honored to be asked and will be there to lead you in the vows no matter when or where they take place," I said to them. After two more pre-marital sessions, we were set. The ceremony would take place at some future date and probably at some chapel on a military post in the United States. "Uncertain certainty," we called it. I saw Gary three days and Annie one day before I left for the U.S.

"See you in a few months," both said. "We'll let you know where and when!"

But the wedding never took place. Gary was about to become a company commander when I left for home. Two months later, on February 8, 1968, he was killed during the infamous Tet Offensive. I learned from a mutual friend that Annie was on duty at 12th Evac hospital when a dustoff helicopter brought Gary in. It was a traumatic time in the trauma unit. They were both 24. Gary had been awarded a Bronze Star with V device the previous July, a ceremony I witnessed. A year later he was posthumously awarded the Distinguished Service Cross for extraordinary heroism during the military operation in which his young life was snuffed out.

Annie never married. In 2007, she died of a massive stroke while attending, of all things, a reunion with her beloved Wolfhounds. I had the honor of doing the eulogy at her memorial service in Charlottesville, Virginia. During the service, I thought about that Sunday morning in Vietnam when she and Gary broke the news of their future plans.

Chaplains who serve with combat troops hear a lot of bizarre things and deal with the unusual and unexpected. Tried and true counseling techniques sometimes have to be cast aside and replaced with something that fits the immediate situation. One day, a soldier came to tell me that he wanted to get out of the army and that he had three ways to do it.

"Three ways? What are we dealing with here? Hardship? Inability to adjust? Compassionate reasons? Conscientious objector? Can you give me a little more about why you so badly need to get out? What are these three ways?" I asked him.

"Chaplain, I just got to thinking that I'd be happier with my friends back home and came up with three things that would get me out. I've put lot of thought to it. First, I could slug an officer. I could just walk right up to him and hit him hard with my fist. Second, I could slug a sergeant the same way. Hit him when he's not looking."

About that time I thought, "O my, what's next? Don't tell me it is going to be, 'I could slug a chaplain'?" But then he got a quizzical look on his face and said, "I can't recall what the third thing is right now." Breathing a sigh of relief, I suggested that maybe two would be sufficient anyway. He said he guessed that was right.

"How about something like this," I said to him. "Maybe you could consider just sucking it up and going on. You are healthy and fit. You can hump it with the best of them. You have already been through the worst part of it, haven't you? That part where the drill sergeants were yelling, calling you worthless nerds and other names you don't hear in Sunday School, right?"

"Maybe I could just suck it up," he said, "At least, I'm getting paid a little bit, and I sure don't have a job waiting back home or a college begging me to enroll."

"Sounds like good thinking to me. One thing for sure, you don't want to wind up in LBJ (Long Binh Jail) for socking your platoon leader in the nose." I printed some words from Ecclesiastes, chapter 9, verse 10 on a card and gave it to him: *Whatever your hand finds to do, do it with all your might.* He folded the card and placed it securely in his helmet band.

"Don't you go slugging anyone now, especially chaplains," I said, laughing as I spoke.

With a grin, he promised not to. I was confident he meant it. It doesn't always work out just as you would like but there are times when you find a way.

CHAPTER 7

Remembering

It is bad for a nation when it is without faith.

—Anonymous

Journal entry, 10 February 1967—"Built memorial wall with a dull saw…late at night."

If you are able, save them a place inside you,
and save one backward glance
when you are leaving the places they
can no longer go.
Be not ashamed to say you loved them,
though you may not have always.
Take what they have left and what they have
taught you with their dying,
and in that time when men decide and
feel safe to call the war insane,
take one moment to embrace those
gentle heroes you left behind.

—Major Michael O'Donnell
Vietnam—January, 1970

By the end of January, just 54 days after joining the Wolfhounds, I counted the major cost thus far. We had lost 27 soldiers. Twenty-seven guys, average age 22 years and one month, would never go home again under their own power. Those two months, less seven days, accounted for more than 50 wounded. Reality struck again and said, "The officer making assignments had it right, this is indeed an outfit that is always in a 'kicking contest.'" The night of February 2 was spent with Bravo Company at a vast tunnel complex. It was a relatively quiet night, but I was awakened at 0200 (2:00 AM) by a thought, something closely akin to a vision. These words kept running through my mind: Memorial Wall! Memorial Wall! Something to remember those men who had died and, perish the thought, others that may die, was what I took the thought (vision) to be.

I went back to base camp on February 9 to assist with a special religious service in the Division Chapel. Due to transportation problems, my plans to go back out again early on the 10th fell through. Remembering that week-old "vision," I located a 4 by 8 sheet of three-quarter inch plywood, borrowed a dull hand saw and began constructing a memorial wall at the back of the Wolfhound Chapel, working from a crude drawing on a piece of cardboard.

My amateur carpentry skills, with some help from Curtis Lerdahl, chaplain assistant, were put to work all that day and far into the night. By midnight, a 3 by 8 foot table-like device was covered with naugahyde. It was placed in plain sight of all those who might exit by the rear screen door. Before going to bed, I went back through my KIA list and visualized how the names would be placed on small brass plates and how they would be attached to the memorial wall. At the center of the wall would be a larger brass plate engraved with the words, "In Memory of Second Wolfhounds Who Gave Their Lives in Defense of Freedom."

The next morning, Curtis and I went into Cu Chi village and located a little shop that specialized in plaques and engraving. Within a week, I began attaching the names, beginning with Tracker Dog Handler PFC Bobby Hudson, Lake City, Florida. Ten months later, SP4 Robert Parker, Delta Company, from

Ponca City, Oklahoma would be the last plate attached. Between those two would be the names of 92 others. Ninety-four men, ages 18 to 45, who made the supreme sacrifice.

Doubts began to creep in after a few days. *Maybe the memorial wall should not be on display*, I thought. It entered my mind that maybe soldiers would look at it and say to themselves and others, "Man, I'll probably be next," or "I wonder if the guys who may see my name on this board will even care?" Such things really bore on my mind. I didn't want to turn the chapel into something that simply reminded soldiers of their mortality.

One day, those fears were alleviated as I observed three soldiers, recently returned from a tough two weeks in the Ho Bo Woods. They stood side by side in front of the wall. If they talked at all it was a whisper. Each would point out a name to the others, then all three would rub their fingers across it. They would just brush fingers lightly across the two square inches of brass. That done, they would move to another name, evidently to all those they had known.

Then I saw something only one time, but seeing it once was enough and very touching. An 18 year-old combat veteran bent over and touched his lips to a name. His friends did not make light of that gesture. Instead they patted their saddened buddy on the back and walked out, momentarily holding hands the way some football teams do in a huddle. As I observed that silent act from behind the hanging beads that separated my tiny office from the sanctuary, I swallowed a couple of lumps the size of golf balls.

The memorial service for 12 men from Bravo Company who were KIA in a command detonated minefield was held in late January. At least half of the 12 were regular chapel attenders, young men I had come to know well in my first six weeks with the battalion. That was by far the largest number I had memorialized in a single day. Genuine rest was evasive that night. Much of it was spent wondering and thinking about ways to adequately honor and remember.

It may be that seeds for that later "vision" were sown that night. From what my assistant told me later, I must have fixated on that project. Once started on the wall, I barely stopped for anything. I measured, sawed, nailed and tried hard to complete it. Around 1800 hours, I suggested that Curtis get some food and call it a day. But I stayed on, thinking about the project, but even more about the numerous letters that needed to be written and mailed to Venice, California; Columbus, Mississippi; Tampa, Florida; Prichard, Alabama; Little Rock, Arkansas and seven other cities where loved ones had already been notified that their soldier would not be returning. My letters would be an attempt to give some solace and assurance that their special family member had been remembered by his friends and close associates in a far away land. All the letters, 94 eventually, were sealed with a prayer that the words they contained might help a little.

Thankfully, sadness doesn't last forever and bad news can be tempered with good. I needed something to get past the loss of so many at once, and I got it in a letter from my wife. "Our son, Paul, was saved this week!" she wrote. That was a report I badly needed, one that turned a deep valley into a mountain peak. He would be baptized a week later. That was memorable also.

Soon after the Memorial Wall was in place and affixed with 39 names, the Division Commander visited the 2nd of the 27th battalion. It was unusual for stars to show up in our area but I looked up and there he was. The 'Hounds were on a three-day stand down and everyone was in. I was gluing Lieutenant Steward's name to the Wall when I saw the Major General's party coming down the walk, which we had constructed from ammo boxes.

He had stopped to read the words on a professional quality sign my assistant had painted and placed on two posts that stood on either side of the walk that led to the chapel. These words were prominently displayed: *Through Here Pass the World's Finest Soldiers. The 2nd (and best) Wolfhounds.* He read the words slowly, nodded his head and smiled. His entourage included the 2nd Brigade Commander, who also smiled.

Later, with some of the staff and company commanders in the O club, I tried to confirm that Brigade Six had smiled. "Yes, he did. I tell you, he smiled." I reported with emphasis. But they, jokingly I think, accused me of coming close to an infraction forbidden in the Bible—telling a falsehood. "You know what one of the Big Ten says," one laughingly remarked, "Thou shalt not bear false witness."

"Well, maybe it was an illusion caused by the sun and shadows," I said.

I followed correct protocol in greeting the general and those with him. The battalion commander (Trojan Six) made the formal introductions to the 25th Division commanding officer, the Second Brigade CO, the Division Sergeant Major and others. Of course I had met the brigade commander previously.

"Chaplain," the Major General said, "I have heard about the means of remembering and honoring fallen soldiers that has been installed in the chapel and wanted to see it while I'm out this way."

"Yes sir," I said, and led the group to the place where the memorial wall was placed on the right side of the rear chapel door. The general stood and silently surveyed the blue imitation leather-covered shelf for a few seconds, then bent over and read some of the 39 names. He wanted to know how I had arrived at the idea of constructing and displaying such a memorial. I didn't mention the "dream/vision," but simply stated that it had crossed my mind one night that these Wolfhounds ought to be remembered with some kind of special monument.

"Over a period of several hours it just sort of came together," I told him. I also mentioned my ambivalent feelings about having it at all after the first few names were attached, and how I had considered taking it down.

"Please don't consider destroying it. This is one of the best on-going tributes I have ever seen, and probably the first one here in Vietnam," the general said. "I appreciate your idea and your work on this special project," he added. "I'm going to ask my G-1 to pursue something like this at our division chapel. I hope, Chaplain Tucker, that there will be no occasion to add even one more name."

Every person standing nearby nodded agreement, and all were surely thinking the same thing: If history repeats itself, there would be more. There were. Many more!

Once on the way, the commanding general's party left as rapidly as it had entered. As they walked out the Wolfhound Memorial Chapel door, Trojan Six gave me a thumbs-up and mouthed "good job," to which I mouthed "thanks" in return.

Turning back to the memorial wall, I placed a piece of masking tape over Lieutenant Steward's nameplate to set the glue a little more firmly. We had met for the first time only about nine weeks before his death. Without asking a single question, I had learned a lot about him during those few weeks.

It seemed strange in a way, because I was the "paid religionist," or "a hired sin hater," as one of my seminary professors used to call the theology students in his class. The reason it seemed so strange is because Steward laid no claim whatsoever to any form of organized religion, and certainly not Christianity, the very thing I had dedicated my life to. Yet we got along like brothers and he appeared to have a great deal of respect for what I stood for.

A couple of times, while he was waiting to be assigned to a platoon, he joined two other chaplains and me for late-night games of pinochle. On one occasion I joined his platoon on the rifle range, where they gone to fire for qualification. Mostly as a joke, I think, Steward invited me to fire his M-16 and was highly impressed that I could place more rounds in the target that two-thirds of his soldiers could.

"How did you learn to shoot like that?" he asked. I made no attempt to explain that country boys in my generation usually had a .22 rifle before they had a bicycle, or that many oil cans and cull green tomatoes were exploded by the hollow-points we could purchase for a penny each.

The better I came to know him the more I felt he never expected to go home alive.

Though he always dug a foxhole in field night positions, he never entered one to sleep or rest. Instead of crawling into the hole he would lean against a tree or nap beside the hole he had dug. A number of his soldiers told me such stories. From his first week in-country (in Vietnam) he rarely retreated to the relative safety of a bunker during a mortar attack, but would lie in his bunk and listen to the explosions nearby.

PFC Powers, a member of Lieutenant Steward's platoon, came by to talk with me on March 4. He was highly disturbed and quite angry. "What is going on?" I asked him.

"Chaplain, I'm having some bad thoughts about wanting my platoon leader dead," he said.

"I'd say such thoughts are pretty bad. What has got you so worked up about him?"

"He is just so by-the-book regulation and won't cut us any slack," Powers said. "It seems like he wants to volunteer us for all the bad stuff. We have lost five men since he took over as platoon leader. Our little platoon has had the last five KIAs in the battalion," he continued. "Also, when we are 'humping the boonies,' he insists on walking point, or at least being the second man in line. In our last fire fight I had some thoughts about taking him out myself. And, Chaplain, I don't like having that kind of feelings."

"I don't blame you. Hopefully no one would be comfortable with such thoughts," I responded. "Is it possible that he walks point because he thinks it will make easier for the soldiers under his command? Is he maybe being tough on the guys to better prepare them for what might happen next? Losing five men in two weeks has to cause him great concern and weigh heavily on his mind. Wouldn't you think that to be the case?"

"Yes sir. I know he is just doing a hard job the best way he knows how, and I am probably wrong in my feelings about him. Right now I promise you that if the lieutenant leaves this place in a body bag it will be a Victor Charlie (VC) that put him in there. It won't be me, Chaplain. I tell you right here and now, it won't be me."

A few days later, on March 9, Slater, 3rd Platoon medic, was wounded in his lower left leg. Also wounded, though only slightly, was Lieutenant Steward, who did not want to be evacuated, but his company commander insisted that he board the helicopter with Slater and about eight more soldiers from other units.

I replaced one of the medics and made the flight to 12th Evac on an over-loaded chopper. I sat on the floor with my right foot on the helicopter skid and my right arm around Steward, who appeared to be a little groggy. The hospital medics cleaned his wound, placed a small sterile bandage on it and released him for duty. He was back in the field before dark.

While we waited for a ride back to the field, Lieutenant Steward told me that Powers had apologized to him a couple of days earlier. Powers wanted his platoon leader to know that in days past he had allowed himself to become obsessed with anger, maybe angry enough to shoot him during a fire fight or to toss a grenade his way. But now, so thought Steward, Powers genuinely regretted that he had ever harbored such feelings and that he had been a divisive member of the platoon. Their talk must have done the trick, because in Lieutenant Steward's mind it was as if nothing had ever happened. Now I hoped it was fully resolved in Powers' mind as well. It seemed to be when we last talked.

The next day an alarming and related event took place.

March 10 began quietly in our field location near the Oriental River and not far from the Cambodian border. At 1600 (4 PM) a call came to battalion forward that elements of Charlie Company had taken casualties. The initial report was that a Viet Cong soldier the company was taking prisoner had blown himself up.

The next report was worse still. Injured, were Specialist Bill Eisensee, PFC Strickland and James Powers, who was in especially bad shape and needed medical help in a hurry.

Then came word about a fourth casualty: Lieutenant Ray Steward was KIA! With that news a thousand things flashed through my mind, among them two names: Powers and Steward. They were the same two names that had appeared frequently and sometimes disturbingly in the recent past.

Close to nightfall, I got a ride back to base camp and went directly to GRO (Graves Registration). Lieutenant Steward's body was already there. I asked the GRO attendant if I could view his body and say a prayer over him. He gave his consent and knelt to unzip the green body bag. Ray had two small wounds in his chest. They looked like entry wounds that might be caused by a very small caliber weapon. On the surface of his sallow chest they looked no more harmful that the little shoulder wound he had received the day before. But it was much worse this time. I quoted a verse he liked from the 23th Psalm, breathed a short prayer and walked out of that solemn place.

The next day I saw the wounded men in 12th Evac and spoke at length with Eisensee. Events of the day before were fresh on his mind and he freely related them to me: The platoon had found a VC in a hole and ordered him to come out. "As the Vietnamese guy was coming out of the spider hole, our 3rd platoon had him almost surrounded, on three sides anyway, because one side was thick underbrush," he recounted.

"I was more or less on the left flank, Strickland was on the right and the lieutenant and Powers were in the middle, side by side, walking slowly toward the VC, who had his hands behind his head. Without any warning, the frightened looking little guy raised one of his hands and literally exploded. He must have been grasping a hand grenade.

"He somehow had himself booby trapped, I guess. The explosion was real close to our platoon leader and Powers and about 10 or 12 feet from Strickland and me. When he lifted his hand I jumped backward and immediately went prone. I think most of the other guys did the same. I don't know if Powers and the lieutenant did or not. Probably not. It happened so fast. The VC practically disintegrated."

Even in the terrible loss, my mind was relieved somewhat. Powers and the officer he had once threatened charges against were on the same side in the final encounter for both.

PFC Powers was seriously injured in the suicide attack but once stabilized and coherent, he was anxious to talk about the episode that would shorten his tour of duty by several months. Even before being evacuated to the hospital at Cu Chi, he was aware of his platoon leader's death. In fact he and Lieutenant Steward were taken out on the same dustoff. His words were that the short flight back to base camp was not a pleasant one. Not only was he dealing with excruciating pain, the haze of morphine and worries about "what next," but also with the knowledge that the body lying beside him, the man he had once hated, would never give another command.

It was with barely focused, tear-filled eyes that Powers gave about the same story Bill Eisensee had given a few hours before: "A squad from the 3rd platoon came upon this 'gook,' he said. "The little guy was hiding in a hole and tossed something our direction. My first thought was that it was a hand grenade, but it must have been a dirt clod or a ball of rice or something to signal that he wanted to surrender.

"We hit the ground and he disappeared again. I think it was Strickland that began crawling toward the hole with a grenade. He was almost close enough to drop it in when the VC appeared above the rim of the hole. It looked like he was giving up, so we held our fire. He came out with his hands behind his head and looked straight at the lieutenant and me. We were standing almost shoulder to shoulder.

"Lieutenant Steward moved his rifle up and down rapidly, a signal for the man to raise his hands above his head. We walked toward him and were only a few feet from the guy in black pajamas when he raised a hand and his head came apart like a pumpkin falling off a truck. Awful thing to see. It became hazy after that. But I do remember falling across the lieutenant and hearing someone call for a medic. Only after we were loaded on the chopper did I learn that our platoon leader was dead," he sort of choked out.

"You already know that Strickland and Eisensee were injured too," I said to him, "but they will recover. And you will probably be heading back to The World soon."

"Yes sir, that is what they tell me," the young soldier said. "Chaplain, I want you to know that the lieutenant and I got everything worked out. I had dumped some pretty heavy stuff on him. But I tried to express regret about some of the earlier feelings I had about him. He told me not to worry about it and consider it done and over with."

"I know. He told me that the two of you had 'buried the hatchet.' That was good news."

"He was really an okay guy. Good leader. Good soldier, too," Powers commented.

"He was all that," I responded, "and so are you. Now the main things you have to do are follow doctor's orders, get better and deal positively with whatever comes next. What do you say we make this pact: I'll remember to pray for your future, and when you think about it, will you remember and pray for your squad members, platoon and the Second Wolfhounds? And I'll get my part of our pact started right now."

I voiced a short prayer at his bedside. The next time I visited that ward Powers was on his way to the United States of America—The World.

While losing soldiers to death was almost as hard as it gets, there was something harder still. At least I found it so. Following the reality of every KIA, my first thought was: Those who know this youngster best are waiting for the next word from him and maybe it will arrive soon, even today, but the next word after that won't be welcome. It will, in fact, be the worst of all potential fears. One stranger in a military uniform would change their outlook and their world in an instant.

What was the harder task? It was being the person who broke the saddest of sad news to wives, parents, siblings and other loved ones. As a pastor and as an army chaplain, it became my responsibility to handle some difficult tasks, but none half so difficult as telling a mother that her son would not be returning, or a wife that the father of her children had made the supreme sacrifice.

In my lifetime I have dug ditches, picked and chopped cotton daylight to dark, swung a pick and a splitting wedge for hours at a time, wept with friends in hospital rooms and conducted hundreds of funeral services. But taking the most distressing of news to family members, especially during wartime, made all the other physical and emotional experiences appear calm by comparison.

Between tours in Vietnam I had the honor of serving at Fort Sill, Oklahoma, as chaplain for OCS (Officer Candidate School). The years of 1968 and 1969 were tough ones for U S troops in Southeast Asia. A large percentage of the more than 58,000 names on the Vietnam Memorial in our nation's capitol died during those years. It was during those 24 months, minus one, that I was "between tours."

Maybe it was because I was considered a combat veteran or maybe my name just came up often, but it seemed that my time to deliver next-of-kin notifications came around a lot. All the other chaplains no doubt thought the same, but we never compared notes or number of trips. Though it was a dreaded assignment, I worked hard at carrying it out with dignity and never tried to beg off.

Even before going out for the first time, I learned that it was going to be an arduous task. That bit of education came on a weekday in the Fort Sill Post Exchange. I entered the door, turned right and walked down a long aisle toward the jewelry section, where I hoped to purchase a watch. As I walked at a deliberate pace toward my PX destination, I noticed that a young woman behind the counter was gazing intently at me. When I was perhaps 20 feet from her, she broke into tears. She tried to hide it, but her emotional stress was obvious.

Trying to act as if I had not noticed her reaction, I turned my gaze from her to the display case and said, "I'd like to look at a wrist watch, please." Upon hearing the words of a shopper, she shifted from crying to near hysterical laughter. If one can sob and laugh at the same time, she was the prototype.

Before placing a tray of watches on the display case, she apologized for her initial response and said she owed me an explanation. She began, "When I saw a chaplain walking rapidly in my direction I just knew it had to be bad news. I anticipated the worst. A lot of things flashed through my mind."

She explained that her husband, a Warrant Officer, was a helicopter pilot in Vietnam. After becoming accustomed to getting letters from him every three or four days, she had not had one in over three weeks. She knew that chaplains in dress green uniforms sometimes bore "the news," and that this time it was going to be for her.

"No," I gladly said, "just something that keeps time, and an earnest wish that you'll never be approached by a chaplain or anyone with an unsettling message." I bought a watch, wished her well and left her a little shaky but smiling.

Two days later I checked by, walking more slowly than normal, to see if she had heard from her chopper pilot. She had. The same day, in fact, she had sold me the watch. That experience prepared me, but only slightly, for less happy endings. A few days later the Post Chaplain gave me the duty of delivering a death message to a family in a small town about 50 miles from Fort Sill. Their son, a soldier with the 101st Airborne Division, had been killed in action two days earlier.

A young buck sergeant, driving an olive drab Army sedan, picked me up at the Artillery Bowl chapel office and we drove north on US 62 toward Anadarko. No one was home at the address I was given. The sergeant and I spotted two men standing in front of a small Assembly of God church and we stopped to make an inquiry. They knew the man I was looking for and told me that he had lived alone, "after his boy went off to the war." "Do you know if he works around here?" I ask them. The church's pastor, the man who did most of the talking, said that he drove a gravel truck for a local company, and told us where he might be working that day.

We were there in ten minutes. There were two huge gravel trucks on the site, and I quickly located the one operated by the man I had come to see. The sedan driver stopped on a dirt road and I got out to wave at the man in the truck. He braked to a stop but did not climb down and I could not make him hear me above the roar of the powerful diesel engine. The driver's seat was at least eight feet above where I stood. When it became more obvious that he was not going to exit the cab, I mounted the metal ladder and went to him. Standing on the top rung, near the open truck door, I introduced myself and tried to prepare for the next words that had to be spoken.

"Is this something about my boy in the army?" he asked with a concerned look.

"Yes sir, it is something about your boy," I answered.

"Something has happened to him, I know it. I know it. Something bad, ain't it?"

"Yes sir! I very much regret to inform you that your son has been killed in the war."

He cut the engine. The gravel pit became deadly quiet. He looked over my left shoulder for a half-minute or so, not saying a word or making a sound. It was like he was trying to spot something out in the distance. Suddenly his head bowed forward into my chest and he tumbled out of the truck. I jumped backward to the ground and caught him before he hit. The sergeant saw all that action and came running to help.

We laid the man across the back seat of our car and I told the driver to head in the direction of town and watch for a hospital sign. Fortunately, we saw one quickly and we skidded to a stop at the emergency room in five minutes. Help from on High, was the way it appeared to me. The emergency room physician and nurses knew the man and how to take care of him. "Weak heart," the doctor said. "He has been here many times. He'll be fine."

We drove back to the church where we had seen the men earlier. I told the pastor what had happened. Learning from him that the man was a member of the local Methodist Church, we drove there and I spoke with that minister. After hearing my reason for being in town and what had happened when the message was delivered, he said he would get to the hospital in a hurry. We stopped by the hospital again on the way out of town. I looked through the Emergency Room door and saw the Methodist pastor speaking with one of the nurses. I hoped his presence would be a consoling factor in the bereaved father's life.

Survivors always wanted answers. How did he die? Did he suffer? Was death instant? When will we see him? Some were angry. They were angry at the military for taking their boy away, and to them, the one delivering the message was the military. Some wanted to know when they would be getting the insurance money. That was something I did not know and was careful to inform them that the Survivor's Assistance Officer (SAO) would contact them soon with answers to all their questions.

Some expressed appreciation, even so much as saying, "Chaplain, I know you are saddened too." To which I would respond, "Yes, believe me I am, but the heaviness I feel can't begin to match what hangs on your soul. I am genuinely sorry to be the bearer of news like this."

It fell my lot to deliver dozens of messages similar to the one mentioned above, and though I willingly performed those solemn tasks, they never became routine. And I never returned from one without thinking that it was more heart-rending than being on the other end—where the soldier died.

Long after retiring from the military and while living in my home state of Arkansas, I made a trip to Iowa as part of a disaster relief team. The volunteer endeavor was to assist people whose homes, businesses and farms had been flooded along the Mississippi River. While filling and stacking sandbags in Davenport one day, Lieutenant Tom Murphy came to mind. He had spoken of Dunkerton, Iowa, where his wife and son were living while he was in Vietnam. "While I'm in the state, why not go to his hometown," I mused.

Early the next morning I pointed my rental car toward Dunkerton, a small farming town not many miles northeast of Waterloo. My first stop was at the town's tiny post office. The sole employee knew I was not "from there," and asked how she might assist me. I told her that I was a retired army chaplain. I explained that I had served in Vietnam with a Dunkerton native by the name of Tom Murphy. "Hopefully," I said to the post mistress, "I would find someone here who remembered Tom, who died over there in 1967."

With a surprised look she said, "I remember Tom. What a good boy he was! His mother still lives in town, not five minutes from here. Would you like me to call her?" I said yes.

We conversed by phone a few minutes and I explained my association with her son a quarter-century earlier. She said that Tom's son Ray was on his way from Waterloo and should be at her house any minute. "Could I come over?" she asked.

In ten minutes I was conversing with Lieutenant Murphy's mother and son, now 33 years of age. They had a lot of 25 year-old questions and I was able to provide most of the answers. After an hour or so Ray suggested that we drive to Waterloo for a meeting with two of his aunts, his father's sisters.

The sisters, both successful business owners, had a lot more questions. They seemed genuinely pleased to speak with someone who had been with their brother in his last days. They had heard that he had died as a result of friendly fire, and wanted to know if I knew that to be true. "It is true," I told them. "One of our Air Force planes had mistaken Tom's platoon for enemy soldiers and fired on them." That matched what they had heard through official channels.

What they had not heard was that I was by his side, kneeling over his lifeless body, just minutes after his death. The sisters were avid Roman Catholic, and certainly knew the prayers and scriptures that I, a Baptist, had said over Tom's body that March day in 1967 did not qualify as Extreme Unction. Yet, they were genuine in expressing gratitude that a priest (minister) was close to their brother when they could not be. Tears flowed on that October day in 1992. And some closure came. They said it was badly needed. I sensed it too, as did Ray.

Ray accompanied me to the cemetery where his father was buried. The dates on the large granite marker matched those in my journal. With lumps in throat, we stood for a while and talked across his father's grave.

"I was only eight when my dad went away," he said. "As I grew older I often wondered what his thoughts of me and mom were."

"Ray," I responded quickly, "I can tell you this. They were good. He loved his family and was not hesitant in letting anyone who would listen know it. I was one who listened and fully understood. Your dad was a good man. A very, very good man."

On the drive back to Davenport I was taken with something akin to "terminal gratitude" for the opportunity to meet the Murphy family. We were all able to close out some things.

CHAPTER 8

Meanwhile, Back At The Flagpole

War is mainly a catalogue of blunders.

—Winston Churchill

Journal entry, 21 October 1967—"They seemed content to live in cleanliness, away from the crud and mud."

Master Sergeant Rutledge was one of the most respected first sergeants one would ever meet. Alpha Company was fortunate to have a veteran of his caliber as its Top. He was an avid supporter of our chapel program and a real friend to lower ranking GIs. So when he asked me if I would accompany him to Graves Registration to assist in making a more positive identification of a soldier, I said yes without hesitation,

The first sergeant had already seen the soldier in question very briefly, but in the chaos of exploding artillery rounds, dustoff helicopters, close support gunships and a large enemy unit that refused to break contact, he was not one hundred per cent sure of the ID. Knowing I had done extensive counseling with the soldier he suspected the KIA to be, he asked me to accompany him. Another Alpha Company soldier, SP4 Hermon, who had received a minor wound in the most recent skirmish was going with us. My thought was that Top invited Hermon simply to allow him a few hours out of the field. He was that kind of soldier's soldier.

Soon after his request, we were on the way to Long Binh in a UH1 (Huey) that had delivered small arms ammunition and .81 mortar rounds. The pilot agreed to make the detour before flying back to Cu Chi. In fifteen minutes we landed no more than a hundred meters from the place no one liked—the Morgue, better known as GRO. After assuring the Huey pilot that the visit would be 10 minutes or less, he consented to wait.

The three of us were admitted to that drab, gray building. Rutledge gave the attending medic the name of the soldier he suspected to be the KIA. He pointed us to a casualty bag on the right about 20 feet away. I had been there before, so had the first sergeant, but it was a first for Specialist Hermon, who had turned very pale and was close to being sick. I asked him if he'd like to wait outside, but because the soldier we were seeking was in his squad and from his home state, he declined. He wanted to go through with it.

The medic unzipped the bag and I looked on the kind face of SP4 Lewis Steinhauser. There was an entry wound on his forehead squarely between his eyes, about an inch above the bridge of his nose. Of course his face was distorted and swollen, but there was no doubt. I looked first at Rutledge and then at Hermon. They both nodded. It was Lewis, a fine soldier and a great young man, who I thought resembled a young Clark Gable. He had a wife and two children back in Georgia.

A lot of recent memories came flooding in. Mainly because of his two physically handicapped children, he had begun paperwork for either a compassionate reassignment or a hardship discharge. Both Rutledge and I thought he was a prime candidate for a hardship discharge and we had worked diligently to obtain the necessary verifying documents to make one a reality. We had received most of them. We were waiting for one more notarized statement from a person who knew Lewis' domestic situation. It never came.

Seven or eight minutes after walking away from the Huey, we headed toward it again. As the engine sounded and the big rotor began to turn I told First Sergeant Rutledge that I needed to make a visit to LBJ (Long Binh Jail) to see an incarcerated soldier. "Since I'm here," I said, "it makes sense to do it now, because I don't like to come to this place more often than absolutely necessary." He knew what I meant. "Tell the S-1 or someone at Headquarters that I'll hitch a ride to Cu Chi later today and be back in the field tomorrow, hopefully by daylight." He thanked me for helping him with the identification and we went our separate ways.

Specialist Hermon and I began our walk toward LBJ, a confinement facility where a Second Wolfhound was serving time that had something to do with a missing weapon and the local black market. We had walked about 15 minutes and were nearing a more thickly populated area that contained office buildings, a large PX, a snack bar and even a handball court. Hermon was startled with all the amenities. I suggested a quick side trip to the PX to see if we might get a Pay Day candy bar or a package of peanuts. "Maybe a soda to wash it down with," I said to him. "I don't usually carry money to the field. But, I have enough MPC (military payment certificate) to purchase a little unhealthy food," I assured him. We walked on.

Near the PX entrance we met an army major on his way out. Creases that looked like they could inflict a wound ran down the front of each leg of his new-looking jungle fatigue uniform trousers. He wore a stiff starched green bush hat, the brim of which pointed slightly up on the right and slightly down on the left. On his right collar was a subdued, embroidered Major's leaf. On the left collar was an immaculately embroidered black shield, which, in its metal version, would have been red, white and blue. Though no jump wings adorned his chest, he wore spit-shined jump boots that looked like they had not seen dust in months.

He stepped in front of SP4 Hermon, the soldier walking with me, and signaled him to stop. Hermon came to a halt two steps from the major and saluted. We both saluted. When the officer finally broke the silence it was to say, "Soldier, you need a haircut! When did you last get one?" He didn't seem to expect an answer. His next condescending words were: "How long have you been wearing those fatigues?" And looking down at his muddy jungle boots, said, in a derisive tone, "Have those boots ever been shined? Or buffed?

Or even had the mud scraped off?" Then he turned to me, who didn't look much better than the young man he had just chewed out, and said, "Chaplain, is this man with you?"

"Yes sir, he is," I said. "We are only minutes out of Graves Registration, where Specialist Hermon assisted in identifying his best friend, who was killed earlier today. We left a place known as The Horseshoe less than an hour ago. The soldiers out there, including this one, sir, have been living in ankle-deep mud for the last three days and nights. Late last night and early this morning they were in heavy contact with a VC force of unknown size. In addition to the man we came to identify, we had three others killed, including a short-timer company commander. I can't tell you how many WIAs there are, and won't know until I get back to the 12th Evacuation Hospital at Cu Chi tonight. I do know there is at least one in that category though. It is the soldier standing here with us now. He sustained shrapnel wounds, though minor, before break of day this morning."

The officer turned his gaze from me back to the soldier, was silent for a few seconds and said, "Carry on!"

We continued our journey into the huge PX, where I bought two candy bars and two warm Pepsi Colas. Five cents, each item. Twenty cents would take care of our late lunch or early supper. As we walked out of the store, I heard Hermon say, under his breath and mostly to himself, "What a jerk!"

I gave no indication that his three-word sentence registered with me, but I knew what he was referring to. And may the great commanders I had the privilege of serving with forgive me for saying that I didn't totally disagree with him.

"I'm about ready to head back to the boonies. What about you?" I said to the still frustrated soldier with me. "I'll come back to the stockade another day." We made our way toward a chopper pad, which was easy to detect. All we had to do was watch the coming and going of helicopters. Dozens of them were either landing or taking off at any given time on that gigantic base. We checked in at operations, told the sergeant on duty where we wanted to go, and thirty minutes later were on our way to Cu Chi aboard a Chinook with a sling load of 105 artillery rounds.

During the short flight, I thought about something I had read or heard during the officer basic course at Fort Hamilton, New York. It was that only about one out of every seven soldiers actually fired weapons and did battle with the enemy. I took that to mean that for every GI on the line, with a pocket full of hand grenades and wielding a machine gun or any number of weapons, there were six in support. They were the people who received and delivered the mail, cooked and served the food, got the ammunition and other supplies up where they were needed, took care of pay, handled mountains of clerical work, sent fellow soldiers on emergency leave, repaired vehicles and kept the lights burning. Every supporting task was and is crucial to the mission, some more than others, and soldiers on the line knew it. Still, it was an eye opener for the grieving soldier with me, and ultimately for me as well, to witness the rear echelon first hand.

While most soldiers were encouraged, when at all possible, to shave daily and utilize his steel pot as a wash basin on occasions, they were pretty much exempt from rendering the right hand salute unless a "full bird" (Colonel) or higher ranking officer appeared on the scene. Take him back to the rear and the soldier would fall right back into military courtesy and dress routine, but in the field, where he lived in a hole at night and in some degree of fear day and night, most of the regulations seemed superfluous.

It was (and maybe is) that same principle that often made it difficult for the combat soldier to return home and live among fellow citizens who barely acknowledged that their country was at war. He thought it strange that his friends "back home" complained about poor TV reception or about the super market being out of their favorite ice cream. He told very few, if any, his story. "They wouldn't believe it anyway, Chaplain, or care!"

I thought back to some meetings in Tan Son Nhut and Saigon, one in particular at the Rex Hotel in Saigon. Those who lived and served there rarely thought of it as a war zone, especially in the early years of the conflict.

One day, Chaplain Dale Moon, who served in a combat outfit much like the Wolfhounds, and I talked during a break at a MACV chaplain's conference. I commented that it was a nice to take a break back in the rear, that the hotel beds were clean and comfortable and that a steak and lobster dinner beat our somewhat normal fare by a country mile. "You know what though, Dale," I said to him, "I miss being out there with my guys."

"I wondered if anyone else was having crazy thoughts like that," he responded. "What is not to like about being dry, eating like kings and showering in warm water? But here I am, in a place that has all the appearances of a secure area, hearing no gunfire, seeing no flares, being in the best of all worlds this side of my own home, yet not liking it very much. Tuck, how do you make sense of thoughts like that? I see some of these guys wearing starched khaki uniforms and boots so shiny you can almost see your reflection in the toes. They are all in this war, I guess. In Vietnam, right? But I haven't seen many uniforms with a patch denoting a combat unit on the left sleeve. Have you?"

"Nope, sure haven't," I said.

He wondered, as had I, about some comments a mutual chaplain friend had made during one of the "Tell-how-your-work-is-going" seminars. He had made a point to tell the rest of us how he was genuinely pleased to live in relative luxury in Southeast Asia, far from home. A hootch maid cleaned his quarters, laundered and ironed his clothes and shined his boots, all for the equivalent of twenty dollars a month.

"Our cooks can really lay it out too. Three great 'hots' a day! Real eggs, steaks, beef roasts, delicious pastries that would rival your favorite bakery back in the USA. Sometimes we have turkey and dressing when it isn't even Thanksgiving. Can't beat it, guys," he said with a laugh.

"Not all is rosy though," he continued with his report, which I still wonder if it was real or imagined. "The biggest problem among my soldiers is boredom. They are bored out of their gourds, and drugs follow that, alcohol too. A lot of alcohol abuse. With so much time on their hands, soldiers in my outfit are prime targets for drugs. I don't know how it is where you are, but at my place drugs can be obtained for nearly nothing."

The "bored" word is what caught a number of us by surprise. Those of us who served with combat units could hardly fathom an environment such as he had described. Our guys were sometimes rowdy, scared, lonely and macho, but rarely, if ever, bored. As to the personal hootch maid and gourmet food every meal, those were as foreign to us as the country in which the conference was being held. Back with the hard-charging troops was where most of us wanted to be, far away from the 'flagpole.'

We agreed that "going native" was a state we could be approaching without being fully aware of it. Above all, I did not wish to become judgmental toward those who served in places of relative safety, rarely heard the sound of a fire fight or presided at a memorial service for a fallen soldier. I was successful in the wish to avoid becoming judgmental, because those at the front knew those at the rear had important jobs to perform, just as those out on the line did.

Having been in the office that made assignments for the Sea Bee school graduates back at Port Hueneme, California during the Korean War, I knew what it was to be part of the rear echelon crowd.

As the saying goes, "someone has to do it." And I did it gladly. But for some mysterious reason, one that may remain forever unclear to me, I felt a driving need to experience the combat soldier's war. Maybe that mentality had its start during World War II when, as a pre-teen, I watched newsreels at the Drew Theater in Monticello, Arkansas and stood in awe of the uniformed veterans returning from places they named: Sicily, Bougainville, Germany, China-Burma-India, Subic Bay and U S Navy ships. They wore the CIB, Twin Dolphins, Jump Wings and rows of campaign ribbons, including the Purple Heart. Some of them had peculiar looking hooks where hands had been and black patches where eyes had been. Heroes! Some of the returnees, maybe six out of seven, probably served "behind the line," but to an eleven year-old they were all heroes.

Journal entry for May 4, 1967: "Showed Ten Commandments in Wolfhound Chapel. It was well received and well attended." That film was one of the few that ever made its way to our battalion. During my second Southeast Asian tour, with the 212th Combat Aviation Battalion at Marble Mountain, film night was a weekly event. Movies were available almost nightly in the rear areas, especially in the larger military installations, but not up our way. However, on Thursday, the 4th of May, I was able to offer the famous Cecil B. DeMille film to soldiers, who patiently waited through four breaks as the next reels were threaded into a .35mm projector. That old flickering projector would be considered a dinosaur in this technologically advanced day. Back then our guys thought of it as a link with home and the movie theaters they once frequented.

The film ended late. At the conclusion most of the guys went back to their sandbagged platoon barracks. A few, who didn't normally enter the chapel much, stayed around to find names of friends on the memorial wall. PFC Tom Clark asked if he could help and I invited him to get the reels into the properly numbered canisters, while I finished with securing the projector.

Mostly though, he wanted to talk and solicit my "advice." Clark was nearing the end of his tour in Vietnam. His company and platoon had suffered a lot of casualties. He had been awarded several decorations, including a Bronze Star with V device and a Purple Heart. His platoon had been involved in some really hairy stuff. "I lost three buddies from my platoon before you started putting names on that little blue table," he said to me. "But I wanted to talk with you about something else, if you have time. I know it's late."

"I have time," I assured him.

"Chaplain, I'm giving some serious thought to extending," were his next words.

"Okay! Some other Wolfhounds have done that. Most of the ones I have spoken with extended or re-upped for other assignments, usually off the line somewhere. Saigon or Vung Tau, for example. Is something like that a part of your thinking?

"At first I thought it might be," he said, "but not anymore. Last week I went to the big in-country headquarters to sort of check out a potential extending job. Chaplain, I did not like it. I got my heels locked four times in those two days, one for non-regulation head gear and three times for not saluting an officer. On the saluting, I just forgot. After these months of not saluting very much, I just forgot about saluting those officers. Once what I had done hit me I apologized and gave them a sharp one, but still got chewed out. Maybe I was wrong, but it seemed that most of the people I spoke with were concerned about things that don't amount to much. I talked with two men who had almost completed their 365 days and had never held a weapon with the safety off. I guess that is a good thing, but it didn't take me long to see that it is not my thing. Down there near the head shed I missed what goes on up here, and I missed the guys in my platoon."

"So," I asked him, "does that mean you are rethinking your request?"

"No sir, I'm going to extend, but stay where I am. I've been on the M-60 machine gun team from the day I set foot in Bravo Company. Before becoming assistant gunner, I was an ammo carrier. First Sergeant told me that if I extend for present duty I'll be promoted to Specialist Four and become gunner. Leader of the team.

"You plan to give Uncle Sam six more months for the privilege of being gunner on the crew you have served with from the start, is that right?"

"Yes sir. That's what I really want to do. I know from my training and from these months in 'Nam, that the machine gun is in the bull's eye. The guys at the other end of that thing want to knock out something that is throwing hundreds of .30 caliber rounds toward their positions. We have been told that our weapon is one of their big targets, second only to the soldier standing next to the one with the whip antenna. But we are a good team. We've learned not to stay in one place any longer than absolutely necessary. Fire some rounds and move. Fire some more rounds and move again. Don't linger in one place long enough for the enemy to put fire where they saw the tracers coming out."

"That is commendable, 'Soon to be Specialist Clark,' I said to him. It is a tough assignment but I know you will handle it well. I wish you the best in this."

Then he said, "I told my mom that I might extend and that if I did, there was a chance I'd have a new job in a safer place. Now I have to let the folks know I'll be staying with my old outfit, because the other didn't work out. That wouldn't be lying, would it? For a fact it didn't work out." I had to agree with his rationale on that.

"One more thing, Chaplain," the seasoned vet, still a teenager said, "would you mind saying a prayer to God about all this, especially that my mom will understand? I don't want her to be sad when she learns I won't be getting a job in the rear."

"I would be pleased and honored," I responded. We stood side by side in front of the communion table, which had been constructed by a Vietnamese carpenter. I prayed first for his parents, asking the Lord to give them assurance and peace about their son in a land so far from them. I prayed that every man on his team and all in his platoon and company would be protected from harm. I prayed that all military personnel in Vietnam might have a hedge of protection surrounding them. "God," I prayed, "help Clark's parents to face bravely the prospect that it would be eight months before they would see him again, instead of the two they had been counting on."

As he walked out the side door of the chapel and toward his bunk, I prayed another short prayer: "Heavenly Father, don't let him go home before completing his extra six months." I pointed my hand, first in the direction he was walking, and then in a sweeping fashion over the entire battalion area, and quoted, as a promise and a prayer, Psalm 91, verses 9 and 10: *Make the Lord, the Most High, your refuge, then no harm will befall you, and no disaster will come near your tent.*

It was midnight when I entered my little house—the Holy Hootch. I did so with a question on my mind: "Who would begin to understand the mentality of a young man who preferred to be here, rather in relative safety near the proverbial flagpole?" I would. And did.

CHAPTER 9

Listening And Learning

I'm tired and I want to go home.

—Old American Ballad

Journal entry, 18 October, 1967—"Harold lost both feet in a mine explosion."

No conference on human relations or highest level post-graduate counseling seminar could ever prepare one to deal adequately with real life experiences. As a chaplain, I quickly learned that the person who feels like he knows all the answers has not heard all the questions. I found this true with the diversity of subjects one might hear in a military setting, especially among those facing dire circumstances on a near-daily basis. Even knowing the impossibility of doing so, I wanted to "fix" everything and get everyone who could do something to help to go ahead and do it. Now! In a hurry! Time is of essence! But patience is a high virtue, though difficult to fully attain.

Anger has to be put aside. If it lingers, it destroys the person who harbors it. Beginning long before my first tour in Vietnam I worked long, hard and successfully on a personal principle concerning that emotion: "If anger pounces, don't let it hang on more than 15 seconds. Life is too short for one for one to spend much of it weighted down with that emotion." So it was frustration and not anger I was dealing with that day in the morgue while helping to identify Steinhauser, whose name came up in the last chapter.

Lewis was the consummate good soldier, one who did what was required and more. He was a dependable young man, but with a lot of problems at home. As stated earlier, I requested letters from five individuals who could verify the hardship situation. The four that responded gave the same story. His two little boys suffered from severe handicaps. Each stated the difficulties the young mother faced. Her sole income was from Lewis' allotment, which was 95 per cent of his base pay.

In varying words, each respondent wrote about the very small mobile home, parked in her parents' back yard, in which she and the children lived. Two of the letters related stories about doctor bills, poor nutrition and inadequate winter clothing for the children. One hand-written letter from a neighbor had a separate note attached with a straight pin. In the note were these words: "Chaplin, please hope this boy if you can. His wife and kids need him bad."

To add to my frustration, the supporting letter that never came was requested from an individual whose profession was the same as mine. After my 15 seconds or less of anger and a couple of days worth of frustration had subsided, other and more gracious thoughts entered: Maybe he never got my letter. Maybe he posted a reply that was lost in the mail.

Maybe he didn't know enough about the situation to respond. Maybe the church to which I had written no longer existed.

There could have been good answers to all my questions, but all I could think of at the time was that if a strong statement had arrived when the others did, Lewis could be packing for the long journey home. Instead, this father and husband had, in the prime of life, been taken to his eternal Home.

From the "lost or overdue letter" episode, I learned a lesson that has stayed with me for more than forty years: When requested to write a letter (or email) of reference for someone, do it quickly. As a rule, pastors and chaplains get a lot of requests to provide references for those seeking promotions, scholarships, entrance into certain colleges and positions and jobs of all kinds. With every request I immediately think back to that 1967 October day in Graves Registration, and how things could have been different. Then, if at all possible, I have an answer on the way in two days or less.

I named my jeep the "Wolfhound Watcher." Those two words were stenciled in six-inch letters under the windshield of that dependable little army green vehicle. There were times when I thought "Wolfhound Listener" might better describe a major part of my role. If one does indeed learn by listening, I learned a lot.

Most of my listening and learning took place far away from comfortable chairs in a nice office. We met where our duties took us: In the bottom of a bomb crater. In the burn ward or triage. Aboard a noisy a chinook, shouting to be heard. Over a meal of cold, rain-soaked field rations. Sitting on two layers of sandbags in the back of a dust-shrouded two and a half-ton truck. And occasionally, during a firefight.

My first heavy contact came on March 1, 1967 in some triple-canopy jungle of War Zone C. At least I thought of it as heavy, though there were only three or four snipers and two .51 caliber machine guns firing on the Alpha and Charlie companies I was humping with that day. Two soldiers from the lead platoon were hit when the shooting started, one in his left leg by a .51 round and the other in his stomach by a sniper, firing an AK-47. We pulled them back to the rear and into a small clearing. Charlie Six (C Company Commander) called for a medical evacuation helicopter. While a squad worked at hacking out a landing zone for the dustoff, I low crawled between the two wounded GIs. One of them was a young man I knew well. He showed up often at chapel and field services. When I called his named, he opened his eyes, smiled and spoke: "Chaplain, I knew you would come!"

That is what he said, "Chaplain, I knew you would come!" Before saying a word to him, a question gripped me: "What if I hadn't?" I wondered for years what was behind his first words that day, and still don't know for sure. Maybe he was expressing a need to see a caring soul by his side. Through pain of a sucking chest wound he kept talking and tried to laugh. He expressed deep concern for the other wounded soldier, who was calling for his mother in one breath and cursing the VC and "this sorry land,' in the next breath. The company medic said his leg wound did not appear to be life threatening. "But the other, Chaplain," the medic whispered, "may not make it to the hospital alive, if we can't get him out of here soon. He needs better care than I can give him."

A small LZ (landing zone) was cleared just in time to receive the dustoff. The wounded soldiers were loaded in seconds while the chopper hovered at about 18 inches.

The pilot had to take it out almost vertical. The soldier with the stomach wound gave a weak wave as they lifted out. I looked his way and prayed with my eyes wide open, thinking that would probably be the last time I'd see him alive.

Just before the dustoff got enough altitude to fly over the tree tops, a sniper begin firing on it. The right door gunner silenced him with a long burst of well placed M-60 rounds and the flight continued.

Late the next day I got a flight back to base camp. I went straight to the hospital, dreading what I might learn. But there was some surprising news. The soldier with what was thought to be the worst wound made it. I found him stabilized and alert in ICU. He remembered everything about the day before, including the Bible verse we quoted together: "*If God be for us, who can be against us?*"

The surgeon came into ICU while I was there and said, "Padre, you're looking at a miracle lying there! Initially, we thought, no way! But, with at least one more surgery, maybe two, this young man is going to be as good as new."

Ironically, the soldier with what the company medic thought were non-lethal wounds died before the dustoff landed at the hospital. Hearing that, made me regret I had not taken more time with him while the chopper was inbound. At the morgue entrance, I knelt in prayer for the family of the dead soldier. Regrettably, I hardly knew him.

Death was the worst news. Seriously wounded was second. But listening to and dealing with some other situations came in very close to the first two. How does one, including "Supreme Six X-ray" (another epithet sometimes given the chaplain), give any hope to an infantry platoon leader whose frequent letters from his wife dealt with one subject only—divorce? Every letter the same thing. "When are you going to sign the papers? I no longer want to be married to you. Give me my freedom, now!"

Rare were the times when the lieutenant had time to talk to anyone except his men and the company commander. But on June 4, while on a short break, he came by the Wolfhound Chapel and we talked. He did most of the talking. I listened intently and learned some valuable lessons. One was how very blessed I was to have a loving, supportive family back home.

"Never in my life," he began, "had I consulted with a chaplain or priest until my wife began dumping the D word on me. We have been married two years. I can't begin to put in words how much I love her. At the same time I want to set her free, if that is the only thing that will bring her happiness.

"Chaplain, you know the responsibilities we face in combat. At present I have 38 good soldiers who expect me to make the kind of decisions that help us win the next fire fight and keep them from being casualties. I consider myself a good leader, too. All the things a good platoon leader is supposed to be, I have worked hard to become. But I find myself thinking about my wife, even in heavy contact with Charlie, when my full attention needs to be on how best to maneuver my guys and finish it off without getting someone hurt."

Most people never see a hard-charging, ground pounding, infantry officer weep. But two weeks later I saw Lieutenant Morrison with tear-filled eyes. "I set her free!" he said.

As we prepared for the latest of the Second Wolfhound's many combat assaults (CA), Corporal Yarbrough came to the prayer altar at the end of a pre-deployment service. He stayed until everyone else had left. "Chap, you got a few minutes?" he asked. "That is a big affirmative!" I answered. He chuckled at "that's a big affirmative," because that was one of the catch phrases going around among enlisted men at the time. I invited him to say what was on his mind.

"Well sir, a few minutes ago in the chapel service you read a verse, I'm not sure where, but I think the Old Testament, somewhere."

"It was," I responded, "the 91st Psalm, verses 5 and 6. Here it is: *You shall not be afraid of the terror by night, or the arrow that flies by day, or the destruction that lays waste at noonday.* Does that sound like it?"

"Yes, sir. That's it. When I heard those words I thought even more about something that has been on my mind for two days. It just won't go away. I keep thinking that something is going to happen on the next operation. I'm not especially nervous about it or afraid to get on that slick (helicopter) tomorrow, even though you can't keep from being a little shaky about going in on the first lift. The CO told us this morning that second platoon will lead the way. That's the one I'm in. Rifle team leader, second platoon."

"Thinking something is 'going to happen' doesn't necessarily mean that it will be bad, does it?" I commented. "Hopefully it means that you'll jump out of that chopper onto a cold LZ, or that the artillery prep has been so effective you'll be picked up with the same number of M-16 rounds you went in with. I'll be living with the hope that something like that is what will happen on the next operation. Maybe those words you picked up on from Psalm 91 were words 'from on High,' as a reminder that you don't go it alone."

He nodded thoughtfully and turned to leave. He picked up a Gideon's New Testament and looked toward the back until he found the words he wanted: *You shall not be afraid of the arrow that flies by day.* "Keep it," I said. He kept it open as he walked toward his company. It was obvious that he was memorizing those words. I returned to my own packing with a thought: "I learn more from these kids, most of them barely out of high school, than I'll ever be able to teach them." (Just so the reader will know, Corporal Yarbrough completed his tour and went home unscathed).

"It looks like I won't be playing any more pinochle with you and the other chaplains for a while." Those were the words of Tom Murphy that January 18, 1967 evening.

"You've heard what happened to Bravo Company this morning?"

"Sure have, Tom. Terrible news. I got back from a meeting in Saigon about 1400 (2 PM) and found 12th Evac teeming with Second Wolfhounds, most of them from one platoon. Evidently Bravo was making a sweep and Lieutenant Gray's platoon got caught in a command-detonated minefield. My latest word is seven wounded and ten killed. The KIAs identified so far, at least when I left the TOC about 20 minutes ago, are Archuleta, McCarty, Provenzano and Workman."

"Lieutenant Gray got it too," Tom said, with a note of urgency in his voice. "I've been waiting to be plugged into a platoon leader slot, so this is it. That's why I won't be able to join you, Sink and McInnes for any Wednesday night get-togethers for a while. I'll be joining Bravo Company in about ninety minutes. Trojan Six is taking me out in his chopper. I just wanted to let you know."

"I'm grateful, Lieutenant Murphy, I really am, because you have many details to take care of and a lot of thoughts to process," Then I asked: "Are you okay with this?"

"It is what I have trained for, and I have no choice. Naturally, I would have preferred to take leadership of a platoon under different circumstances. Replacing Leonard at the end of his six months on the line would have been a lot better, but things don't always work out the way we'd like them to, not in a place like this."

"You'll have your work cut out for you. With so many losses at one time, morale is no doubt about as low as it can get. I remember when we first met. Wasn't that at Camp Alpha? Or on the bus from Tan San Nhut? I can't believe that was only six weeks ago. It seems like years. We talked about families, backgrounds and how people in your Iowa home state raise corn for a living much the same way many here in Vietnam raise rice for their livelihood. You told me about Ray, your son, and how you wanted to be a good father to him and do the things that would make him proud. Now here you are moving to a job, one I've heard a number of O-5s and O-6s say is the ultimate for hands-on leadership. I wish you well in this challenging new position."

I hitched a ride on the same C and C that took Tom to his assignment with Bravo Company, and dug a shallow sleeping hole next to the CO, Captain McCarthy. Even after losing so many people, he was completely in control of the tactical situation and his emotions. That evening, over hot chow, prepared back at Cu Chi and flown to the field, he made a solemn observation: "Chaplain, Operation Cedar Falls has been rough on us!"

A week later, SP4 Otis Jones, age 22, from North Little Rock, Arkansas, was killed while he and another soldier were setting up an ambush near Phu Hoa Dong. It was Bravo Company again! And the same platoon that had lost so many a few days earlier. It was also the day Lieutenant Tom Murphy took his platoon, which had gotten some replacements but was still vastly under strength, out for the first time. Grim initiation.

Annie Cunningham, the 'Hounds favorite nurse at 12 Evac, attended the 2/27 chapel service on the last Sunday of May. By her side was First Lieutenant Gary Jones, the officer she had fallen for. They had fallen for each other, as has been reported in an earlier chapter. At the close of the 8:30 service she, with Gary, stopped by to speak and deliver a message. The message was from

PFC Rodrieguez, one of our Dog Handlers who was admitted to the hospital on Thursday. He was improved but still a very sick soldier when I saw him late Friday evening.

"I spoke with him about 7:00 this morning," she reported. "When I informed him that I was on my way to his battalion for chapel, he asked me to tell you that he needs to see you soon, today if possible."

Of course I'll go see him again very soon, but he probably wants to see a priest," I said. "Or did he say the Wolfhound chaplain?"

"He called your name. Would you ask the Wolfhound Chaplain Tucker to see me when he gets a chance?" Annie said.

Just as soon as the 10:30 chapel service was over I jumped in the Wolfhound Watcher jeep and drove to the hospital. I found PFC Rodrieguez resting, with his eyes closed but awake. His lower legs were wrapped in several layers of bandages. A cast covered his left arm from shoulder to wrist. He opened his eyes and smiled when his name was softly called. "You look better than you did two days ago," I said to him. "I hope you are feeling better as well."

"Not too bad now. The doctor says it will take a while, but when everything heals up I'll be walking as well as before. He told me my wound is the million-dollar kind. So it looks like I'll be going stateside soon," he rather weakly said. "But chaplain, I want to talk with you about something else, something that has been on my mind since the day I got hit. It won't take long. Do you have a few minutes?"

"Take as long as you like. I can be here until the nurse runs me out," I assured him.

He continued: "That day, I think it was last Thursday, two other Dog Handlers and I were on an AP (Ambush Patrol) with Charlie Company. We were near the village of Xom Moi. Everything was quiet and kind of peaceful when all of sudden there was a tremendous explosion. I am not sure, but my dog may have been killed. I know my dog-handler buddies were hit.

I remember hearing them moaning and calling for the medic. I recall lying on the ground with a lot of people around me, and being loaded on a helicopter. But what I remember most is being afraid, not of dying but of not being ready to die. Chaplain, I couldn't get it fixed in my mind that the God of Heaven would accept me, and I didn't know what to do, except call out to Him. And I couldn't think of enough words to even make a decent prayer. So over and over I kept saying, "I want to follow you, O God! I want to follow you, O God! I think I was whispering it."

Together we looked at the story of Nicodemus in the Bible, and he asked questions of me, as Nicodemus had of Jesus, about the meaning of being "born again." He listened intently as I read from the Gospel of Luke the episode of the Prodigal Son, who eventually went back home to his father. The bed-ridden soldier said that he wanted to go back to the Father. In the 16th chapter of Acts, he identified with the frightened jailer who cried out, "What must I do to be saved?" And with tears in his tired eyes, he agreed with the answer the jailer received. I left him smiling and seemingly happy.

When I returned from the hospital all the mess halls were closed. I had homemade cookies from my wife's kitchen for lunch. I digested about ten of them and the recent bedside lesson at the same time. Both were very good!

During my two tours in Vietnam, and in many other military settings, I listened to hundreds of heart breaking stories. But none left me with a more helpless feeling than one I heard from a soldier who had been with the 2/27 only a month. I was leaning against a tree writing a letter when he sat down beside me.

After some words of greeting, he said, "Chaplain, did you hear about the soldier that was killed just outside the wire at base camp four days ago?"

"Yes I did. We'll have a memorial service for him next time his company is in Cu Chi. Evidently he was killed by friendly fire," I said to him.

"It was friendly fire that got him," he said. "Charlie didn't get him. It was me, Chaplain, I'm the one who done it. I killed him. I been here just a real short time and the man I killed was about the only friend I had."

"Hey Daniel, what do you mean you killed him?"

"It was about 0200. I was on guard in my sector of the bunker line. I heard a noise not far outside the wire. It was movement, getting closer. I was shaking like a leaf, but when the movement was real close I called out the challenge—Smoky. I expected to hear the password—Mountain. He didn't say the password. All I heard was someone talking real fast in a high voice. Squeaky sounding words that sounded like 'sojer' and 'came in' and 'merica, merica.' Something like that! Then, Chaplain, the noise got closer to the wire. I thought it was some VC getting ready to overrun us. So I popped the Claymore. The noise stopped. At daylight we made a sweep and found the GI my friendly fire had taken out. The CO said he must have gone out to relieve himself, gotten disoriented in the dark, wandered outside the wire and got completely lost. The captain said it wasn't my fault."

Heavy load for a teenager to carry! There are some lessons you'd rather not learn.

The author conducting a field service with Wolfhound Recon Platoon

Chaplain Carter Tucker's steel helmet doubling as a field altar

Chaplain Tucker and Captain Tom Brewer in Vietnam, 1967 –
Captain Brewer was seriously wounded a few days later.

Chaplain Tucker and Captain Brewer 39 years later at
the Wall in D C. Tom Brewer wrote a very good book
about Vietnam entitled *Searching for the Good*.

Chaplain Tucker accompanying troops through
rice paddy. A typical and frequent scene

Setting up for the night

Chaplain Tucker with Vietnamese children. Kids love the
Americans, referring to them as "Numma One GI"

"Ye Holy Hootch" - the chaplain's house at Cu Chi Vietnam

Helicopter ride to reach the Wolfhounds

Chaplain Tucker with a duster crew on the Oriental River

The Memorial Wall, constructed by chaplain to honor Wolfhounds who gave their lives. (I lost 94 during my first tour in Vietnam)

Wolfhound Memorial Chapel next to Cu Chi base camp chaplain's quarters (Holy Hootch)

Memorial Chapel (sign) painted by one of the 2/27 soldiers

Memorial service for soldiers killed in action in the Wolfhound chapel

Memorial service in chapel

Soldiers and a Tracker Dog operating in water–three of
the soldiers and the dog were killed a few days later

Memorial service that included remembering
Prince, a faithful tracker dog

Chaplain handing out "goodies from home." One of
the recipients was killed that night in 1967. I refer
to him under a fictitious name in the book.

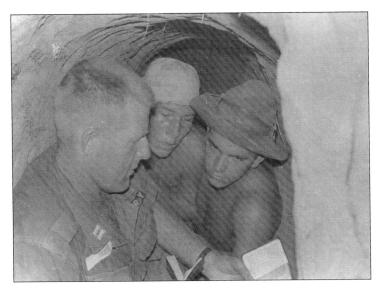

The author conducting a service for "tunnel rats" in one of
the tunnels they searched. (Dangerous and scary work).

The 2/27 Wolfhound "tunnel rats" with Lieutenant Harold Graves

Chaplain baptizing Specialist Bill Spafford in 1967

Chaplain in field with Vietnamese farm children

Chaplain Tucker with Bible in helmet band (This photo appeared in every major newspaper in the US in the Spring of 1967 under caption, "Chaplain keeps his powder dry"). It is an AP photo.

CHAPTER 10

Laughter And Tears

Even in laughter the heart may break.

—Proverbs 14:13

Journal entry, 29 October 1967—"He hesitated...the woman shot him."

Like most young people I've known (and once was), the soldier can and will come up with anything, especially the unexpected. Stand up comedians, who are supposed to say and do funny things, do not begin to match the humor of an innovative young soldier, and he isn't even attempting to be humorous. If ever there was one who could "make lemonade when life gives you a lemon," it was the American soldier.

That was never more obvious than on a day when I was accompanying two companies of Second Wolfhounds on a sweep near Trang Bang. The forward elements of Alpha Company began taking sniper fire from a canal line near the village. I was with one of the mortar teams about 200 meters behind the lead element when a report, that later proved to be erroneous, came back that Alpha had at least one WIA. I began working my way toward where one of our M-60s was firing, alternating between walking in a crouch and low crawling. About 50 yards behind where the lead platoon was temporarily pinned down by the sniper fire, I heard strange human sounds. They sounded like a mixture of snorting, howling, crying and hysterical laughter. Thinking I was near one or more wounded soldiers, I turned that direction and quickly discovered the source of the unusual noise. Behind a low berm two 18-year old combat vets were lying side by side reading a Tom and Jerry comic book. Kids in front of their TV on a Saturday morning could not have laughed harder or louder than those two young men did while only 50 yards away a machine gun was sending lead into the canal line. I lay for a few minutes behind the berm and congratulated them on their choice of literature, glad that their voices had echoed glee and not pain.

Heading back to my spot with the mortar guys, a thought hit me, as it has many times since: "Nobody but an American Soldier! Nobody!"

When Lieutenant Neptune was critically wounded on March 15, 1967, the same round that almost did him in took out the 100-kilowatt generator that provided electrical power for much of the 2/27. Except for flashlights, a few candles and a couple of old-timey coal oil (kerosene) lamps, most of the base camp was in nighttime darkness for more than a week. Engineers and electricians began work on the generator the same night it was knocked out, but the damage was severe and needed parts were difficult to obtain.

Two sergeants and a warrant officer were working on the generator when I returned from two days in the field on 22 March. Very much needing to prepare for Easter, which was only three days away, I made my way to the O-Club with hopes of scrounging some candles. On the way I stopped by to speak with the three men hard at work on the generator. "Making any headway?" I asked. Mr. Gray responded that they were getting close and would soon be ready to "see if this monster will crank." I wished them luck and continued my short walk to the little officer's club.

Upon entering the screened side door of the structure, I spotted two lieutenants sitting at a crude table in the semi-darkness. One had been slightly wounded and was on light duty while waiting to rejoin his platoon. The other had been in country only two weeks and was waiting to be assigned. Montgomery, the 21 year-old lieutenant who was recovering from his "easy Purple Heart wound" (his words), said, "Chaplain, can't you do something about these lights?"

"Oh," I said, "you want light?" Then, with my arms held high, and in my deepest possible ministerial voice, said, "Okay, let there be light!"

What happened next defies description to this day. The same instant I spoke those innocent words that undoubtedly bordered on sacrilege, the mechanics chose to see if the generator engine would start. It would and did! The word "light" was barely out of my mouth when the bulbs in the O-Club flickered a time or two, then completely dispelled the darkness. A hundred yards away we could hear a gasoline engine hesitate a few seconds before catching on and setting that generator to doing what it was designed to do. The young lieutenants stood slowly and, with wide-eyed wonder, looked at one another, then simultaneously swiveled their heads slowly in my direction. They did not speak a word. Their looks spoke for them: "What just took place here?" I knew it was simply a coincidence that after many days of work on the electrical power-producing machine, the men decided to try it the same moment I went into my little unrehearsed act.

The three of us shifted our gaze from one to the other for a few seconds and then, like kids pouncing on a loose football, just fell to the floor in laughter. Those two ROTC graduates were laughing so hard they were literally gasping for breath. Both of them lay face down, beating their fists on the plywood floor. I was kicking my feet in the air like a six-month old baby and probably making sounds like one. If a senior officer had happened by while all that hilarity was taking place he would have probably called the guys who deal in straitjackets. I got up first, now laughing more at the antics of the lieutenants than the event that had prompted them.

I paid ten cents for the Pepsi I obtained from the now running but still warm refrigerator and headed toward the Holy Hootch. I yelled back to the guys inside: "Don't forget. Easter in three days! See you in chapel." They were there, still amused about the let-there-be-light episode.

The Brigade Five, 2nd Brigade executive officer, would have been the mostly likely one to look askance at two junior officers and the battalion chaplain rolling in laughter on the floor of the battalion officer's club. He later became notorious for something that had nothing to do with tactics and combined arms.

Rather, it was for a nickname by which he became known in the 2/27 Headquarters Company. It started in the mess hall, spread to other sections, and finally became well known to the enlisted men of the entire battalion. Maybe to some of the officers too, but none dared to let on they knew anything about it.

One early morning the Five came to the 2/27 for breakfast in HHC's mess hall. Everything went well until he came to the toast, which had been placed several layers deep in an insulated container that was often used to take hot chow to troops in the field. The toast near the bottom of the container was not at all crisp and it was from there that the Five got the piece of bread that eventually gave him a new name: Soggy Toast. In modern day parlance, he went ballistic, and loudly commanded that the mess sergeant stand before him! "Get him here on the double," he shouted loud enough for most in the 2/27 base camp to hear.

The mess sergeant came running when called and stood with heels locked, while the officer, who wanted crisp toast, ranted and raved. "Do you expect soldiers to fight a war on food like this? How skillful does one have to be to provide decent toast? If ever I come to this mess hall again, and it will be soon, and find soggy toast in this mess hall you will be looking for you another job! You are very close right now to joining the 11Bs (Riflemen) in the field. Do I make myself clear, no more disgraceful stuff like this soggy toast not fit for a pig's slop bucket?" The longer he talked the louder he got. Soldiers seated in the mess hall, suddenly decided they were no longer hungry and slipped out. News spread in a hurry: "The Brigade Five doesn't like the kind of toast that folds over like a wet wash cloth."

From that day forward he was known in much of the 2/27 battalion as Colonel Soggy Toast. The stories were rampant and numerous: "Soggy toast in the HHC mess hall may cause America to lose the war." "We should drop a ton of soggy toast in the tunnels of Cu Chi and the bad guys will go back north in a hurry." "When the Brigade Five is promoted to O-6 he'll probably pin a piece of soggy toast on his collar rather than the silver eagle." "Someone ought to send word to his wife that serving soggy toast may be injurious to your marriage."

Those were some of the more complimentary statements.

For a couple of months the epithet was used so much that even I, who never called him by his nickname in the presence of others, almost made a slip one day. At the close of a Brigade staff meeting, which I attended in the absence of the Brigade chaplain, the Five made a point to express gratitude for a memorial service eulogy I had delivered the week before. So ingrained was the "Soggy Toast" title that I came within an inch of saying, "I very much appreciate that Colonel Sog…." Fortunately, I caught it in time and said, "I very much appreciate that Colonel, Sir!"

Somewhere I read that laughter, even when forced, results in beneficial effect on us, both mentally and physically. That being so, the Second 'Hounds were healthy.

Captain Chris Dudley was one of the most efficient and loyal company commanders I ever knew. But when the time came to take things less seriously he could do that too. In fact he was a master at that skill, and I sometimes wondered why he, not a "churchman," so readily shared things with me. Maybe it was because he knew I would keep his confidence, something I've always been careful to do and something I'm doing now, because the name "Chris Dudley" is not his real name. But the incident was very much real.

One day Captain Dudley and I ran into one another at 12th Evac Hospital, where we were both visiting with some of the same injured soldiers. He wanted to know if I had time to talk a few minutes and I said yes.

We sat in my jeep and conversed for almost an hour. Mostly, he wanted to tell me a story and I encouraged him to have at it, because he could tell a story like no one else.

"You were in the Horseshoe with the battalion last week, weren't you?" he asked.

"Sure was, part of the time anyway. As always, I try to get back to Cu Chi for Sunday morning and back to battalion forward by dark. Sometimes it works and sometimes it doesn't."

He continued: "Brigade Six was out there more than I'd ever known him to be. Every time we made contact I expected to look up and see his chopper, and often did see it. Did you know that two weeks ago he landed and relieved a platoon leader he thought was moving too slowly and led the platoon himself for a half-hour? You have to do something to get that Silver Star, right Chap?

"One day last week my company was in light contact. There was a lot of firing and I reported a 'possible' drop of blood on a leaf and continued to look for more."

"I remember, I was with the Battalion Three and heard that transmission," I said.

"Closer examination revealed the red spot on a leaf was not blood. But Brigade Six interpreted my report as a 'blood trail,' and radioed that he was coming in. He wanted to see the non-existent blood trail. There was a field nearby where he could land, so I had to think and work fast. I took the radio from my RTO, gave him 20 piasters and told him to go the farmer's house about a hundred meters back and purchase a chicken. The farmer was pleased to sell one of his old roosters for that good price and the RTO was back in less than a minute.

"The old bird gave his life for a good cause that day, Padre. I ran through the woods for about 50 meters, letting rooster blood drop on the ground, on twigs and waist high on the bark of small trees. The trail ended at a stream and I sent the dead rooster back to the farmer by another soldier while my RTO and I rushed back to where the 'trail' started.

"We were kicking around and searching intently when Brigade Six landed and rushed out to where we were conducting our search. I showed him where the trail began and he began to plod through the brush, his head turning right and left. 'Look here,' he said, 'there is more. And here is some on this sapling. It must be on his hands, one of them at least.' We lost the trail for a few minutes, then my RTO found it again: 'Over here, sir, there is a spot on the ground almost as large as man's foot.'

"But the trail ended at the stream and we deducted that the person losing that blood must have crossed the water and disappeared into a tunnel complex. The colonel was pleased to see an actual blood trail and I was most pleased to be able to show him one. The Six had a good day, one he could tell his children and grandchildren about. Was it my best day? Probably not, but you know the saying: 'If mama ain't happy, ain't nobody happy.' Substitute boss for mama and you got it. If the old man left happy, then so did I. Besides that, we won the heart and mind of a farmer who was paid 20 piasters for a rooster he got to eat for supper."

There must have been a happy ending to that story. Ten years later I saw Chris at a major military post in the states. He was a battalion commander, a Lieutenant Colonel (P). That meant he was on the list for promotion to full colonel. I didn't mention that day in 1967, but sort of wondered if some platoon leader or company commander might some day have a laugh at his expense. They remain capable of such things.

When the soldier goes for days without a hot meal he tends to get irritated, especially if he is told one is forthcoming and then disappears. That scenario was almost played out on an especially hot and humid day in August. The three line companies had been patrolling for three days, living on C-Rations and warm water, diluted with purification tablets. About an hour before sundown the third day we arrived at our night position. A platoon nearest the woods stripped off and began taking a bath in a small canal near the sector they would be responsible for that night. The word had spread that they would be eating hot chow that night and that some blocks of ice were being flown out to cool their soft drinks and tea. Morale soared with that news. As squads took turns bathing in the narrow canal, inbound helicopters could be heard. Hot food and cold drinks were on the way. When the slicks (UH1 helicopters) were in sight a couple snipers opened up on them and the landing was aborted. The choppers pulled right, away from the direction of fire and left the area.

When the firing started I, like most others, dropped to the ground. From my position on the ground I witnessed a sight that remains vivid. I saw a squad of Wolfhounds jump quickly out of the water, pull on their army green boxer shorts and jungle boots, don steel pots, grab their M-16s and take off across the open field toward the snipers. With loose boot laces curling about their ankles and helmet straps flying by their ears, they ran and fired.

The company commander was going nuts, calling for the soldiers to come back. But they didn't stop. The snipers did though. They must have faded into the surrounding woods, and five minutes later, when the helicopters made a second attempt to land, they came in unhindered. The company commander cooled down, laughed with everyone else, and the boxer shorts-clad squad members got to go first.

During chow I sat on the ground with the squad leader and we talked about their charge across the field. He assured me that it was not planned and they could not explain how it happened or who started it. Nobody yelled, "Lets go get 'em!" He said getting to his weapon was the first thing he thought about when he jumped out of the water.

"I suspect," he continued, "that if the first squad member out had gone to ground others would have done the same, but I grabbed my rifle and steel pot, so did Philips and we just took off. We were on our way as if by command.

"I would think that not one of those guys hesitated a second to consider that he might get hurt. Just some nutty kids doing stuff, Chaplain, getting caught up in the excitement of the moment."

In the battalion staff meeting that night the S-2 suggested that the shooters in the woodline may have passed out from fright as they watched eight soldiers speeding their way, rifles blazing, John Wayne style. No wonder young people are called on to fight the wars!

War Zone C was known for its thick, almost impenetrable jungle, much of it triple canopy. Inside those thick woods was almost like being in a large warehouse with no lights, so dark was it, even at high noon. Because of the three layers of foliage, like a small tent inside a fifty foot high tent, inside a 150 foot high tent, the jungle floor rarely got a direct ray of sun. There were unverified reports that 500-pound bombs most often detonated in the tree-tops or on the second layer of foliage, rarely falling all the way to the ground.

It was in War Zone C that the entire Second Wolfhound Battalion was operating in the early spring of 1967. Alpha, Bravo, Charlie and Headquarters companies were part of a huge S and D (search and destroy) mission. The Battalion Commander and his staff were ground-pounders for that mission, because the Command and Control helicopter was of little value in terrain where visibility was so limited.

It was difficult, even in daylight hours, to keep the men on your right or left in sight, though they were normally no more than 15 feet away. It was a perfect place for booby traps, ambushes and the enemy's firing lanes, as we would find out during those days.

On that particular day Charlie Company was in the lead. Headquarters Company was next in line, with the battalion staff in the middle. Following, were Alpha and Bravo. I chose to hump it with Headquarters Company that day. I learned during an early morning field worship service that, due to some recent losses, the medics were vastly understaffed, so I chose to spend most of the day with the "docs." In addition to my combat chaplain kit and rucksack, packed with field rations and extra socks, I carried a litter and sometimes a rigid container of extra medical supplies. But my load was nothing compared to that the mortar and machine gun crews had to carry.

The morning was hot, humid and free of action. Though every soldier had at least two canteens of water, by noon most were out of water and extremely thirsty. Resupply was next to impossible, so most had to refill canteens in small jungle streams and stir in purification tablets. Hundreds of those little pills were in the container I was carrying for the medics. One HHC soldier, who in former times had been suspected of malingering, complained of heat stroke symptoms, but with some water on his face and head and some convincing that getting out of there before we reached our night location was almost impossible, he moved on. To lighten his load, I carried one of his three bandoleers of .30 caliber ammunition for a couple of hours. Occasionally the 'Hounds found and destroyed some items that would assist the enemy, notably rice caches, a few weapons and clothing hidden in shallow holes and short tunnels. Dogs generally sniffed out those caches.

Shortly after noon things turned from tedium to high excitement, and strangely enough, it was then that the "laughter" caught up again. Suddenly, two (it sounded like a dozen or more to me) .51 caliber machine guns opened up on Charlie, the lead company. I was still with HHC and the medics, about a hundred yards from the Chi Com (Chinese Communist) heavy weapons. When shooting starts one's natural inclination is to hit the ground, getting as low as possible. I hit the ground and wished for a way to get even lower. The .51 calibers were spraying the area where Charlie and Headquarters were. Rounds were thudding into large trees and penetrating the 6-8 inch diameter trees. Up front, our guys were returning fire, but they had no real targets. Through the medics I got word that two men had been hit, both pretty bad. (I wrote about these two men, one of whom died later, in an earlier chapter).

As I lay on the ground and unsuccessfully tried to scoop out some dirt with my hands in order to get a little lower, Alpha Company began passing through HHC to help bring relief to Charlie Company. I looked into the face of a young soldier I had come to know well. When possible, Philip was always in chapel services, whether in base camp or the field. About 18 inches from my face, buried as deeply as possible inside that helmet with a Gideon New Testament in the band, he recognized me and stopped. With a surprised look on his peach-fuzz face said, "Chaplain, what are you doing here?"

"You know something, Phil," I said, "I was just lying here asking myself that same question." And as we spoke that hurried greeting a round cut off a three inch limb about eight feet above ground. What was left of the tree branch hit the soldier's boot.

"I've got to get going," he said. "See you Sunday!" And he continued his mission.

Ten feet into his journey, just before entering thick brush and disappearing from sight, he stopped again. He pushed his steel pot back an inch or so, looked me in the eye, and, with a wide grin, said, "Ain't this a bunch of fun!" And with a wave from the hand not gripping his M-16, he crawled on toward whatever was out there. By then the wounded guys were pulled back to a tiny clearing 50 meters away and I began working my way to them. While doing so I kept thinking about Philip's words: "Ain't this a bunch of fun!"

Who wouldn't be pleased to serve with soldiers who can find something to laugh about while dealing with situations that were anything but funny?

Just before dark I conducted a field service with Alpha Company. Philip was there. We didn't mention our strange meeting in the jungle. I've wondered if he ever again thought about his cheerful statement before moving on to help silence the heavy machine guns. Probably not! But I did. I thought about it a lot.

Seeing a soldier take an out and out spiritual stand is always impressive. The same could be said for any young person, high school or college student, or any person who has to contend with peer-group pressure. So when a soldier stated a desire to not only follow and serve the Lord, but to be baptized as well, I tried my best to accommodate him. It was not always easy, because baptismal pools or other places to carry out that ordinance were not readily available. Still, as with all things worthwhile, there were ways, and we were fortunate to find them.

About half way through my second tour in Vietnam I had the privilege of getting to know Staff Sergeant Nolan, senior mess sergeant for the 212th Combat Aviation Battalion at Marble Mountain. I had met and spoken with him many times over the months, but one late morning, upon return from a sleepless overnight in Chu Lai, I went by the mess hall for a cup of coffee. SSG Nolan was alone and sat down to join me. We chatted about army chow and other small-talk subjects for a few minutes before he brought up a subject that was obviously weighing heavily on his mind.

"Chaplain Tucker," he began, "I'm 42 years old and I know it is time to get serious about my relationship with God. I've gone to church off and on for years, but it never did add up to very much. But lately, in our little Wings of Freedom chapel, I've begun doing some heavy thinking. One Sunday, I think three weeks ago, you talked about the boy in the Bible who left home and went into the far away country. I looked it up later and read more about it. The Prodigal Son, isn't that right?"

"That's it exactly. The younger son left home and found things were a lot worse away from home than were at home. So he returned to his father and asked forgiveness."

"Chaplain," he said with emphasis, "that is what I have done. After a long time away, I have come back to the Father, which I take to mean Jesus. In a far country in Southeast Asia, I have come back to God, my father. Now I would like to be baptized and I'm hoping you can do it. Do you think we can do it around here somewhere?"

"I'm sure we can," I replied. "We will find a way."

The following Sunday afternoon Captain Gary Tucker (no relation), WO3 Williams, three cooks, Staff Sergeant Nolan and my chaplain assistant Jerry Logue got in (and on) my jeep and drove to China Beach, on the Marine side of the Marble Mountain military base. Gary Tucker and Williams, avid Christians, attended chapel services regularly. They agreed to be witnesses at the baptism, which was to take place in the South China Sea. All of them joined Nolan and me as we waded toward deeper water on the beautiful, isolated beach. We waded out about a hundred yards and the water was still less than knee deep, so we moved on another fifty or sixty yards. Even that far out, the water barely came up to my knees.

"Want try it here?" I questioned Nolan, and he said yes.

It was then that I learned something: Nolan was afraid of water. At least he feared having his head under water. He did fine until I placed my right hand behind his head and started to lean him back into the water. When the water reached a point where it was about to submerge his shoulders, he would kick one of his feet in the air, yell loud, "WeeWhoo," and break loose from my hold. He would apologize, both to me and to the small congregation in the water, for "being such a baby." He told us that he never liked to have his head under water.

After a few minutes we tried again. "Sergeant," I said, "I'll take you back until the water is up on your chest and I will stop. We'll stay like that a few seconds and with this wash cloth I'll grip your nose lightly to keep water out, then very quickly I'll take you under—bloop, bloop—and right out again. Your head will be under water no more than one second, and even during that one second I'll have a firm grip on you. Deal?"

Again, it worked well until that final in–out, bloop–bloop. And again the foot kicked high as he yelled WeeWhoo and broke away. By now he was almost in tears. He wanted to be immersed as an outward testimony to his faith, but fear kept him from doing it.

I was about ready to give up on getting it done that day, until I looked to my right and saw a large wave forming. Surfer's wave! From on high? Those who had come with us were facing out to sea and saw it too. Nolan was facing toward the shore and was unaware of what was developing 200 yards out.

"Okay, Sarge," I said, "what do you say we try it one more time? Okay with you?" He nodded yes. "So once again, I'll take you back into the water and stop dead still when the water covers your chest." I kept glancing out to sea as the wave got higher and started to roll in.

The onlookers could hardly contain themselves because they knew they too were in for a drenching, but they didn't speak a word or do anything to alert the sergeant to my scheme.

I talked him through it for the third time. "Here we go then! Close your eyes. Slowly and deliberately back. Water up until it covers your chest. Stop. Hold your breath. Grip your nose lightly with my left hand. No water in your nostrils. Half second in, half second out. No danger to anyone."

And the wave hit! Much larger than it first looked to be. It was over my head. Gary, Williams and the others were wet to their necks, and Staff Sergeant Nolan got baptized in ways that none of us had expected.

We laughed while wading back to the jeep and on the short ride back to the U S Army side of Marble Mountain's airstrip.

Even Nolan, feeling a little tricked but mostly blessed, joined in. As Jerry Logue parked the jeep in front of the chapel, who should be walking by but our commander Colonel Hickerson? Looking at our soaking wet fatigue and Nomex uniforms, he said, "Have you guys been swimming in your clothes?"

"Sir," I answered, "it's a long story." He laughed when we told the short version.

It was at Marble Mountain, near Danang that I met Pastor Le Van Tu. Pastor Tu had a church, school and orphanage. Our chapel provided money, building materials and clothing to support his many areas of ministry. Soldiers from my aviation outfit would often go to the orphanage just to play with the bigger children and rock the little ones, many of whom were half-American and pretty much disowned by the families of their young mothers.

After many months of association with Pastor Tu, I was invited to his house for a meal. A number of American missionaries and military chaplains had also been invited. When we entered the dining room I was directed to a chair at the head of a long table. An Alliance missionary, who had been in Vietnam for many years, sat to my left. The pastor's wife and small children began serving, and I was served first. On my plate was a pile of white rice, easily as large as half a volley ball. Squarely on top of the large mound of rice was a chicken head. Actually it was a rooster's head, very large with a long red comb. The rooster's head with comb on top stood up at least three inches above the huge serving of rice.

All the guests were served large helpings of rice, but no one else had a rooster head. With food in front of them, Pastor Tu and other Vietnamese pastors looked my way and smiled, as only people from that part of the world can look at you. As quietly and discreetly as possible I asked the American missionary why I was the only one who had a chicken head.

"You are the guest of honor," he said in a whisper.

Just as quietly I said to him, "If you'll be the guest of honor, I'll give you my plate."

"This is their way of saying thanks to you for the many things you and your soldiers have done for their church and community," he informed me. "They are waiting for you to take the first bite so everyone can begin eating. That is their custom."

I picked up my fork, smiled at everyone, nodded to Pastor Tu and took a big bite of rice. That set the tone. The table became a veritable beehive of activity. While everyone was busily occupied with talking and eating, I slid the rooster head to the edge of the plate and covered it with rice. I never learned if I was supposed to take a bite of that thing. If it was edible, Pastor Tu and his family had some wonderful leftovers.

My first tour in Vietnam was barely underway when I began to get boxes of "goodies," especially homemade cookies. Among the hundreds of soldiers in my "congregation," cookies, if offered, didn't last long. I always offered. I have a mental picture of PFC Jerry Don Everett and his Charlie Company platoon in the back of a deuce and a half (Two and a Half Ton army truck). They were going out for the night, as I understood it, to serve as a blocking force for Alpha Company. PFC Everett was seated next to end, right side.

"Say guys, I have two big packages of homemade cookies from Arkansas. Want some? Pass these around."

Everett said, "Chaplain, this puts me in mind of my grandma's home cooking, back in Desha County. She wrote me one letter and said we're gonna have all kind of everything I want to eat when I get home. So I told her to just fix it all. Get all the recipes out, then double them up and that ought to about do it."

The other soldiers in the truck had various responses to those words, including, "Amen. Amen to that! Bring on the home cooking!" I kept doling out cookies.

PFC Everett continued, "Yes sir, when she hears this soldier done dropped in at the Little Rock bus station, she know ain't much more'n two more hours to Dumas, then the next stop Tillar–smaller than Dermott but bigger than Reed."

"That's where you're from?" I said. "Tillar, Arkansas? Close to McGehee, Rohwer, and Winchester. Not too far from Back Gate?"

"Hey, Chap, you know that country. You from somewhere close to there?"

"Pretty close. Monticello. Up in the hills." I answered.

"I'll be going home soon. Maybe you can come over to Tillar when you are over to see your Monticello folks."

"You got it. We'll have us a Wolfhound reunion down in the cotton country."

It's good when a plan works out. Better than scoring the winning TD. This one didn't! Not on earth, anyway. Jerry Don and several squad mates got it that night. Halloween.

CHAPTER 11

Come As You Are

They shall renew their strength

—Isaiah 40:31

Journal entry, 24 September 1967—Conducted five services today...
on the go!

Sometimes it was in a twenty-foot diameter bomb crater. Five times it was in thatch-roofed village schools, which were simple open-sided, brush arbor type sheds, no larger than the living room in an average American home. On occasions it was near the raging waters of the Oriental or Saigon Rivers, or on the broken remains of a blown-up Buddhist pagoda, which had been destroyed by indigenous populace as a warning to those in nearby villages. Frequently it was in eight-foot high, trampled down elephant grass. Sometimes it was in an open field with attendees huddling the best they could under a poncho.

Such were the "churches" and "chapels" where soldiers assembled to worship and pray in combat situations. Austerity and field expediency personified.

At first I thought, "How very unusual and different!" Then it became routine and even preferred. My thoughts during the first two or three field services were something like this: "This time last year I was concerned about comfort of the congregation in the beautiful country church I served as pastor near Eldorado, Arkansas. Was the thermostat too high? Too low? Hopefully, neither too warm nor too cool! Is the sound system set right for the average worship participant? Is lighting adequate? And I thought about dress. Nobody inspected, but "Sunday best" was the unofficial rule. Coats and ties and dressy dresses were accepted, though not required. It was that way, "back there."

Now it was different. Dress was not an issue. Muddy boots. Smudged, sweaty faces. Hand grenades hanging on web gear. No padded pews in this outdoor sanctuary. Sit on the ground with M-16s by your side or across your knees. Wear your steel pots or sit on them, it's up to you. Come as you are. Private, Sergeant, Captain or Colonel, all are welcome and during these moments all are on level ground. For a few minutes we'll reflect, sing a verse or two of "Amazing Grace" and "On a Hill Far Away." We'll pray silently and audibly, nod agreement to a brief message about the Lost Sheep or The Rich Young Ruler, and return to foxholes and fighting positions to face what the night may bring.

Lieutenant Chuck Glasscock, Recon Platoon Leader was nearly always there, the mission or tactical situation permitting. So respected was he that most of his platoon members attended field services with him. These many years later I can almost see Chuck, all six foot two and 160 or so pounds of him, making his way to the improvised field altar, where we'd meet at the announced time to turn thoughts to things higher than war.

"I'm sort of ashamed to admit it, but I've never been much of a church-going person," he said to me one day. "Suits, white shirts and ties just didn't seem to fit me correctly. I felt out of place wearing them and felt out of place in church without them. But out here it's different. You, our preacher, wear the same jungle fatigues the rest of us do. Most of us are usually a little on the scroungy side, needing a haircut much of the time and nobody cares. Nobody is looking down on anyone else. I don't know why, Chap, but Jesus seems to be more real when you don't have to worry about appearances or 'singing off key.' Maybe that doesn't make any sense at all."

"It does. It makes big time sense. And the longer I serve with troops in combat the more sense it makes. It will be a sad day if ever we come to think that God will not receive the one dressed in faded jeans, scuffed boots and soiled fatigue pants," I said.

Lieutenant Glasscock was pretty typical of those who possessed a deep faith in God and had experienced the same New Birth that Jesus explained to Nicodemus in the Gospel of John, yet were not totally sold on the institutional church. They did not oppose it and even gave in support of it, but didn't involve themselves personally in it with much consistency.

Maybe it was from him, or one of his contemporaries, that I first heard this: "I have come to the point where I like Jesus better than the church!" I've heard similar testimonies since those days in the jungles and mud of Southeast Asia. Words like this: "Jesus, yes! Church, no!" I hope our future generations will get beyond that saying.

Two memorable events during those days serve as reminders that even those who had never outwardly placed much stock in organized religion in general or the church in particular may turn to it when things seem dark and almost hopeless.

During my second tour in Vietnam, at Marble Mountain, near Danang, I met PFC Grayson in an unusual and unexpected way. Shortly before 2200 Hours (10 PM), at the conclusion of a rocket attack on the 212th Combat Aviation airstrip, I entered the front and only door the Wings of Freedom chapel for what I hoped would be last time that day. The entire area was still completely blacked out. The only illumination was the intermittent light from flares about 300 yards away, just outside the battalion perimeter.

As I stepped through the door, the dim light from a distant flare revealed what appeared to be a person sitting on the left side front pew. That was unusual because all personnel not on duty were supposed to be in or just leaving the safety of bunkers.

"Hey. Who is there?" I called out. There was no answer and no movement from the seated figure. My second call received no response either.

Stepping into my tiny chapel office I placed a red lens in my crooked-neck flashlight and began the 50 foot walk toward the barely visible person, calling out as I walked. Still no answer. In the dim red light of my flashlight I could see the person was a soldier. His head was leaning on the back of the hard wooden pew, his face turned upward like he was gazing at the ceiling. His arms were hanging over the bench on which he was seated, hands pointed forward.

"Hey, soldier, this is the chaplain. Can you hear me?" I said to him.

"Yes sir, I can hear you." And he began to weep.

"What is your name? Can you tell me your name? Are you okay?"

"Grayson. PFC Grayson," he said. "I don't think I'm okay."

Then I noticed it. There were wet spots on the floor under each hand. I forgot about blackout and replaced the red lens with a clear one and discovered that he was bleeding from both wrists. The spots on the chapel floor were blackish red.

I wrapped my handkerchief around his right wrist and gripped it tightly with my left hand. With my bare, and certainly unsanitary, right hand I gripped his left wrist and got him to a standing position. "Can you walk?" I asked him. He said he could. Walking backward and gripping both his wrists, I guided him out of the chapel and to the battalion aid station about 50 yards away. The medic on duty began work on him immediately and discovered his wrist wounds were superficial, little more than scratches but deep enough to cause some bleeding.

Within an hour Grayson had been cleaned up and bandaged, and he was apologizing for being a bother and getting blood on the chapel floor. I assured him that the chapel floor was the least of anyone's worry.

Grayson's company commander got to the aid station about the time the medics finished with him. I suggested that Grayson spend the rest of the night in my hootch, a neat little two-room house a Vietnamese carpenter had built near the Wings of Freedom chapel. The commander agreed, saying, "I hope you can do him some good."

By then it was midnight. We talked until 0300 (3 AM). During those hours I discovered that his home life had not been the best. He had no parents who cared (his words), no church and, of course, no pastor. About the only real tie he had left was a girl friend back in Missouri. Reba Jean, age 18. Now he didn't even have Reba Jean. It was the dreaded "Dear John" letter from her that had sent him into the chapel with bad thoughts and a dull razor blade.

Grayson and I talked about many things before getting a little sleep between 3 and 5 AM. His upbringing did not include church attendance. "Chaplain, I've been in the army seven months and have never entered a chapel, but you are going to see me here from now on," were his words about 2:30 AM. I explained to him the meaning of verse 16 in the third chapter of John's gospel. He had never heard of it. He had never heard of a Bible character known as the Philippian jailer, and was carried away with the exchange that took place between the jailer and a man named Paul. He was so enthralled with the words of Jesus (printed in red in the Bible I gave him) that he could hardly stop reading. He found faith and direction in the wee hours of the morning following the darkest night he had known in his 19 years. As I drifted off to sleep I thought about field services two years earlier in another part of Vietnam. It was the same both times: Come as you are.

Not all the stories ended as happily as PFC Grayson's did. Private John McCollum's didn't. I met Private Mack, as he preferred to be addressed, several years later in Germany. He desperately wanted to find a faith to guide him and enjoy a life of freedom from chemicals. We spent many hours talking and praying, and it sometimes appeared that victory was just over the horizon. But debilitating things also invite people to come as they are. John found out which pull was the strongest. Regrettably, I did too.

On a Saturday in late October we met for at least the 20th time in a little building that had once been used as a conference room by the German Air Force during World War II. A small steeple had been erected on the roof and it served as an ecumenical chapel for the U S Army. My office, with a desk and two straight chairs, was in one corner. It was in front of the desk that John fell to the floor that Saturday afternoon and called out to God.

For more than two hours I watched him beat on the floor with both fists and cry out for deliverance. "Oh, God, in the name of Jesus the Christ, deliver me from that which binds me and bind me to yourself. Break me of this habit that is killing me. Lead me to take up the habit of living for you, praying to you, serving you, worshiping you."

On and on he pleaded for a new life and a spirit free of all shackles. He would call out and beat on the floor for a while, then sit up and read from the Bible for a while. Once, while sitting with his back against my gray metal desk, he began thumbing through an Armed Forces Hymnal, as if searching for something he knew was there.

Suddenly he turned to me and spoke: "Listen to these words from this song book." And he read them to me: "Just as I am, though tossed about with many a conflict, many a doubt, fightings and fears within, without. O Lamb of God, I come! I come!" John stared at me a few seconds and said, "Did you hear that? Those words are talking about me, Chaplain, about me! Did you hear them? 'Though tossed about with many a conflict…and many a doubt, fightings and fears within and without.' Those words describe me better than anything I've ever heard."

"John, there are a lot of voices vying for our attention and a lot of things to deal with. Among all those voices a man has to be sure he is listening to and following the right one." I asked him to hear words from the 30ᵗʰ chapter of the Old Testament Book of Isaiah and see if he might be able to find something in them that applied to him: *Either way you turn, to the right or to the left, you will hear a voice behind you, saying, "This is the way; walk in it."*

After pondering those words a minute and reading them silently, he fell on his face once again and began beating the floor, begging to be freed from that which had bothered him for so long. Had I not known better I might have thought he was a man who had taken leave of his senses.

At last he went silent and stood. With the smile of a winner on his face, told me he had won. "It is over. I'm delivered. I have won!" he said. "God has promised it and I have claimed it."

It was dark and we had missed both lunch and dinner. John said he was going to the snack bar for a sandwich and then to let three of his friends know he wouldn't be doing any more junk with them.

The latter sounded like an excellent course of action. It would take some real intestinal fortitude. He was sure the guys would be pleased that he had won the battle. I hoped he was right.

But John had not won!

A few minutes before midnight I received a call from Colonel Fincham, his battalion commander, with word that John was in the medical clinic in very bad shape. I dressed in a hurry and rushed to the clinic. As I entered the emergency room I heard what sounded like a pro-longed exhale. It was Private John McCollum's body undergoing some sort of involuntary reaction. He was dead when I stepped to his side.

Early the next morning—Sunday—I went to John's room on the fourth floor, not a half block from where we had spent most of the daylight hours on Saturday. Three of his buddies, fellow drug users as it turned out, were there. I knew them all. "What happened?" I asked the one I knew best. "What happened last evening when Private McCollum came to see you guys and tell you something?"

"Chaplain, he came to tell us his life had been changed, that God had cleaned him up and that he was going to pay off all his drug debts and not use any more," his buddy told me. The two soldiers with him nodded agreement. "So we came up with a celebration plan," he continued. "One of the guys pulled out some pills he had bought over the counter in town. He suggested that we go to John's room on the fourth floor and have a last big time together to help celebrate John's release from the old life and his new life with God. That is what we did.

"Starting about ten o'clock, we smoked some, took a few pills and took a few drinks. We got with it pretty heavy. John did too and all the while he was saying it would be his last time. Around eleven or so he opened the dormer window and stepped out on the roof. He extended his arms and began waving his hands, like he was waving at someone on his right and left. Then he yelled out loud, like a wild man, 'I can fly. I can fly. Everybody look at me, I'm going to fly.' And he jumped. But Chaplain, he couldn't fly, except to the concrete walk four stories down."

The chapel service, held in the same place John and I had spent so many hours the day before, was somber. Most of those in the congregation knew the soldier who now lay in the morgue, most of his bones broken. For several weeks he had been a Sunday morning chapel volunteer, greeting people as they entered, handing out bulletins, being friendly and doing his best to serve. All the while he was fighting a terror within.

As has been reported, chaplains in Vietnam had to hitch rides to reach their field units. You'd catch a resupply helicopter, a med evac and very infrequently, one whose pilot needed to get in some flight hours. When "hitching" you stood the chance of visiting some unexpected places. On May 23, 1967 I jumped on a chopper headed for Duc Hoa, where two 2/27 companies were then operating. Enroute, the pilot got a call to do a non-emergency medical pick up at an artillery fire base. When he set down, I jumped out to speak to some soldiers while the door gunner helped with the evacuee.

One of the first men I met was the Bravo Battery Commander of the 1/8 Artillery. He noted the chaplain cross on my steel pot and thought I had come to do some counseling and hold a service for his soldiers. I didn't have the heart to tell him that I was going to jump on that bird and fly out again in about 60 seconds.

After getting assurance that the pilot would let one of the Wolfhound company commanders at Duc Hoa know my whereabouts, I agreed to stay with the artillery battery a while. Of course I didn't know any of the artillery soldiers and they didn't know me. But that didn't seem to matter. The first sergeant got busy getting the word out that "the chaplain" was in the field and would offer a field service at 1400 Hours. I had 20 minutes to get something together. At least half of the soldiers on that fire base attended.

The Battery Commander said it had been weeks since they had a religious service of any kind. I'd never seen a more appreciative bunch of young men, not even among my beloved Second Battalion guys.

That pilot had agreed to pick me up again in two hours, "unless he was tasked with another mission in the meantime," in which case he would attempt to get someone else to get me out of there and on to the companies at Duc Hoa. Two hours and 12 minutes after jumping off among a bunch of strangers, I was on the way out again with the same pilot. I expressed gratitude that he didn't leave me stranded, especially since I was there with no field gear or extra socks (necessities). But my trusty combat chaplain kit nearly always contained a few cans of C-rations and a warm Pepsi or Ginger Ale. And, like most field soldiers, a P-38 (can opener) was always at the ready on my dog-tag chain.

"Where do you want to go now, Chaplain?" the pilot asked. I told him that my original destination was Duc Hoa and that I still needed to go.

"Then Duc Hoa it will be," he said. We were there in 20 minutes.

Two other slicks (UH1 helicopters) landed just ahead of us. They were loaded with hot chow, iced-down drinks, and mail. Talk about Christmas in May! Now that was just about it—Hot food *and* mail call.

Because I arrived at the same time, some of the soldiers helping with unloading thought I must be responsible for their double good fortune.

"Sorry, guys," I said. "I'm not Santa Claus coming early. Can't take credit for this. But someone is looking out for you and for that I'm grateful."

I still didn't have any field gear except for a poncho. Though sleeping with it wrapped around you was like sleeping in a steam room, it had to do. I used a borrowed entrenching tool (little folding shovel) to dig a shallow foxhole, and after chow and a late evening field service with Bravo Company, I took to that 2 by 6 trench like it was the best room in a fancy hotel.

While thinking about home and the activity filled day, it occurred to me that it was the first time I had had the privilege of holding services with two Bravo units the same day—Bravo, 1/8 Artillery and Bravo, 2/27 Infantry. I didn't suppose that would be anything earth shaking to most people, but it was worth a daily journal entry.

So was what happened at breakfast the next morning. I was having warmed over pancakes with Alpha Company soldiers, including SP4 Lou Diamond As we ate, I noticed his boots. He had worn his jump boots to the field and they were coming apart. The stitching was literally disintegrating in the heat and humidity.

The sole of his right boot was completely detached from the upper leather from the toe to his instep. He had wrapped heavy green tape around the fractured boot but that repair job didn't fare well with constant activity. Nor did his attempt to repair it with a boot lace a squad mate had given him.

"What size boots do you wear?" I asked Specialist Diamond.

"I usually take a 9W. Wide so I can wear two pairs of socks," he said.

"This is your lucky day. That is my size and for the double socks reason. My green and black jungle boots are broken in well, and they are yours."

"Oh, Chaplain, I can't take your boots," he said.

"Yes you can, because I'm heading back to Cu Chi on the bird you hear inbound right now. I'll tell the supply sergeant a sob story and get another pair, 9W. So you take these."

Take them he did, and I boarded the Huey in my sock feet. I don't think the door gunner, crew chief or either of the two other passengers even noticed. My assistant noticed when he picked me up at the chopper pad and made one comment: "It would have been something if your chopper had gone down in enemy territory, leaving you to walk to Hanoi barefoot."

"Thankfully, that part didn't happen. Get this little vehicle to Headquarters Company in a hurry, I need to see the supply sergeant."

CHAPTER 12

Commitment

If your sword is too short, add a step to it.

—Anonymous

Journal entry, 15 July 1967—Dog tired. Our guys need a rest and a good foot drying.

PFC Grayson, whom you met in the last chapter, made one of the most dramatic turns I had ever witnessed, or have since. When we stopped talking about 3:00 AM, he slept soundly on the wooden bench I had built to double as a couch in my 180 square foot hut near the chapel. I checked on him every few minutes to be sure he was still there and that his wrist-slashing episode was over and done with.

After a very short night we walked to the mess hall at 6:30 for some breakfast. Some of his company personnel were there, but they seemed unaware that anything untoward had taken place with him. Rolled-down sleeves of his fatigue blouse hid the gauze bandages on his wrists. We never mentioned our strange meeting again.

Between mouthfuls of scrambled powered eggs and Canadian bacon, Grayson asked some questions that I detected were straight from the heart: "Chaplain, do you know any way I can do something for someone? Maybe at payday give money to a good cause?"

"You probably don't know this, but the guys here in the 212th give to the support of an orphanage not far away," I responded. "But you might want to send a money order to your church every month and designate it for missions, hunger relief or something like that."

He answered: "The thing is though, I don't have no church. I think my mother used to go once in a while, but I never went with her after I was eight or nine. I just never knew anything about God and Jesus before we talked last night. So, I don't know where I could send something that would do any good.

"But helping the orphanage might be something I could do. What do you think?"

"I think it would be great. I'll take you out there sometime soon, maybe next Sunday or the week after. It was started and is run by a small group of Catholic nuns from France and this country. Many of the dozens of children are half-American, fathered by GIs. Some of the kids were rescued from the street, where they had been abandoned by mothers, who could not take care of them or by the mother's parents who didn't want them.

"A little five-year old boy, who has become a favorite of our guys, lost his right arm above in a rocket attack when he was three. At least that is how the nuns tell it. Many others have lesser wounds, but they are all happy kids. They love the soldiers and the soldiers love them. You probably will too."

He looked toward the next Sunday the way a child looks for a birthday party. My jeep, loaded with more soldiers than the MPs would normally allow, got to the orphanage about 2:00 PM. I quickly introduced Grayson to the nuns and they introduced him to children, who were starved for attention. The other guys, cameras at the ready, began their weekly visit with the happy children. For Grayson, it was love at first sight.

I discovered the depth of his love and commitment the next time he was paid. He brought me an envelope stuffed with MPC (Military Payment Certificate, which, in an attempt to keep American dollars off the Vietnamese economy, was how we were paid). It contained $160.00. He wanted to give all of it to purchase food and clothing for kids in the orphanage.

"How much did you get paid this month?" I asked him.

"A hundred and sixty dollars," he told me.

"So you want to give your entire month's pay to the orphanage this month?"

"Yes sir. I want help those kids with food and some better clothes to wear."

We ran his gift through the chapel offering on the Sunday it was designated for the orphanage. After changing it to piasters (South Vietnamese currency) I gave it to the diminutive and grateful administrator. The amount was more than double any monthly gift the Wings of Freedom chapel had ever made.

Next payday, Grayson brought me another fat envelope. This time it contained even more–$168. And I asked him if that was the sum total of his pay that month, to which he answered in the affirmative.

"Grayson, this is more commendable that I can express to you. Two months in a row you have given everything you drew." I asked him if someone in the states was sending him care packages or money to purchase the things he needed. His answer was that the only thing he ever got was a half-page letter from his mother about once every three or four weeks.

We talked some more about his desire to help others and his commitment to the kids in the village. At last he was able to see that he might not be considered a miser if he kept a little for his own needs. Things like shaving soap or cream (he had begun shaving with cold water and no soap since his first visit to the orphanage), deodorant, a new pack of razor blades and even a soft drink and a candy bar from the China Beach PX on occasions, might be "permissible." He agreed, and took back eight dollars.

Combat chaplains and other spiritual leaders I know readily testify that not all episodes they encountered had such happy endings. But rewards came along, and there were (and are) enough of them to make their efforts worthwhile.

As with so many dedicated servants of God I met among soldiers over the years, I often wonder what happened to Grayson after he served his time in Uncle Sam's army. If he continued on the path he began following shortly after receiving his devastating news, he gave to numerous worthy causes, including his life in committed service.

The military has never been portrayed as a fraternity filled with angels. I found it an organization that is an extension of our society, neither wholly angelic nor wholly vile. I also found that when one of those youngsters, enlisted and officer alike, made a conscious decision to commit his life to God and to spiritual principles it was for real. It had to be real, because there were so many detractions to deal with.

A simple poem, which dealt with faith and the soldier, appeared in the Pacific *Stars and Stripes* during operation Junction City in 1967. Though the verses will never rival Frost, Kipling or any real poet, they spoke to many a youngster out on the line. It is entitled simply, *The Faith of a GI*.

> There is a man, hardly more than a boy,
> Who through this strange land does plod.
> He's a man who will fight
> For the one solemn right
> To bow down and worship his God.
>
> He loves and cherishes life,
> Though reality tells him he could die.
> But somehow you just know
> he was ready to Go.
> Because he had the faith of a GI.

Do not despair for this young man's soul.
For the "On High" command he does wait.
And to all he would say:
"By night and by day,
In the almighty I have anchored my faith."

Do I really know this man? Yes!
I've seen him in the swamp and the dry.
His weapon held close and with care,
his lips uttering a silent prayer,
I've seen the faith of a GI.

Shortly after reading those simple verses, which I have kept these past 45 years, I met SP4 Don Harrelson. Don, at age 25, was five years older than the average rifleman. His wife of two years lived in Ohio. That was where he wanted to be, and not in Vietnam.

Those two subjects came up with frequency in our formal counseling sessions as well as in the many informal conversations we had. Don loved his country, had a firm belief that he should "do his part," got along well with and loved his fellow soldiers and was a "flag-waving," patriotic young man. But he missed his wife and wanted to be home in Ohio. Even as he shared those feelings he did so with some tinges of guilt, and readily acknowledged that probably his thoughts about home and family were not unlike thoughts every soldier away from home was having.

"You are definitely right on that subject," I said to him, as we shared a homemade brownie on the edge of a bomb crater. "Most of the youngsters in your company would much prefer to be somewhere else. So would ninety-nine percent of those in every combat unit in this country."

"I know, I really do know that but if they want it as badly as I do, there are some hurting and really frightened guys in this place," he said. "Is there any avenue I can pursue, Chaplain? Anything that will result in my get transferred to the states? I know it is a long shot, but it is on my mind all the time, even more since learning my wife is having some serious money problems."

"Without documentation for hardship or compassionate reasons, it is almost impossible. You've seen others leave in a way you surely don't want," I said.

Every few days he'd drop by to talk a few minutes. He would try hard to dwell on other things, but if we were together for more than five minutes, the same subjects surfaced—fear and home.

I felt deeply for him, as I did for all those facing the terror of war, but all I could do was pray with him and try to offer some reassuring words. In the meantime he continued to be a good, very dependable soldier, even as he fought a fierce internal battle.

Between 3 August and 7 October, 1967 Specialist Harrelson and I met for a few minutes after nearly every worship service, whether in garrison or the field. During our conversations about spiritual matters and biblical principles I learned that he gave ten percent of his pay through our chapel offering every month. *How dedicated is that?* I thought. Here was a man whose pay had dropped to a third of his former civilian salary, with a wife who was having a difficult time making ends meet, and yet he was careful to tithe his income every month.

By the time I took a few days for Rest and Recreation (R & R) to Thailand on the 7th of October Don seemed to be less worried about his situation. Getting back into Vietnam late on the 12th made it necessary to stay in Saigon overnight. At 0900 the next morning I hitched a ride on a chopper bound for Cu Chi.

There were a lot of letters to read and "goodie" packages to open (and share with perennially hungry GIs). But something else I learned upon return was especially welcome. My journal entry for 13 October stated it: "Learned that none of our guys had been hit while I was in Thailand. Not even one dustoff. Great news!" News like that usually doesn't hold for long in war. It didn't then.

On Monday, the 16th of that month, I was back in the woods and rice fields for field services with Headquarters and Charlie companies. After a night battling mosquitoes, the 2/27 began a sweep of an area where VC had been sighted.

I joined up with Delta Company, which had become part of the battalion in mid-August. Being with them for a couple of days would provide an opportunity to get to meet some new soldiers, who had not yet felt they were genuine Wolfhounds.

The good news I learned on the 13th turned bad on the 18th. While "humping the boonies" with Delta, I learned that another Wolfhound company, on a mission near the Cu Chi perimeter, had detonated an anti-tank mine. There were casualties. Specialist Don Harrelson was one of them. The soldier, with whom I had spoken so often and who wanted so badly to be home, now lay wounded, or worse. Which, I did not know.

I jumped on the first chopper that resupplied Delta and flew back to 12th Evac Hospital. It was with a feeling of deep dread that I anticipated what might be found upon landing at the hospital. "If he is even alive, what would I say to this soldier who talked with me so often about 'getting out of here?'" I kept thinking.

Jumping out before the skids touched down, I ran to the emergency room, a place that was well known to me. A nurse, who occasionally attended worship services at the Wolfhound Chapel, was on duty and attending an injured soldier. "Can you tell me if Specialist Don Harrelson has come through here?" I asked, and she pointed in the direction of triage.

Upon reaching triage, a very busy place at the time, I saw a gurney near the entrance. On it lay a someone covered with a white sheet. I could see no boots. Where the lower legs should have been, the sheet lay flat on the gurney. I moved closer for a better look. I knew the soldier. It was Specialist Harrelson. Both legs had been blown off below his knees. His badly mangled left arm was wrapped in bandages.

Now the dread was even more pronounced, but I moved to within a foot from him and quietly called his name. He was highly sedated, but recognized me. His grime-covered face broke into a weak grin. Before I could form enough words to express regret for what had taken place it the last three hours, he reached out his good right hand, lightly gripped mine and, still smiling, said, "Chaplain, I'm going home!"

All I could say was, "That you are, soldier. You are going home!" He went to sleep as I stood beside his gurney. The morphine had taken over.

It took several days to get him ready for a flight out. His left leg was amputated just below the knee, the right, half way between his knee and ankle. I made a point to see him as often as possible before he was evacuated to a hospital in Japan. He was in amazingly good spirits the day after becoming a double amputee. He made a request: He wanted to become a member of First Baptist Church, Okmulgee, Oklahoma, where my wife and I were members. I wrote the pastor and asked him to bring his request before the church and vote on it. That was before the days of texting and instant communication, so it was long after Harrelson had left Cu Chi that I heard back from Pastor Stanley White, that the church had overwhelmingly, and with profound gratitude, approved his request for membership. I knew what the outcome would be and assured Don of it. That request involved a special word—Commitment. But there was more.

On October 25, 1967, my last day to see him and the day he boarded the medical evacuation plane, he requested one more favor, which I gladly granted. He had received pay that was due him—$333.00. He asked me if I would purchase a money order for that amount and send it to his wife. Before I could leave the ward with his money, he called out, "Sir, wait," which I did.

He wanted t expand the instructions concerning his last payday in Vietnam: "Would you please purchase two money orders? Get one for a tithe to my new church in Oklahoma and another for the balance to my wife?"

While driving to the APO, I shook my head in awe of what I had just heard. I took his $333 and purchased a money order for $33.30 to the church he would probably never see, and a second one for $299.70, on which I wrote his wife's name. Ten minutes later they were posted to the respective parties. No stamp was required. "Free," printed on the upper right corners of the envelopes got them on their way. I went aboard the plane with him and prayed for a safe flight. Also, that his greatest home-coming fear, which was that his wife might not love him as a cripple, would be unfounded.

The day he left, I learned that PFC Shaun Hebert had died during the night at 45th Surgical Hospital, near Tay Ninh. News of his death reawakened all kinds of memories and visions of commitment with a different slant.

Hebert, though an E-3 (PFC), had been a sergeant more than once. He was a unique, happy-go-lucky person, which often led to trouble and loss of rank. He once told me that he had fought against the Viet Cong with the French Army. He was 10-12 years older than most of the American soldiers he served with, but joined with them as if the same age.

I saw him as a man of contrasts and knew him to be one of varied experience. With the news of his death, I thought about an event that had taken place a few days before, when Hebert was tasked with transporting a suspected VC detainee to the interrogation people at another location. A few minutes into the transport, a shot was heard in the direction the guard and detainee had walked. "The VC broke and ran," PFC Hebert reported to the officer investigating the incident, "and I had to shoot him!"

It was the word of one against another, but I could tell the S-2 people thought he had simply assassinated the prisoner. The main reason they thought that was because in the same area, just two days before, two medics from Hebert's company had been killed in a well-cleared firing lane as they attended wounded soldiers. A third medic had been wounded before the company commander forbade anyone else to enter the firing lane until the sniper could be dealt with.

That incident created a dilemma for those of us who thought the detainee's death was probably an act of revenge. What does one do? The dilemma ended, officially anyway, with Hebert's death.

The title for a later chapter will be, "War is what they say it is!" It is that. The same day the older medic died, another of our soldiers shot himself in the leg. "Probably self-inflicted," the investigative report said.

When Ralph Smith, who went to Vietnam as a PFC and left a year later as a Staff Sergeant, was awarded the DSC (Distinguished Service Cross) for heroism, I took some time to really consider what it is that drives a person, especially one in combat? What is it that makes one drive on when the danger of being killed is extremely high? I wondered, and still do.

One would never expect to meet a more laid back, non-heroic type than Ralph. He was among the first to show up when chapel call was announced and the first to drop something "in the plate" when humanitarian needs were announced. The calm, good natured, champion-of-the-under-dog guy. I thought of him as the consummate Christian disciple. Every pastor dreams of filling his church with servants like him. Yet on a given day in 1967 the small-town youngster from North Carolina defied death and did things that most people can't begin to fathom.

What causes such action that turns out to be heroic?

Patriotism? The flag? Apple pie and motherhood? A medal for bravery? Maybe no one knows for sure, but probably none of those. Not at the time anyway. It is doubtful that the one who performs such abnormally courageous acts knows what the motivation is. But commitment comes close to defining it? Commitment to the guy on the left and to the guy on the right. As I saw it, to the soldier it was, "get the job done and move on." It is the best of all good things when the commitment points two ways—to God and mankind.

When this subject rises I always think of another dear friend, one who gave his life on Halloween Day (actually the night before), 1967. His name was Riley Leroy Pitts. When I met Captain Riley Pitts he was Commanding Officer of Charlie Company, Second Wolfhounds, 25th Infantry Division. On October 31 his company was alerted to go to the aid of another company, which was in heavy contact with a large NVA unit. Riley, a man blessed with deep compassion and a strong religious faith, led his guys into the fray. He fired his CAR-15 (compact version of the M-16 that many company commanders and platoon leaders preferred) until all his magazines were empty. His attempts to silence the enemy fire continued with a government issued .45 caliber pistol, until all the rounds in it were gone as well.

Next, his RTO told me later, Captain Pitts hurled one of his hand grenades, which hit heavy brush and bounced back among the platoon he was moving with. The instant it fell among Charlie Company soldiers, Riley threw himself on it, as history reveals that so many others have done. But the grenade did not explode. It was a dud.

In five seconds he was up again and continuing the attack through thick underbrush, firing an enemy soldier's weapon he had found on the battle site. Less than a half-minute later his earthly life ended. The soldier who saw his last seconds of life said that Riley could not have known what hit him. He was moving one second and down the next.

A lot of heroic acts took place in the last few minutes of Captain Pitts' life, but the part about wrapping himself around the ricocheting grenade is what was most firmly stamped in my mind. When one performs such an act there is obviously no time to think about it. No time to say, "Well, this device has the potential to take a lot of lives, so maybe I can do something so that it takes only one life—mine." Who knows what the last thoughts of the self-sacrificing one might be, but probably not something like this: "I care about these guys and they don't deserve to die in this foreign land, so I will."

Still, in there somewhere is an emotion known as love. At such a crucial point, love and commitment seemed to be closely aligned. I was pleased to witness those two words played out as a pair many times, and never ceased to be amazed.

Captain Pitts received the Congressional Medal of Honor for deeds performed on that day/night before Halloween. A few months later I heard that he was the first African-American officer to be awarded the MOH in Vietnam.

Thoughts of the memorial service conducted for Riley Pitts and three more of Charlie Company's soldiers—PFC Chapman, PFcEerett and SP4 Miller—remain vivid. Noise from torrential rain on the chapel's tin roof was so loud the words Lieutenant Colonel Walter Adams and I spoke could hardly be heard above the roar that early November day. I recall thinking, but not saying, "these great guys gave their lives in the noise of a horrendous fire fight and here we are honoring their memory in the noise of nature." And, though there would be sadness for a long time in four more homes back in the United States, there was peace for a commander and three soldiers he deeply loved. The sounds of battle would buffet their eardrums no more.

At first I found it ironic that, after seeing close friends and squad mates become casualties, soldiers often volunteered for duty that appeared to be even more dangerous than they had endured thus far. There was (and probably still is) something in the human spirit, and certainly the youthful human spirit, that makes the rest of us shake our hands in wonder. Maybe it was an attempt to prove something or answer the call for adventure, but in many there seemed to be a need to do more than they had done so far. Admittedly, after a dangerous and death-dealing encounter, a few might seek what they thought would be safer havens. But, from my perspective, those who acted conversely were more numerous.

There continued to be youngsters like PFC Ellis. After an operation in the Filhol rubber plantation, dealing with almost unceasing fire from snipers, he had about reached a decision to volunteer as a tunnel rat. "What do you think about that?" he said to me.

"A lot of guys do it," I said, "and you surely have the build for it." (He was five inches short of six feet and a wiry 120 pounds). "Has anything happened to make you think seriously about such a decision?" I asked him.

"In a way, I guess you'd say it has. A friend I've been with since basic training was a 'rat.' He tripped a booby trap in a tunnel. Now he has only one eye and scars all over his arms, chest and face. I volunteered to go down and get him out," the soldier said.

"I saw him in the field that day after he got hurt and again in the hospital," I said to Ellis. "So, did that trip below the ground convince you to become a tunnel rat?"

"No, I don't think so. It was scary as all get out down in that hole. But, sir, I want to do it for him. I have his flashlight. It should have been destroyed by the blast. You would think, anyway. It didn't take a single hit and was still burning when I got to Stan. If I do it and make it out of here, maybe we'll be able to talk about it someday."

I sat in head-shaking wonder over a reason like that, and could only wish him well as he exemplified commitment to a close friend. He submitted his request to the First Sergeant and within two weeks became a full-fledged tunnel rat. His resolve was amazing.

That same spirit in soldiers became evident as they volunteered to become LRRPs (Long Range Reconnaissance Patrol members), better known as "Lurps." Knowing that they would be called on to operate with small teams, usually out of range of artillery support, existing on cold canned food, moving at night and lying dead-still in the daylight hours, sometimes only a few feet from trails traveled by well-armed enemy soldiers, they still volunteered. Was it the excitement? Was it the danger, over which they hoped to win? Was it dedication to a cause? Whatever it was, it was to be admired.

It was present in those who reenlisted (re-upped) for present duty. Time and again I saw it. While it was possible to re-up for a rear echelon job, they often did so for "present duty," or for a job that was even more dangerous, like a door gunner for a chopper outfit that ferried soldiers on combat assaults and eagle flights. Or the one who got only a mild taste of combat a few hundred yards back, extended to serve on a .30 caliber machine gun team. Maybe it was for the excitement and adventure, but I thought it something deeper.

Tim Workman was a recipient of an unusual kind of commitment from a senior NCO, who had been in the army more years than Tim had months, and the younger soldier never knew how his good fortune came to be.

Private Workman had been with the 2/27 only a month and was still a Private E-2, one small step above the lowest paid rank in the army. Fresh out of the field after his first combat operation, he came to me with a letter he had received just minutes before, but the news it contained was eight days old. With a trembling hand he offered me the letter. His just barely 18-year-old voice said, "Chaplain, would you read the first few lines? It is from my father."

I read it aloud: "Son, as you know, your mom was not in good health when you left. Now I am sorry to tell you that something else has happened. At only 40 years of age, she has had a heart attack. The doctor told me today that she might not make it much longer. He cannot say for sure, but he says 15-20 days may be about all she has left. Do you think there is any way the army will let you come home? I know you'd like to see her before she passes on and she'd sure like to see you. I would too."

His eyes looked pleadingly into mine as I handed the letter back. "Okay, son," I said to him, "lets first go to your company and let them know I'm taking you for a ride in my jeep. We'll ask

Red Cross to send a wire to verify your mom's condition, and if it still looks as bad as your father indicates you ought to be able get home on emergency leave. I'll walk with you through all this. Okay?"

On the way to the Red Cross office Private Workman told me something that I was not at all surprised to hear: One dollar was all the money he had in the world.

"Don't worry," I told him, "your CO can help you can get a month's advance pay and Red Cross will, I am quite sure, help with a plane ticket once you get to the West Coast. Very soon we will be able to see how it all works out."

Early the next day verification came back through Red Cross. His mother's condition was critical and she was expected to live only a few more days. Tim's company granted him fourteen days emergency leave. Finance gave him a month's advance pay, which amounted to less than $140.00 dollars. Red Cross gave him a grant to assist with his flight across the United States. Some of his platoon members, who hardly knew him, took up a collection that amounted to eleven dollars. Even with all that, he would likely wind up hitchhiking part of the way, with little or no money for food and lodging.

While Workman was making arrangements to get to Camp Alpha and a space available flight to the USA, his company began a field operation that was scheduled to last eight days. The First Sergeant had gone with his company and the Field First, a Sergeant First Class (SFC), who normally accompanied the unit on field operations, stayed back. It was with him I spoke.

"Sergeant," I said, "I guess Top told you that Private Workman is going on emergency leave? I'll get him to the afternoon convoy, but I'm concerned about his finances. I really don't think he has enough money to get him home and back again. If he can get there maybe his dad can help him with return fare, but that is not a given, because he will be facing some serious hospital and funeral bills. I guess we'll know in two weeks."

"That is tough," the sergeant said, "maybe I can help some. Chaplain, would you come back to my quarters a minute?" I followed him to a dark, sand bagged room adjacent to the company dayroom. Under his cot was a green army footlocker, which he pulled out and opened.

The locker's tray had two sections. One section contained neatly rolled socks and underwear. The other side contained money. Rolls and rolls of money. At least 25 rolls, and possibly more. It was Military Payment Certificate (MPC). He took one of the rolls from the tray and handed it to me. "Would you give this to Private Workman?" he said. "Don't let him know where it came from. It is a gift and not a loan. All he has to do is get it changed to American dollars and get to that airplane."

While still in his presence I laid the money out flat and counted it.

One thousand dollars! In 1967 the average enlisted soldier did not make that much in five months. Having made an allotment to my wife for most of my pay, I drew only $150 a month. So I was holding big money in my hands. Rolling the bills back up and replacing the rubber band, I gave the sergeant a look that he must have been interpreted as a question, which it was.

"Chaplain, this money has nothing to do with the black market. In no way did I obtain it illegally. I know you must wonder, but you'll have to take my word on it," the senior NCO said with emphasis.

I gave the money to Private Workman. "It is not from me," I told him. "Take it to finance with your emergency leave papers and get it changed to American dollars. Go home, see your mom and dad, spend your money wisely and come back in two weeks." He was overwhelmed. Like me, he had never seen that much money in one stack. "The only thing I can say about this is that Santa Claus came early this year," I told him.

He got home two days before his mother died and returned to Vietnam a day early.

Though I felt ambivalent about the gift, I also felt something else was at work in that emergency situation. A committed benefactor was driven to help one in need.

On that subject, PFC Joe Lewis and PFC Grayson, who after coming to Jesus in faith, surely got it right. Lewis: "I can't quit smiling." Grayson: "I can't quit giving."

CHAPTER 13

Fear And Courage

The man who knows no fear is a biological impossibility.

—Rotor

Journal entry, 31 March 1967—"It was payday though; that helped some."

There was a slight quiver in his voice as he spoke and in his hands as he used his P-38 to open a can of beans and franks. But his smiling face mirrored triumph and victory. PFC Roukoski and I were sitting on the ground next to a large tree. I was using Sterno to warm my last can of roast beef and gravy. He was taking his cold. I encouraged him to continue his story.

He asked me if I knew what day it was and I told him it was Saturday. "First day of April." He said he knew it was the year he'd go home: "Eighty eight days and a wakeup."

"Wow," he said, "April first! But this is not an April Fools' Day story. On Thursday, all three line companies were doing a re-con by fire, it just seemed like a regular old stop and go battle, but Sarge said we were re-conning by fire.

"Alpha was the last company in line and my squad was bringing up the rear. I thought all the danger was up ahead, but suddenly there was a stinging sensation on the right side of my neck. It felt like someone had raked me with a coal of fire. I fell to the ground beside a small log and reached for the burning spot with my left hand. There was a little blood, but very little.

"I didn't know it then, but a bullet had grazed my neck, barely enough for a Purple Heart. I could hear my platoon sergeant yelling for us to stay down. I wanted to move to better cover, but every time I'd move even one meter in any direction a bullet would hit the log or out in front of me about a foot. Chaplain, I was scared out of my wits, thinking that the next one would have my name on it. I've been in 'Nam a long time and been in some close scrapes, but I had never been that frightened before. Here I am two days later, happy to be alive, but still shaking."

"Was time registering with you? Do you know how long you were pinned down?"

"It seemed like an hour, but it was only minutes, maybe about three. One of my buddies, who had better cover than I did, spotted the shooter in a tree and took him out with a short burst from his M-60. The guy, dressed in green and black, was hard to spot among the tree foliage. He had tied himself in the tree. His rifle fell to the ground and we policed it up, but we made no attempt to get the sniper down."

As we finished off our unusual breakfast meal, he told me that his friends had spoken sympathetically with him about his near-death experience. Quite nonchalantly, he had said to them in return: "It ain't no biggie!" "But, Chaplain, I was scared, scared, scared."

I knew some of which he spoke first hand, but didn't let him know it. I wanted to hear his story and he needed to tell it. I had joined the battalion in the field at 0800 just before the re-con by fire kicked off at 0900. Snipers began their harassing tactics right away. The area was criss-crossed by canals, and we waded across some that were neck-deep, muddy and working with leeches.

Roukoski got hit about 1030, but had continued with the company, a band aid on his superficial wound. By 1200 the battalion had reached a large cane field and set up a perimeter.

Sniper fire became heavier as we waited for boats to get us across a canal that was at least 50 yards wide. Chinooks delivered the boats a couple of hundred yards from where the snipers were concentrated. I continued to stand in awe of those pilots and of the gunship pilots who tried to silence the enemy fire while the Chinooks landed.

The choppers were not out of sight when a firefight broke out and the crossing was delayed about an hour. Then the shuttling began, a platoon at a time in each of the three large boats. I crossed with 2nd Platoon, Charlie Company. Heavy sniper fire continued, even as our guys on both sides of the canal dropped mortar rounds into the most likely hiding places.

As my boat eased across the canal I was reminded of an account I had read about American soldiers crossing the Waal River in Netherlands, not many weeks after the Normandy invasion. I recalled reading that the defenseless soldiers suffered numerous casualties in their flimsy canvas boats that late summer day in 1944.

Unlike the crossing near Nijmegen and Arnhem in eastern Holland, we didn't take a single hit. Still, a slow trip across a body of water while bad guys are sending AK-47 rounds your direction, takes a real toll on the fear factor. We ducked low in the boat as if to be protected by the thin metal sides.

On the 31st the Wolfhounds continued to move while snipers continued to remind us that they had not gone away. Specialist Sullivan's war ended that day with a bullet through his heart. We circled up and dug in under fire. It appeared that we were in for a rough night. And we were.

It was Friday and I hoped to get out on a resupply bird to prepare for three base camp chapel services on Sunday. But, because of the heavy and unceasing sniper fire, no helicopters could get in. C-Rations again, or what was left of them. Word was passed to dig in deeper than usual because of an expected mortar attack. Maybe some rockets as well.

The perimeter was attacked in Alpha's sector but not overrun. Charlie Company got three BC (body count) in an ambush just outside the perimeter. Sleep came uneasily and in short spurts. There was no chance to conduct a field service that evening, but I had a lot of opportunities to crawl near soldiers in their fighting positions and say a prayer, which I did several times. Some rewards come in strange packages!

Though considered men by military standards, many of the jungle fatigues-wearing youngsters I could think of only as little boys, and if not little, at least boys. Especially at first, though most became men in a hurry. Some had graduated from high school at age 17 and arrived in Vietnam the same year they graduated. Their bodies had been hardened in Basic and Advance combat training, but nothing could prepare them for what they would see in close combat. Most did well with it. Those who had the good fortune of being assigned to units with knowledgeable and caring NCOs did best. The sergeants, beginning with the Top on down to squad leader, were the keys. They could defuse macho attitudes and feelings of invulnerability the "newbies" might have. Usually. One day I saw First Sergeant Green in the 12th Evac, where we were both visiting patients. He asked if I'd talk with Private Bolden, who had been in his company about three weeks. I told him yes.

Later in the day Bolden, two months into his 18th year of life, came by the chapel. After talking a few minutes about his family, home state and how he came to join the army, I asked two direct questions: How are things going with you right now? What is your greatest fear right now?

"Well, Chaplain, things are not too good, at least for me they aren't. I get so scared just thinking about going out there where people are shooting at one another I can hardly stand it," he began.

"You have been out, how many times now?" I asked him.

"Only two," he answered. "The first time we stayed out four days. We had no contact. Didn't see a single Victor Charlie (Viet Cong) or hear a shot fired. But the flares drifting down and making weird shadows had me shaking like a leaf. I don't know if the other soldier in my foxhole noticed it or not but if he did he must have thought he was linked up with one scared bunny."

"So you've been out twice? Was the second time any better?"

"Maybe a little bit, but it was on a CA (Combat Assault) and the very word 'combat' made me want to run away as fast as I could and not board that helicopter. But there was no place to run. Also, I really didn't want to be the only coward in my squad. Anyway, we jumped out into a rice field and ran to some woods. Nobody shot at us. It was what you call a cold LZ (Landing Zone). After about an hour we were picked up and taken on another CA. The LZ was cold again. We stayed out there one night and came back in the next day. The guys tell me I've been lucky so far, because before long we'll be landing where it is hot," he said with an anxious look on his face.

"Be assured, Private Bolden, that every soldier on that chopper was concerned during the flight and about what might happen when they jumped off in a Combat Assault. It is not fun and games out there, and they all know it. At the same time, you and I need to remember that we are surrounded by people who know what they are doing and who will do everything possible to see that our people don't get hurt. They may talk tough and even act like they don't care about you, but it is only an act. They will be beside you every step of the way, even when the steps are scary," I said in the most comforting voice I could generate.

"Sir, I have to tell you something. It has been on my mind almost from the first day I got here. Maybe I don't think as much about it now as I did last week. But for a while I thought about shooting myself, maybe in the foot or leg, and make it look like an accident. That is not very good thinking, is it?"

"Not good at all," I responded. "Like all the others you see walking around and getting ready for the next operation, you just have to be sure things are right between you and God and move on. Pay close attention to your leaders. Learn from them and apply what you learn to your own situation, and I will be praying that in eleven months you'll leave this place with your head held high. But those who take that other route you were talking about will have to face themselves in the mirror some day. And it will be hard to do. Son, isn't that right? Is that kind of the way you see it?"

"Yes sir," he said, his chin quivering ever so slightly.

As he stood to leave, I said, "The battalion will be going out again soon, just as it always does. I'll be out there too. There is no telling where I might show up. If you see me, give a high sign and we'll talk some more." He promised to do so.

"Soon" came quickly. Three days later, in fact. Most of the 25th Infantry Division began an operation with another infantry division and a separate brigade. A battalion staff meeting revealed that it would be the largest joint operation the war had thus far seen.

Four days into the operation most of our soldiers witnessed a phenomenon that reminded them, several told me later, of how the world may someday end.

It was an Arc Light, code name for a B-52 strike. My ringside seat was a berm on the south side of a rice field that encompassed more than a hundred acres. Nothing closer than a half mile obstructed my vision or that of a half-dozen soldiers seated close by. Though the impact area was more than five kilometers away, it sounded much closer.

The planes that delivered the bombs were so high we could not see or hear them. The first thing we saw was a cloud of dust or smoke, appearing first in the north and spreading higher and higher as the cloud moved east. A few seconds later a sinister sound reached our ears. It started as a low roar, like distant thunder warning that more was to follow. Then the sound grew louder and deeper, like a giant bowling ball rolling across an uneven floor. Baroom! Baroom! Baroom!

The sound reminded me of the one time I had seen a thoroughbred horse race. The race track chaplain and I were on what is known as the back side of the track and about sixty yards from the starting gate. When the starting gate opened sixteen thoroughbreds charged our way. At first there was a lot of dust, but little sound. Then the sound became a roar as 64 hooves pounded the sand and sawdust. By the time the inside horse passed about five feet from where I stood the noise was deafening. I'm confident my heart was beating much faster than normal. The power of those animals was astounding.

Arc Light, though much farther away, was like that. First the sight, then the sound, then two thoughts: 1) What awesome power! 2) What living thing could remain a living thing in the face of it? Captain Lloyd, our S-1 and a student of the Old Testament, made a memorable statement when the sound had dissipated: "That reminded me of what must have happened to Sodom and Gomorrah when destruction fell on those people." As I watched the slowly settling dust and smoke, disagreeing with his analogy did not seem to be an option. Talk about fear! Those who were five kilometers north of where we sat must have experienced that emotion in ways I could only imagine.

Before week's end I officially met Corporal Yelvington, though I had seen him often in the area. He came by my little sandbag covered foxhole and asked to speak with me. "You don't ever have to ask," I said, "Say on!"

He began: "I ain't never had no real fear and always done my job and more. But tonight, Chaplain, my squad is going to set up an OP (observation post) about two hundred meters outside the wire. I don't think we are supposed to shoot nobody; just look, listen and report back to the company, or maybe the battalion, somebody like that. It won't be the first time my squad has been on things like that. It is always a little scary out there with just a few men. You have to be real quiet and never shine a light. Tonight just don't seem right. I keep thinking that tonight could be my last on earth. If I don't come back, would you send this letter for me? It's to my grandmother. She raised me and she is about the only one I ever hear from, except my little sister once in a while." He handed me a thin envelope. After some words of encouragement and a prayer with him, I promised to post the letter if I had to.

Fortunately, I didn't have to. A few days later, back in base camp, I looked him up and gave him the letter, which he tore to shreds. I congratulated him on a good move.

Much later in my tour another soldier approached me with a similar request, except that he had not sealed the letter, rather he wanted me to read it. He handed me the letter and said, "Chaplain, would you do me a favor and mail this letter tomorrow after my platoon has been air lifted to Xom Moi, wherever that is? You can read it if you want to."

"Conroy," I responded, "the thing is, do you want me to? I really don't make a practice of reading other people's mail, but if there is a special reason I'll read it."

"I'd really like for you to read it, and see what you think," the soldier said.

It started as it should have with, "Dear Mom," and continued: "I'm pretty sure this will be my last letter. Tomorrow I'm going on an eagle flight to a place by the name of Xom Moi. It is a very bad place with a lot of booby traps and snipers and other things to bring death to American soldiers. I'm taking a rucksack filled with grenades and two extra magazines for my rifle. I plan to go down fighting, and I hope you will be proud of me. Be sure to tell everyone hello. The chaplain is mailing this letter for me. Remember to pray for your son in 'Nam."

"Private Conroy, you don't want your mom to get a letter like this. Can you imagine what it would do to her? You can leave the letter with me if you wish, and when you come back from your eagle flight we can read it together and laugh. I know that you can get someone else to mail it, or you can just take out that chaplain part and mail it yourself tonight. But I can find nothing to be gained from putting this kind of worry on your mother.

Do you know anything positive that might come from it?"

"No, I don't," he said, "except…"

"Except what?

He looked at the floor and continued: "Except it might make her see some of the fear that I go through, and maybe send me a goodie package like a lot of my buddies get from their moms."

That left me nearly speechless for a moment. Finally I said, "How about I write your mother a letter to tell her that you and I have met, that you are healthy, that you have a lot of friends, that you are a good soldier, that you attend chapel when possible, and that the soldiers over here love hearing from home. And that they really appreciate packages, especially home-made cookies?"

He grinned as only a happy teen can. "Would you do that?" he said.

"Consider it done. It will be in the mail tomorrow while you and your platoon are on those choppers. By the time you get back it should be over the Pacific Ocean and half way to the United States of America. Do we have a deal?"

We did. We had a deal.

CHAPTER 14

Tunnels And Trip Wires

Out of the depths I cry to you O Lord!

—Psalm 130:1

Journal entry, 2 February 1967—"Unable to catch last slick...spent night at a vast tunnel complex."

Specialist Four William Lowry had been running tunnels for three hours when he came up to get some food, water and new batteries for his flashlight. Lowry and some other "Tunnel Rats" were working the underground labyrinth while two companies up above were making sweeps in the area and interrogating people in the village where the tunnel entrance was found. The "rats" had thus far located some medical supplies, a few small bags of rice, one weapon (a rusty pistol), some official looking documents and several pairs of black pajamas. They had also, without injury to themselves, located and removed a half-dozen punji stakes and disarmed two booby-trapped Chicom grenades.

I spoke with Lowry as we enjoyed the hot chow that had been prepared in the rear and flown out to the two 2/27 companies. "How many guys are working the tunnel?" I asked him. He said there were four. Three were taking a short rest in a small room between two narrow tunnels while he came up for a few minutes.

"You know something, Specialist Lowry," I said, "I conduct field services in the boonies all the time, but have never held one in a tunnel complex, down there where you guys are facing uncertainty in the dark. About that room you mentioned, would there be enough space for the five of us to meet for a brief chapel service?"

"I estimate it to be about 4 by 6, and maybe five feet high," he answered.

"Might be a little tight, but we could do it," I said. "Do you think the other guys would object to the chaplain going down for a visit?"

"Sir, I think they would love it. It would about blow their minds to see the preacher come crawling through that tunnel, but they would love it. I know you are slender and in good shape, but it will be hard just getting there. I almost quit after a couple of hours the first day I tried it, and was about ready to say, 'this sure ain't no way to make a living,' but I hung on and now it doesn't bother me, not much anyway."

"Give me a quick rundown on what we'll need to do," I requested of him.

"A six-foot ladder gets us to the tunnel, which is about three feet in diameter in some places and about two feet in others. The hole is a little bigger at the bottom of the ladder, giving you some room to get on your belly and get started down that dark alley. Once you are a few feet from the spider hole it is inky black. In the narrow places you can't crawl and have to scoot. The people who dug those things must have been midgets. The distance from the entrance to the first little room I was talking about is somewhere around 60 feet, maybe a little longer. We haven't seen any rats, except tunnel rat GIs in this one. But quite a few spiders crawl around on the dirt walls." The latter I found to be true. Spiders with long legs, but not as big as tarantulas. Nor did they attempt to bite.

"Let me know when you get ready to drop back in that hole," I said to SP4 Lowry.

"I'm going to be right behind you."

After six minutes of crawling, scooting and digging the toes of my boots into the hard soil, I arrived at the widened place. Lowry, more accustomed to such adventure, had beaten me by at least a minute and alerted his buddies that the light they saw snaking closer was the Wolfhound Chaplain. When I entered the tiny earthen room, there they were practically sitting atop one another. Four wide grins on the faces of Lowry, Ellis and two others, whose names I never learned, told me they were surprised and pleased that the chaplain had come to see where they worked. I thought about the verse in the 18th chapter of Matthew: *For where two or three are gathered together in my name, there am I in the midst of them.* We'd do fine, I thought.

There were five of us. It was the most crowded church I had ever been in. I gave each of them an Orange Crush soft drink, which the mess sergeant had given me for that very purpose. They were grateful for the unexpected liquid nourishment and guzzled them down. Though it was eight days after Easter, I selected a crucifixion/resurrrection theme and read from the gospel of Luke about Jesus' burial in the private tomb of Joseph of Arimathea. My small congregation agreed that it seemed a fitting scripture: *And he took it* (Jesus' body) *down, and wrapped it in linen, and laid it in a sepulcher that was hewn in stone.* During the five-minute session, we thought together about how Jesus would not stay in that tomb. Just as they would soon come out of the tunnel and appear to their friends above ground, Jesus would appear first to Mary Magdalene and then to many others. Those young volunteers caught the analogy. They knew the Lord's Prayer, which we recited together and I shuffled and crawled back to light of an April day in Southeast Asia. Four GIs followed in less than an hour, their work underground completed.

It was years later that I came to realize the significance of Psalm 88. Many biblical scholars think the words of that Psalm point to Jesus' incarceration in a dungeon in the house of the chief high priest while waiting for his pre-crucifixion trial to be completed:

> For my soul is full of trouble
> and my life draws near to the grave.
> I am counted among those who go down to the pit;
> I am like a man without strength.
> You have put me in the lowest pit,
> in the darkest depths.
> I am confined and cannot escape;
> my eyes are dim with grief.
> Why, O Lord, do you reject me
> and hide your face from me?
> You have taken my companions
> and loved ones from me;
> The darkness is my closest friend.

The tunnel rats came out for a few minutes then went back in again with several blocks of C-4 and rolls of detonation cord. In twenty minutes they surfaced from the large tunnel complex for the last time. Everyone, including soldiers and occupants of the village, was herded a safe distance away. A senior NCO yelled, "Fire in the Hole," and set off the explosives. There was a muffled sound from beneath.

Smoke belched out the tunnel entrance and several other well-hidden holes that had not been discovered. The earth caved into the more shallow tunnels creating sinkholes that resembled graves. The tunnels would be unusable for a while. Bravo Company's CO turned to me and said, "What about that, Chaplain? Did anyone ever blow up the church right after you finished with your service?"

"Thankfully, never before," I responded.

Cu Chi became notorious for its tunnels, something the Vietnamese knew and the Americans had to learn. The 25th Infantry Division moved into a huge area near Cu Chi village in late 1965, not knowing they were encompassing many tunnel entrances and spider holes. Twenty years later Tom Mangold and John Penycate wrote a revealing book entitled *The Tunnels of Cu Chi*. It gave an exhaustive account of the tunnels and the dangers American troops faced in dealing with them.

Even after a year in place, the 25th units dealt with late night explosions of unknown origin. It eventually became common knowledge that most of those disturbances were created by enemy soldiers who had entered the base camp through tunnels, surfaced through well hidden spider holes, tossed a hand grenade or a satchel charge near an American unit, and disappeared back into the hole. They did little real damage, but it was enough to make people edgy and even trigger-happy. The Dog Platoon, located in the Second Wolfhound's sector of base camp, helped immeasurably to finally rid the area of inside-the-wire tunnels entrances. Once found, they were destroyed.

Alpha Company's SP4 McCray learned quickly of a double danger that existed even when no enemy soldiers were to be seen. Twice in one day he encountered both and shared news about them with me.

On a Search and Destroy mission with Alpha Company, he was bringing up the rear, the very last man in line of march. Moving as quietly as possible he spotted movement about three meters to his left and stopped dead still. A Viet Cong, evidently thinking the company had passed, emerged from a spider hole to take a few shots at the unsuspecting American troops. As he lifted his weapon to fire he glanced to the right and spotted McCray standing not ten feet away. Before shots could be fired by either soldier, the VC dropped back into the hole and was gone. A grenade in the hole and a quick search by an impromptu tunnel rat revealed nothing but a skillfully dug cave that seemed to be endless.

Later the same day, Specialist McCray, still bringing up the rear, spotted something in a tangle of vines that didn't look right. One of the vines, while the right color, did not seem to fit. Upon closer examination he discovered a wire that was rigged to resemble the vines. Miraculously, his entire platoon had walked close to the wire without snagging it. In silence and with high anxiety he traced the black commo wire to an explosive device, a very powerful one. It was a 250-pound bomb, which had evidently been dropped by an American plane but failed to explode.

He called to the soldier in front of him. Soon the platoon sergeant was by his side viewing the trip wire and bomb. They did a little "shaking" together and some "thanking" as well. Within minutes they had packed C-4 around it and blown it in place. Had the trip wire been snagged earlier, a lot of soldiers could have lost their lives, although they were trained not to bunch up. A 250 pounder would have cut a wide swath, even among men separated by 12-15 feet.

"Maybe I'm now living on borrowed time," McCray said. "Twice in one day I could have 'bought the farm'. And I wasn't even walking point."

"It makes one count his blessings, all right," I said with a grateful heart.

CHAPTER 15

Please Write

If you can't come, write!

—Old Country goodbye.

Journal entry, 12 February 1967—"Paul was saved this week. Very happy to get that news."

"Chaplain, there hasn't been no letter at mail call for me since I don't know when." He was not complaining. It was just matter of fact to him. That was simply the way things were with 19-year old Sergeant Wayne.

"At least a month," he continued. It was unusual for him to say that much, but on that particular day he became talkative. This fine, trust-worthy soldier and I had spoken many times. He was seeking to learn more about Christian discipleship and I was doing my best to assist him in that endeavor. His journey into faith had taken several weeks.

Wayne's word about rarely receiving mail came in response to questions I asked him:

"Are there people back home who are pleased that you have committed your life to God? Do you get some letters of encouragement?" He said his mother wrote a few lines every few weeks but mostly to tell him how short money was. "My daddy, I never hear from him. I don't know how things are going with him. It really don't much matter, but when the mail clerk starts calling names I nearly always know he won't call mine."

Just two days earlier I had received a letter from Mrs. Annie Summers, a lady I did not know and would never meet. How, I would never know, but Mrs. Summers' letter had reached me with this incomplete address on the envelope: Chaplain Tucker, Battalion chaplain, Vietnam. Even though the address contained neither unit nor APO number, it made its way to the Wolfhound Memorial Chapel, Cu Chi, RVN. Her letter stated that she was a long-time classroom teacher, an active member of the WMU (Women's Missionary Union) in her church, a widow and a grandmother. And she wondered if there were any "soldier boys over there she might help by writing and sending them gifts along, just to let them know there were people back home who cared from them. If so, could I give her a name or two?" Wayne's name and address were on the way as soon as I could write her a note.

About two weeks later Sergeant Wayne saw me at a field service near Xom Moi and was excited about sharing some news. "I got a letter from this neat lady. She told me about her family and how she was praying for me, and all the other soldiers over here in 'Nam. She even sent a little poem that one of her students wrote."

"That is good news, Wayne. Thanks for telling me about that," I said.

As a squad leader in Charlie Company, Wayne was extremely busy, but he often found a few minutes to seek me out and talk a few minutes, sometimes only two or three. A few days after the initial report about his new pen pal, he gave me more news. It was that "the lady in Alabama" had sent him one package of homemade cookies and another containing three pairs of socks and a little bible with his name printed on the front. Also, he had gotten two more letters, one of them signed by all the kids in her class.

"Sounds like you hit the jackpot," I said. "I know the guys in your squad will help you with those goodie packages." He nodded agreement.

Watching his 6-foot, very slim form saunter away, I called out to him: "Wayne, I know Mrs. Summers would like to hear from you. I hope you will write her when you get a chance." He stopped, and looking back at me said with a wide grin: "I done did!"

"I done did!" His three-word sentence struck me as humorous, but over time it has become sort of an epitaph. Those words, radiating happiness, were the last I heard him speak. On that mid-November day he "went home." Sergeant Wayne, along with three others in his squad and eleven Wolfhounds from other 2/27 units, had the dreaded three letters, KIA, affixed to their names and became part of one of the most traumatic days I had ever known, or have known since. (That trying day will be discussed at length in a later chapter entitled Some Days are Dark—Dealing with Loss).

Did Mrs. Summers know why Wayne wrote her only one letter? I didn't have the heart to let her know that he had been killed. She was a stranger who never met that "soldier boy." Maybe she thought he got transferred, which, I guess in a way he did. Her concern created a lot of joy for him, including hearing the mail clerk call his name.

Pay call (payday) was the most anticipated event in a soldier's life, and no doubt still is. A close second was mail call. This saying was once prevalent among military personnel: "When I see a line I just naturally get in it, because I know it must be for pay, mail or chow, and I am pleased to get all three."

The greatest morale booster for a soldier was a letter, especially one written on perfumed stationery, and if it had S W A K printed along the sealing flap so much the better. The perfumed ones often made their way among squad members, who were sometimes even offered the opportunity to read them. If a soldier got a handful of letters and another got none that day, it was not uncommon for the soldier with the handful to share with his buddy. "Here is one from my mom, one from my sister and one from 'my other' girl friend. You read them if you like while I read these others, then we'll swap." And they would do it. It seemed sort of strange that a soldier from Fordyce, Arkansas would be remotely interested in what was happening among strangers in Muleshoe, Texas. But that was not the point. The point was that he was reading something that had originated in the United States.

A soldier who had been with the 2/27 only six weeks brought a letter and asked me to read it. I was reluctant to do so and said, "Son, can't you tell me what you'd like me to know from it. I'm a little uncomfortable reading another person's letter."

"It's from my wife's mother, Chaplain. Please read those three lines I've underlined there in the middle."

He handed me the single sheet of lined paper and pointed to the underlined sections:

"Jerry, things are a mess here. As you know I didn't much want you to get married, with her still being in school and all. This daughter of mine that you married is messing around with a beatnick disc jockey. Just like always, she tells me to mind my business and goes on with what she wants to do, which is not good, Jerry. It is not good."

"And you are how old now?" I asked the soldier.

"Eighteen. Had my 18th the same day I left the states."

"And your wife is?..."

"Sixteen. She is supposed to start in the 11th grade in the fall, but I don't think she will ever go back to high school, not with her running around with that guy. She'll probably wind up dropping out like I did."

"How long were you married before you shipped out?" I asked.

"Four days. We got married on Saturday and I took off for San Francisco on Wednesday. I think now I should have paid more attention to my dad. He thought it was not a good idea for us to rush into something so important."

The soldier didn't want to try for an emergency leave. His word: "I don't think she cares much about me anyway. There is probably nothing I could do, and I sure don't have no money to travel on."

Much to my sorrow, I encountered many similar cases. So much of it must be going on, I thought. Many of the wives were mere girls, 17 or 18 years of age. They lived with their soldier husbands for a week or two, then faced a year of separation. There had been no chance to even learn the meaning of commitment and how to put each other first.

One soldier left his wife with his widowed mother. Most of her letters dealt with the problems his wife was having with her mother-in-law. "I can't stand it anymore," the latest letter stated. Mail call for him became a time of dread. He hated to open a letter from his wife because he knew what the contents would be.

One of the most clean cut and shaped up soldiers I had ever seen came by my little mosquito net covered sleeping hole and requested a few minutes of my time. "You have it," I said. And we sat on the ground alongside a shallow canal. He pulled a crumpled letter from his shirt pocket. I could tell he had been over it many times and wanted me to read it, which, reluctantly, I did.

My journal for that day says this about it: It was a horrid letter. I read silently: "I have been unfaithful to you and have been since the day we got married." (That was one of the many reasons I didn't like to read other people's mail). When I looked back at him there were tears running down his cheeks. It was a minute before he could speak. Finally he said: "To make it even worse, Chaplain, I got this letter on our first anniversary. We have been married a year and five days."

I wrote him a strong letter of recommendation for compassionate leave and two days later learned it had been granted. "Thank you, Lord," I said in one of the world's shortest prayers. While on leave he requested and received a compassionate reassignment. My part in the story ended there. Whether or not they were able to patch up things and move on as husband and wife, I would never know. Still, hope reigned.

There were times, only a few to be sure, when I had to renew my thinking and take notice that many of the soldiers I served with were boys. "Think about it," I'd try to remind myself, "if they were still at home and involved in their church program they would be in the Youth Department. This time last year they were juniors in high school, some were driving on learner's permits, and had never written a check. Boys, having to become men in a hurry. Men they became, armed with enough guns and ammunition to reduce an average-size house to splinters in minutes. But there was still enough juvenile in them to get excited about what arrived in the mailroom.

"Yea, I got five letters and three of them smell like heaven." "Can you believe it? A package of Brownies from Mrs. Kelly and a squashed birthday cake from my mom." "Look at this, Chaplain, a letter from my little sister. She just turned five. Look at what she says: 'The last letter you wrote me was in cursive. Watch that!' You can read it right there. She prints good.

"Two big letters and a box of peanut brittle. Want some? The brittle part doesn't hold for long in this high humidity, but it is from my aunt's kitchen, and she knows how to make it."

"Would you look at this? A letter from my old basketball coach. Listen to what he says: 'I sure hope you are doing well. The guys on the team miss you. Stay safe and come back to us in good shape.' Can you believe that? And I always thought coach hated me!"

Generous people in the United States sent things to be shared with the Vietnamese people, especially the children. All a chaplain had to do was ask and the items began arriving. The shoe shine kids of Cu Chi get their first Easter outfits through the 2/27 mailroom. No Can Do, the little girl who sold pineapple and bananas to GIs, got her first pair of shoes from a children's Sunday School class in Lawton, Oklahoma. Huge boxes of clothing arrived in care of the Wolfhound Chaplain's office and were distributed to children and adults alike during longer field operations. The children were ecstatic with T-shirts, jeans, swim trunks, sneakers and frilly dresses, just their size. The diminutive women tried on dresses that were more than twice their size and thought it was hilarious. They took them though, indicating in sign language that they could take them apart and use the material to make clothing that would fit. One day the headquarters company mail clerk laughingly said to me: "Chaplain, your friends back in the states are keeping my little room full of boxes, but I'm happy to be part of it." Soldiers had a great time giving clothes and toys to hundreds of peasant children.

What other combat chaplains' experiences were, I cannot say, but I wrote a lot of letters in support of and for soldiers. One of the latter came as a result of a visit to 24th Evac, a hospital in the area of Long Binh. Around 2300 (11 PM) the night before, an Alpha Company patrol had been hit by a single VC with an AK-47. SP4 Madland was KIA and Sergeant Stroud was WIA.

Stroud was lying in bed, his right hand and arm heavily bandaged and in a sling. He asked if I'd write a letter to his parents. I told him yes, thinking he meant to let them know that I had seen him and that he would write later. But he wanted me to write a letter as if he was writing it and sign his name. I located a piece of writing paper and an envelope. "Okay," I said to the wounded sergeant, "your secretary is ready. Tell me what you want to say to mom and dad." I was surprised at the way he started and questioned him to be sure it was what he really wanted them to hear.

"Dear Folks, I did something super dumb last night. My squad had set up an ambush about 300 meters from Alpha Company's field location. We set up claymores and a few noise makers and lay prone on the ground, facing out as we always do. Soon we heard some movement in the brush and tried to get even quieter, barely breathing. The rustling in the brush continued. It sounded like it was 10 meters or so from us but coming closer. We knew it was either an animal or a person walking.

"In a minute or two a guy appeared in a small opening no more than ten steps from where I was hugging the ground. It was very dark but I could tell the person was an enemy soldier, a VC in dark clothing. He was holding a rifle at the ready position. And here is the dumb part.

"I stood up and yelled right out loud: 'Chieu Hoi.' That was a call for him to surrender. What I should have done was pop the claymore that was five feet away, pointing right at him. I had the activator in my hand. But I didn't pop it or fire my M-16. I challenged him instead. Maybe I reverted back to my raising and the thought that everyone needs a second chance. But he didn't Chieu Hoi. He shot me. I don't know how he missed my head and chest, but he did. He hit me in both arms and in my right leg before the other guys in my squad took care of him. Tell everybody hello. I hope to see you in four months, when my tour is up, unless this right hand wound gets me out of here earlier. I'll let you know how that works out. Love, your boy in the army."

I read it back to him and suggested that his letter might put his parents in a high state of anxiety and worry. But he wanted the letter to go. I signed his name and added a note: "I am your son's battalion chaplain. He dictated and I have written the exact words he spoke. He is looking well and is in good spirits."

In this day it would be texting and emails, I suppose, but then it was letters. And it was then that I saw how very important and crucial it was to respond in a timely manner. Today if possible, even yesterday or last week. The necessity for quick response hit me first when I was working with PFC Lewis Steinhauser, who was a top candidate for a compassionate reassignment or a hardship discharge. As reported in chapter eight, letters that verified what was going on with his family came quickly and were placed in his file. But one letter had not arrived. Without it the first sergeant could not legally pull Lewis off the line, although he badly wanted to and had decided that he take the heat and do it anyway after the "next patrol." But it was on that one that the soldier's life was snuffed out by a sniper who was good at his trade.

That episode taught me a valuable lesson. I don't know if anyone ever benefited from what I learned, but I did. It taught me to respond quickly to requests. During and after my years as an active duty chaplain I received numerous requests for letters of recommendation in regard to character references, college scholarships, job opportunities, military transfers and the like.

Some of them may not have been exceedingly important, except to the person making the request. I made it a practice to quickly do what the person making the request asked. Except in very rare cases, the response was in 24 hours or less. And never have I written a letter or made a call on behalf of the person who asked for it without thinking of Lewis and of how one more letter might have made a difference in what happened to him. Maybe it would not have made an ounce of difference, but you still wonder.

Thinking back, I am reminded of how most people—wives, children, parents, former classmates, fellow church members, and the like—really worked at doing something useful and memorable for service personnel, especially those in war zones. That came to mind as I recalled an incident near Danang, during my second tour in Southeast Asia.

One day Captain Morse, a Mohawk pilot with the 212th Combat Aviation Battalion came by my little office in the Wings of Freedom chapel. Morse was not one who liked to hang out in the O Club when he was not on a mission or shuttling a plane to Thailand, so it was not uncommon for him to drop by either my office or living quarters. But on that occasion he had a question for me: "Do you like watermelon?"

"Do I like watermelon?" I exclaimed, "Captain Morse, I was practically raised on Black Diamonds and Dixie Queens back in Drew County, Arkansas. Why do you ask that on this cold and rainy day?"

"I have one, a thirty-pounder. How about if we go to your little house and cut that South Texas Delight? I'll get Gary and Mr. Williams, and maybe your assistant Logue, if you think he'd like to join us, and have a watermelon cutting in the dead of a Marble Mountain winter."

"Wonderful! Guest list and all. First though, I have a very important question. Where did you get a watermelon?"

"My wife sent it. Got it in the mail a few minutes ago."

"You got a watermelon through our battalion mail room? Mailed from the U. S.? The package must have been half the size of this file cabinet."

"Pretty big. She wrapped it good and packed sawdust all round it. I couldn't believe it, but it arrived looking like it had just been taken from the patch," he told me.

"It must have weighed 40 pounds," I said in an unbelieving tone.

"Fifty-two."

Five of us, three combat pilots, a chaplain and a chaplain assistant, enjoyed that out-of season treat. I still marvel at all that was involved in mailing it to Vietnam.

CHAPTER 16

Dealing With Loss

I have no pain, but I have peace, I have peace

—Baxter

Journal entry, 16 November 1967—"Waiting for news...I'm sure it won't be good."

Getting word about WIA (Wounded in Action) was bad enough, but getting word about KIA (Killed in Action) was worse. When either of those three-letter acronyms was brought to my attention it always resulted in a feeling of emptiness and remorse. And, as on many previous occasions, I heard them both on March 21. It had been a relatively quiet morning at Duc Hoa, where I had choppered in to spend some time with Charlie Company.

Upon arrival at Charlie's CP (command post) I learned that Bravo Company had been hit up near the river. Initial word, which later proved to be true, was that five 'Hounds' had been wounded and two had been killed. The helicopter I had taken from Cu Chi to Duc Hoa was still there, taking on some supplies. I ran back toward it, frantically waving my arms, as the pilot revved up for takeoff. He saw me and delayed until I could jump aboard.

"Can you drop me off at Bravo's location?" I yelled above the noise of the engine and turning blades. He nodded yes and pointed to the concertina wire and axes he had taken aboard, indicating that those items were to be dropped off at Bravo. I sat on the metal deck near the pilot and co-pilot for the two-minute flight, praying for the KIAs and wondering who they might be.

A minute after landing I found out. Captain McCarthy, Bravo's CO, told me as I approached him with a questioning look. Before I could say a word he said, "Rosenberry and Murphy. Cline is really bad and may not make it."

"Murphy?" I questioned Bravo Six. "Would that be Lieutenant Tom Murphy?" He nodded and quietly said it was Tom. This was hitting Captain McCarthy hard. Just two months earlier his company had lost ten soldiers in a minefield. Seven had been wounded on that terrible day in late January. I asked where the KIAs were and he pointed to a swampy area southwest of his CP. A green poncho was visible about 150 meters away and I knew it was there to cover one of the bodies. "Is that Tom?" I asked. Another nod.

In dread, while recalling the friendship we had developed the previous four months, I waded through the ankle-deep mud and water toward the rubberized rain gear on a tiny knoll. I knelt close by in several inches of water and pulled the covering from his face. I recognized him right away, although the attending medic had removed his ever-present glasses and placed them in his fatigue blouse pocket. I took the New Testament, which also contained Psalms and Proverbs, from my helmet band and read the 23rd Psalm. Then for some reason I felt a need to read the Beatitudes from the Sermon on the Mount in Matthew. Coming to the words, "Blessed are they that mourn, for they shall be comforted."

I thought about his family and the news they would be getting soon. After pulling the cover back over his face, I sat in the mud by his still form a short time, reminiscing and praying. After perhaps three minutes I knew it was time to move on and locate Rosenberry. Looking up to get my bearings, I saw Trojan Six—

2/27 Battalion Commander Lieutenant Colonel Ed Peter—on a little hill about fifty yards to my left. He no doubt thought I was administering last rites, and maybe, in God's eyes, what I did was the same thing.

I pushed from the swamp to higher ground and passed within three feet of him. His almost imperceptible nod seem to say it all. That, and his eyes, watery and red.

As I walked on to an identical poncho that covered the body of Specialist Rosenberry, a thought hit me: How does the commander deal with loss? Deep concern for the loss of two more men was written on his face. He needed to grieve too, but he could not let it stand in the way of his present and future responsibilities.

By nightfall I was planning a memorial service for three more whose lives had been taken from them. Trojan Six, with his staff and company commanders, were fine tuning plans for the next mission. Though genuinely concerned and saddened, they had no choice but to push on.

Forty years later, long after I had retired from the U S Army, I broached the question with a dear friend and former commander I had served with in Vietnam: How did you deal with loss and do the job expected of you? He first said that was something from the past and he didn't much want see it surface again. Two days later he sent an email that answered my question. I share some of Tom Brewer's thoughts here.

"For me, dealing with loss as a result of combat operations evoked a complex and often conflicting set of emotions. On taking command of an infantry company in Vietnam, I believed that the enemy we were engaging was comprised of patriotic individuals, who were fighting for their beliefs, just as we were. I could think of those guys as targets, not people with faces and families, so as to keep my emotions at bay.

"As a company commander I had to set the example. I also believed that when we suffered casualties I had to keep a stiff upper lip and stay focused on the mission I was tasked with performing. I could not let grief or despair cloud my judgment or affect my leadership responsibilities. The grief and despair never went away completely and I often feel guilty that I made it back when so many others didn't. My emotions were difficult to control in combat, but I knew they had to be controlled.

"In the heat of battle there was nothing but overt brutality. And as I saw more and more casualties, I could only see the enemy as brutal murderers of my men. So it became impossible for me to do anything but hate them and do everything I could to get them before they got more of us."

Other combat commanders I've read about say pretty much the same thing, even if in different words, such as these: "The most dramatic example might be when your RTO takes a sniper round through his temple and is dead before he hits the ground. You might want to stop and weep, but you can't. There are others depending on you to lead. If you break down, what will they do? Well, they will feel even more vulnerable if they see a long-faced, weepy leader. So you sling the radio over your shoulder and move toward the next objective. In another place and at another time I will grieve, as I have many times before. I will be deeply sorry, and I will feel tremendous hostility toward the sharpshooters who killed my soldiers. But when the stuff is flying, you can't stop. You can't allow fear and grief to overtake and immobilize you."

Colonel Charlie Rogers (later Major General Rogers), who had commanded an Artillery Battalion in Vietnam, was commander of the unit I served as chaplain in Giessen, Germany, until he received his first star. By the time we met, America's role in the Vietnam War was close to entering the pages of history.

Charlie Rogers and I had served two tours in that land. During his second tour he earned the Congressional Medal of Honor. After we had been friends for several months I felt comfortable enough with him to ask questions about the events that led to his MOH and to several other awards for valor that his soldiers had received. I was aware that his firebase had come under heavy attack by wave after wave of enemy soldiers, and that his unit had suffered heavy casualties. Some of the gun crews were down to two men, not enough to operate efficiently. I also knew that Colonel Rogers had personally assumed the position as gunner on the "hottest side" of the perimeter, and, that as fast as he and a vastly depleted crew could load them, had fired fleshette rounds from the piece like it was an oversized shotgun.

"Mortar rounds were falling inside the small firebase. A number of enemy soldiers penetrated the wire and tossed satchel charges before being cut down by our security people. The cacophony of .51 caliber machine guns, AK-47s and exploding mortars was deafening. All that is now public information."

"Is there a word to describe your feelings as you and a slim crew manned that big gun in the face of intense fire?" I asked him.

"Chap, probably it would be numbness. I think my mind just became blank to almost everything else except attempting to 'do something.'"

"Normally, you would be on or near the radio in your CP (command post) when an attack was expected or in progress, right?"

"And that was where I was when the sit rep (situation report) changed from 'movement just outside the wire' to 'attack underway.' We were hit on all sides at once, but the hottest spot was on the side that faced a woodline about a hundred meters away. An ammo handler made the frantic call: 'All of our guys are wounded. I'm pretty sure two are dead. Send a medic! Send a medic! We can't fire.' I tossed the mic to my XO (executive officer), and two medics and I took off in a run. The PFC, scared but performing well under tremendous stress, was still on the horn (radio) when I slid into the gun pit, surrounded by a circle of sandbags two feet high. The gunner and assistant gunner were dead. I knew them both well. Good men!

"As a Christian, I wanted sit down between them, express deep sorrow and pray. But I quickly dragged them out of the way, began lowering the big gun to horizontal, and yelled for the ammunition handler to start bringing up rounds faster than he ever had before. He did it and was soon joined by a couple of soldiers from Headquarters Battery.

"Though they had never been a team, they performed as one that evening. Even now I stand in awe of what they did that day. The attack slowed after what seemed like hours but was only minutes. Then things went quiet, except for supporting fire from other batteries several kilometers away. They were dropping HE (high explosive) rounds all round us.

"The still trembling enlisted men and I just sat and looked back and forth at one another for a few seconds, feeling the heat from a howitzer that had fired too many rounds in too short a time. The medics began moving the casualties out, first the wounded, then the KIAs. Their gruesome task served to awaken me from my temporary reverie."

"And then, knowing you as I do, you mourned for the dead?" I quietly asked.

"That I did, Chaplain. I finally had a few minutes to think about it, and grieve over it, and ask the Lord to receive them in His house. There was no time for anything but fighting back until then. But when it hit, it hit hard. It always does. No matter how many times you face it, you never get used to it. You know that, too. You've been there."

"Yes sir," I said, and thought back to a journal entry I would not read again until 30 years after making it. It was that January 18, 1967 event referred to earlier. Following is a portion of it: "In my seven weeks with the Wolfhounds I had come to know them, at least casually and by sight. Some of them I knew personally, and well. Regulars at chapel. This is the rough part. The KIAs are 1LT. Len Gray, Jesus Archuleta, PFC Gary Brennan, SP4 Roger Bryant, PFC Jerry Humphries, PFC Paul McCarthy, PFC Dennis O'Neal, SP4 Bob Provenzano, PFC Patterson Scott and Specialist Timothy Workman, a medic from Headquarters Company.

My initial thought was to name this chapter, 'Some Days Are Dark,' because of a sentence that concluded my journal entry for that day: "All in all it was a dark day for the Second Wolfhounds." Every leader, from Bravo Six to the Battalion Commander would have to search deeply for ways to deal with it. As usual, they did.

But not only the leaders. Soldiers at the site where buddies died suffered too, maybe even more than senior leaders. How did the fellow grunts deal with the violence and loss? How did the company medic? The point man? The man who was wounded by the same projectile that dealt death to the man beside him? There are probably as many ways to face loss as there are people forced to face it.

I heard an 18-year old, survivor of an ambush and first time under fire, express thoughts on it: "My AIT training made it pretty clear, but out here you learn in a hurry that the bad guys want to take you out. They have real bullets that can do the job. The GI by my side didn't wake up from the one that hit him. It will be hard to sleep good tonight and maybe for a long time. But, Chaplain, I am grateful to be standing here right now talking to you."

On how to cope, his answer was close to one by Robert Leckie, in his book, *Helmet For My Pillow*: "If a man must live in filth, go hungry and risk his flesh, you must give him a reason. It is easier to lose if there is a reason; you must give him a cause. We had to laugh at ourselves; else, in the midst of the mechanical slaughter, we would have gone mad."

To a man, the veterans I served with and talked with, those who lost buddies and close friends in combat, identified fully with the part that says, "We had to laugh at ourselves or go crazy."

After several months with the Wolfhounds, I began to see that the soldier dealt with loss in four ways, which I eventually identified as Four *R*s.

First, there was *Relief*—It was not I who stopped the bullet! I was close to him when he got it, and I can't explain why I didn't get it too. I deeply regret that he won't be sleeping in the bunk next to mine any more, and if possible I'll go see his mama and daddy someday. But I'm alive. Alive!

Some of those who experienced relief that their number didn't come up experienced survivor's guilt as well. An ex-soldier gave testimony to that in an email message 40 years after we served together in the 2/27 Battalion: "I have guilt every day of my life. Even though I still suffer physical and mental anguish as a result of combat so many years ago, I came home whole. I ask myself over and over, 'Why did this one lose an arm, or leg, or eye? Why did so many friends come home in pieces? Why did some have to make the ultimate sacrifice?' All of us who made it back alive hurt for those who did not. Like most, I think that because we are in one piece it means we didn't do enough."

Fortunately, time erases most of those feelings. If they didn't forget, they at least learned to push the sad events into the background.

Desiring to see how other men in other wars dealt with loss, I talked at length with two World War II veterans, one a Second Lieutenant Platoon leader, the other an enlisted squad leader. One fought in the Battle of the Bulge. The other landed on Utah Beach during the Normandy invasion. Both were wounded, and both saw their units suffer tremendously high casualty rates.

And both, age 90 when I spoke with them, expressed thoughts in almost identical words: "You dared not take the opportunity to hesitate and be sad and certainly not show your sadness. If you took the opportunity anyway, you set yourself up to be next. All you could do was hurt for them, hurt for their families, give them a special place in your heart and return home grateful that you didn't die in that land far away. But part of you will always be there with them."

Second, there were feelings that some did not like but were unable to shake—*Revenge*.

That word has dominated the psyche of soldiers and would-be soldiers for years. It has appeared in thousands of books about war and I saw it worked out where the next battle- field was close by. "You got some of us today, but wait 'til tomorrow." History is replete with it: "Remember the Alamo!" "Remember Pearl Harbor!" "Remember 9/11/01!"

When Lieutenant Steward died from the grenade that was dropped in front of him by a VC who appeared to be surrendering, PFC Powers was exceedingly angry. Powers, a soldier the reader may remember from chapter 8, was the soldier who had once hated Steward and entertained thoughts about fragging (killing) him. After a memorial service for Lieutenant Steward, Powers asked if I might have a few minutes to talk with him. He wanted to say again that he had come full circle with his Lieutenant and that he felt a need to avenge his death. "Chaplain, maybe it ain't right to say, but I really want to get me some 'gooks,' for the way they killed my platoon leader. I want revenge on those suckers."

"Well, Powers," I said, "armed combat is about killing. As much as we may not like it, that is what war is about. So you will probably get your chance to take aim at some guys who are pointing weapons your way. I hope you will take great care to not let feelings of revenge blind you. Don't go out there with rage dominating your thoughts and actions. If you do, you won't be at your best. In no way do you want to do something stupid that might cause even more danger to your squad than it will be facing anyway. Remember, the VC that caused KIA to be placed after our friend Steward's name was killed also. I was told that some of his own grenade fragments probably took him out, but a bunch of rounds from American M-1s made sure. So, when and if you take revenge, it won't be against your lieutenant's assassinator. I don't know if this makes any sense to you or not. I guess what I really mean to say to you is, don't let revenge blind your actions. Try to stay in control of your emotions and be the good soldier you are."

"Yes sir, it makes sense. But I'm so sorry that we lost him," he said.

"We all are. Believe me, we all are. He was a good one."

Retreat was a third way. I always wished it did not have to be, but a break from front line combat was often accompanied by some heavy drinking. As a lifetime total abstainer I have never understood the need for alcohol, and I never entered the EM (enlisted men) clubs for the purpose of chiding or shaming those who were imbibing.

After a long field operation, especially if there had been KIAs, I knew the youngsters were displaying their manhood among peers and trying to forget, if only for a short time. But many were the times when I entered the brush-arbor type buildings or large tents where the boisterous, stand down celebrations were going on. A Pepsi or Ginger Ale in hand, I walked among and greeted battle-tested soldiers, some of whom were experiencing alcohol in such gigantic portions for the first time.

Many of them, usually one at a time but sometimes two close friends together, would come to where I was standing or sitting. Seeing them weep was not uncommon. With glazed eyes and speech more slurred than should have been coming from 19 and 20-year old mouths, they would talk about the recent past.

"I lost my friend out there in the mud two days ago. Jason and me, Chaplain, we had talked about getting together back in the world sometimes. There was this girl I wanted him to meet and he said he'd like to. That is never going to happen, 'cause now he is gone. Do you reckon he went to heaven, Preacher, do you reckon he did? I hope he did. I hope I do, too."

Some would sit in silence and stare into the dark Cu Chi night, seemingly lost in thought. Others would talk about how disappointed their mothers or grandmothers would be if they could see them in their present state. I don't know how behavioral science experts would sum up what was going on in those brief respites from war, but I called it retreating and doing what they could to cover the hurt for a little while.

The soldier also dealt with loss by remembering his friends and honoring them. After the initial shock subsided he was pleased to remember. I saw that in the way soldiers responded to the name plates on the memorial wall at the back of their chapel. I saw it in the reverent way they solemnly stepped forth to salute the jungle boots and steel pots during a memorial service. That fourth R—*Remembering*—became even more evident when I finally visited the Vietnam Wall many years after that war had ended. I stood for almost two hours in one place and watched middle aged men, wearing bits and pieces of military uniforms, stare at a single name.

Then at the Korean Memorial I saw other men, some in wheel chairs and others moving slowly with the aid of walking sticks, fix their gaze on a single life-like figure in the memorial. The day was warm but I saw some vets shiver as with a sudden chill. Faces of the figures in the statues reflected extreme fatigue and brutally cold temperatures. The survivors were thinking back. Thinking of when they were there and of friends who died there. Remembering.

On Sunday, November 12, 1967 I had the honor of conducting three worship services before lunch. They began with the Wolfhound chapel at 0830, and even though two companies were engaged in eagle flights, attendance was good. At 0930 it was the 12th Evac, at the invitation of Captain (Nurse) Ann Cunningham. The third stop of the morning was Row Bravo, a place where another 2/27 company was undergoing some training. Big crowd there also. Everything was looking good. The horror of Halloween, now 13 days in the past had begun to ease ever so slightly.

Now I wanted to get back to whichever mess hall what operating for some chow before flying out to Bravo Company, wherever they might be. Riding back to the chapel in the Wolfhound Watcher (jeep) I opened my green, and now very dirty, combat chaplain kit, took out my journal and made an entry of four words: "Two more to go!" I looked at my assistant and held up two fingers. He knew the meaning. Two Sundays to go. "Yep," he said, "you're short enough to sit on a dime and swing both feet."

On my way to the mess hall I stopped by the TOC to check on possible transportation to the field and to learn how the eagle flights were progressing. I walked into an activity filled place and a lot of radio traffic. The Battalion executive office was there and saw me as I entered that huge sandbagged complex. I knew things had taken a bad turn when, with a serious look on his face, he motioned for me to join him outside.

"Which company?" I asked. "KIA?"

"Bravo." And he gave me a name.

"Any more?" He said there was one more, so far, and spoke another name.

I forgot about food and walked back to the Holy Hootch. What had been a good morning thus far had turned sour. I unpacked my chaplain kit and pulled out the journal to make a second entry of the day: "Now Captain Chuck Springer is dead!" After hesitating a moment to reflect on the immediate past and collect thoughts, I wrote again: "Elzie Sanders is KIA too."

Eagle flights had begun to take a toll on the 'Hounds. Just two days before two men—Eastburn and Samuels—from C Company were seriously wounded while participating in a similar operation. And now the K acronym applied to two more.

Twenty-four hours earlier Chuck had admired a little box I had built to ship some souvenirs home. "Say, Padre," he said, "I'd like to have a box like that. That would handle a Chi Com rifle I hope to leave here with. Just the right size."

"Maybe I can build you one like it, if I can locate some more plywood and three hours spare time," I said to him. "That is a slim maybe, Captain Springer, no promises." I had spent a lot of time in the field with his company. One felt better, even safer, by simply being in his presence. He was a great friend to enlisted men, and they loved him. I found him to be among the half-dozen best

MEN WHO FOUGHT...BOYS WHO PRAYED |

liked and most respected officers I met during my 20 years in the military. We hated to lose people like him. Or anyone.

Elzie Sanders died alongside his commanding officer, Captain Springer. My journal entry about him was: "Elzie was one of the finest Christian young men I have met in Vietnam. Duty permitting, he never missed chapel, whether in base camp or the field." Had I been asked to predict what he would become when his army days had ended, I probably would have said, "A minister, a missionary or a businessman who would dedicate at least half his income to missions or charity."

Traffic at Tactical Operations Center remained heavy and I checked by often during the afternoon. I tried to work on letters to next of kin, but the TOC, only a few meters away, kept pulling like a magnet. Bravo Company continued to be the main subject. Before the day was over more names were written on a piece of paper and given to me.

Gregg Goslin and Staff Sergeant Jacob Ortiz were two of the names, both KIA. When dustoff choppers were finally able to begin extracting casualties I headed for the 12th Evac. Three WIAs from Bravo were inbound, I was told. I got to the chopper pad just ahead of them. Specialist Brown and Specialist Dula were the first in. Not far behind was medic Ronald Detmer, who, I learned later, suffered serious wounds while tending Captain Springer and SP4 Sanders. Detmer was that kind of guy, the kind that ignored the danger and performed his duty under terrific odds.

I had first met Ron back in July. I don't remember the details, but they had something to do with the Red Cross and his grandfather. I saw then that he was a youngster driven by dedication. He, along with hundreds of other soldiers I came to know under combat conditions, reminded me of a quote I later read from Detriech Bonhoeffer, a German minister and scholar who opposed Nazism. He was incarcerated at Buchenwald only to be removed just ahead of the liberating allies and hanged near the Czech border only days before the war ended. The quote, from the book, *Bonhoeffer*, is this:

> It is for us as soldiers, who go to the rear (safer place) or on leave from the front (danger, action) but who, in spite of all our expectations, long to be back at the front again. We cannot get away from it any more. Not because we are necessary or because we are useful (to God) but simply because that is where life is, and because we leave our life behind, destroy it, if we cannot be in the midst of it again.

November 12 left the entire battalion stunned—again. I began to think about another question to accompany the two I been pondering. "How does the commander/leader deal with loss? How does the soldier deal with it?" It dominated my thoughts far into the night, *how do I deal with it?*

Earlier in the evening and after chow, which I still didn't want to eat but did, we had an evening service. The chapel was packed. Soldiers filled the pews and sat on the concrete floor down the center, in front of the six-inch high stage and even on the stage. Though it was six weeks before Christmas we sang "O Come All Ye Faithful," and "Joy to the World" like a high school chorus out to win a contest. It had been a sad day for the 2/27 in general and for Bravo in particular. Trojan Six, Lieutenant Colonel Walter Adams, even though he must have had a hundred things on his mind, attended. We needed to think about something else, and for a few minutes we did.

I didn't even mention the tragic events that had spoiled the day. We would do that later at a memorial service. Near the end of a half-hour service I read the 23rd Psalm and we sang a final song: "Mine Eyes Have Seen the Glory of the Coming of the Lord." Those guys all stood, as if instructed, and began marching in place, their jungle boots pounding in time on the Wolfhound Chapel floor, and sang to the top of their voices: "Glory! Glory, hallelujah! Glory! Glory, hallelujah! Glory! Glory, hallelujah! Our

God is marching on." It was 'awesome,' as a future generation would say. Not many things more memorable remain. I can almost hear them singing the chorus of that great hymn as well as hear the sound of about 400 boots striking the chapel floor.

After the Lord's Prayer, they left quietly. On the way out, a few rubbed their hands across the brass plates on the memorial wall. It was not planned that way, but no one said a word. Colonel Adams made a point to shake hands with those nearest him. Some waved to me. And they walked out and toward their respective company areas, thinking about home and wondering about the future.

Somewhat washed out, sad and happy at the same time, I walked the five or six steps to my little hut, wrote a fast letter to my wife and was lying on my cot by 10 PM. It had been a long and very trying day. But sleep did not come as quickly as expected, for I began thinking about the question mentioned above: "How do I, the chaplain of this hard-charging outfit, deal with loss? I had faced it often over the past eleven months, but the question had taken on even greater meaning in the past 13 days. Of course, unknown to me at the time, it would whack away at my thought process even more in just three days. The 2/27 and I, their chaplain, still had to face 15 and 16 November 1967.

On the 15th I received word that my replacement would be in a week from that day. I hardly had time to acknowledge the word from S-1, because another message came in about the same time, with news that Charlie Company, which was on a combat assault in the Hobo Woods, had casualties.

The tracker dog handler was killed almost as soon as he jumped off the chopper, but because of heavy fire, dustoffs could not get to him. Bravo went in to relieve the pressure on Charlie Company and was immediately pinned down. That situation continued pretty much unchanged until the early hours of the 16th.

Close air support and artillery failed to suppress the enemy fire. To make matters worse, base camp was hit by mortars twice during the night, the first time at 2000 (8 PM) and again at midnight. A mortar round hit Ward C-11, killing one patient and several more received injuries on top of those that had caused them to be there in the first place.

I was returning from the chopper/dustoff pad with a jeep load of slightly wounded soldiers when the second attack began. The rounds were falling close so I turned into the hospital and herded my eight passengers into the relative safety of an X-Ray room. One of the soldiers, who had departed from a hot PZ (Pickup Zone) only minutes before, whispered, "Good grief, Chaplain, ain't no place safe in this sorry land. It don't seem right that they'd shell a hospital."

The mortars stopped firing about 12:30 and I ventured out of the lead-lined room to check my jeep. Luckily it had not been hit. The same bunch of soldiers jumped back in and on the Wolfhound Watcher and we took off for Wolfhound country, driving without lights. I dropped the eight guys off at their respective companies, parked the jeep next to my hootch, sat on the single step, ready to jump into the nearby hole if the shelling started again. Everything was blacked out and eerily quiet. I was startled to hear a voice calling my name: "Chaplain Tucker, are you there?"

"I'm here. Who is that? How do you respond when I say Austin?"

"Texas," he responded. "I'm the Colonel's runner. He'd like to see you."

"Is he in the TOC?" I asked.

"Yes sir, he's in there right now."

"If you get there before I do tell him I'm on the way," I said.

Thirty seconds later I was there. "Sir, you called for me?"

"Yes, chaplain, thanks for coming so quickly. As you know, we have been in some bad stuff the last few hours. We think the enemy has finally broken contact. There has been nothing but light sniper fire the last hour or so, probably some guys covering the retreat. But mainly I wanted to talk with you about tomorrow morning, or later this morning I should say.

"You aren't planning to go out there, are you? Before you answer, let me say I don't want you out there. I know you like to be with the troops and they like to see you, but come daylight there is going to be a lot to do here in base camp, especially in the 12th Evac area. We already know that four tracker dog handlers are dead. I pray to the good Lord not, but there could be multiple KIAs in Bravo and Charlie. Contact has been lost with a lot of soldiers. The number of casualties won't be known until a relief company can make a sweep shortly after first light."

I resumed my position next to the one-man foxhole, trying to imagine what those guys were going through out there in the dark. Knowing that death could come at any second from any direction had to be terror personified. I sat without moving for almost two hours and moved inside to my bunk just before 0400 (4 AM). But sleep still evaded me in the wee hours of November 16. I went to the TOC twice more before daylight, but being there made it even worse.

I learned ammunition was critically low. Half of their PRC 25s (radios), indispensable in situations like that, were inoperable. Most of the soldiers were out of water. One medic was known to be a casualty and those still performing were out of emergency supplies.

On and on those surprisingly calm voices reported from Hobo Woods. I forced myself to vacate the Tactical Operations Center with all its bad news and wait for daylight to arrive alongside the battalion S-1, who couldn't sleep either.

News about what had really happened the previous 20 hours did not start coming in at daybreak as expected. It started at 1030 when one unidentified body was evacuated to the hospital morgue. The dustoff co-pilot confirmed the fears that most of us had about the dog handlers. Of the six on the team, four had been killed. The faithful alert dog, a favorite among 2/27 soldiers, was also dead.

At 1200 the TOC began receiving reports from the company that was making a sweep of the battle site. Their reports added to the gloom: Bodies, some of them stripped of clothing, were being found. One wounded enemy soldier, evidently overlooked by his unit when contact was broken, was detained and interrogated.

The POW revealed that the Wolfhounds had encountered two battalions of well-trained and equipped Viet Cong soldiers. Not good odds. An hour later the WIAs began arriving at 12th Evac. There were usually three or four on each chopper. Some were walking wounded, with T-shirts wrapped tightly around their heads or upper arms. Others were barely clinging to life.

At least that was the way things appeared to me. I was obviously not capable of making medical diagnoses. The hospital's landing pad could not handle all the sudden traffic and the dustoffs and slicks began landing on the road about 50 meters away. I grabbed a litter from ER and ran with it to the first chopper that set down on the road. An attending medic and the crew chief slid a wounded shoulder onto the litter while a cook from Bravo Company and I held it at deck level. They deposited him quickly and with great care on the stretcher, and we took off in the fastest walk possible.

The soldier was alert and recognized me. Fear was on his dirt-covered face and he mouthed barely audible words: "Thank you, Chaplain! Thank you. O God! O God! O God! O God!" Eyes filled with tears, he was looking at me but appeared to be staring through me as his refrain continued. We set him carefully on the floor beside another wounded youngster. I patted him gently on his head, notified a nurse about his presence, grabbed another litter and repeated the drill. The cook and I made three trips before the flow of wounded stopped.

At about 1500, helicopters started appearing again. I watched three as they began their approach. Something about the sound of them seemed different, as if their engines were being handled a little differently and that maybe the pilots were taking extra care. It was almost reverent. As stated in an earlier chapter, I sensed why.

They were just Hueys, like hundreds of others I had seen and heard. But these three made a different sound from those I had met with the litters. It was their cargo. They were transporting something precious—2/27 soldiers, Wolfhounds who had given it all in a place called Hobo Woods.

First to land was Trojan Six, Battalion Commander. His C and C ship dropped off two KIAs before refueling and flying back out to continue his command and control duties.

Hospital and Graves Registration personnel were at the open door of the chopper before the skids touched down and I was with them. It was while the two young soldiers were being off loaded that I discovered it was the Colonel's bird. He had a look of one who had lost his dearest friend. He acknowledged my presence with a slight wave of his hand and I returned his greeting with the same gesture. In just seconds his pilot had the C and C on the way to a refueling point. Duties in the Hobo called him.

On that 16th day of November I was close to becoming a "single digit midget," the time when there would be less than 10 days to go! Lieutenant Gary Jones had even given me a swagger stick he had purchased in Cu Chi. The swagger stick was a foot-long ornamental piece of wood that guys sometimes carried to indicate short-timer status. Carrying it that day didn't seem the right thing to do. I placed it on the litter of a badly wounded soldier, who was obviously shorter than I was, but for a different reason.

The other two dustoffs unloaded quickly also, and flew back the way they had come. On that fateful day I had been with the battalion two weeks short of a year, and had come to view the enlisted soldiers almost like sons. My own son would be in their age category in a few years. Watching and helping close to 20 WIAs get into ER and triage was bad enough, but nothing like what came next.

I jotted their names down as they were taken off the choppers or when they were transported to Graves Registration. (Other personal information was added later). Not knowing how many to expect, it seemed they would never stop.

Near the end I was praying—more like begging—"O Lord Jesus, please no more! No more!" For no particular reason I touched the left shoulder of every one of those guys:

SP4 Robert Brede, Combat Tracker Team, Alexander, Minnesota
SP4 Arnold Johnson, Combat Tracker Team, Rochelle, Illinois
SP4 George Koon, Combat Tracker Team, Baltimore, Maryland
SP4 Mark Howard, Combat Tracker Team, St. Louis, Missouri
SP4 Jessie Conner, Charlie Company, Statesboro, Georgia
PFC Lindaberry, Charlie Company, Middle Valley, New Jersey

Somewhere in the midst of all the gruesome reality of the late afternoon, the senior chaplain for MACV (Military Assistance Command, Vietnam) showed up. He was making a courtesy call on some of his chaplains in outlying units, and the 25th Division Chaplain was on his agenda.

For some reason he was dropped off at the hospital and I was the first chaplain that crossed his vision. I was sitting on my helmet and staring at the ground when he, unaware of what had been going on the last 24 hours or of what was going on then, stopped in front of me and called my name. I jumped up and apologized for not acknowledging his presence. He immediately sensed that trying circumstances were in force. "I could see it in the slump of your normally erect frame," he said. I gave him a two-minute rundown on recent past and present events.

"Sir, my assistant can drive you to the Division Chaplain's office, but I need to wait here for the next dustoff," I said. "There will probably be many more."

"This is not one of your best days, is it?" he said, with a voice of deep concern.

"No sir, there have been some trying days in the past year, but none worse than this," I said to him. My words were probably barely discernible, but it was all the volume I could muster, or wanted to. Speaking softly just seemed right.

He decided to end his visit to outlying units there in front of the entrance to 12ᵗʰ Evac and jumped on the next flight to Saigon. I saluted him as his chopper gained altitude. As his helicopter headed south I heard two coming in from the northwest. Were more Wolfhounds aboard? Yes. The list continued:

> SP4 Glenn Wylie, Charlie Company, Saxonburg, Pennsylvania
> SGT Wayne Adams, Charlie Company, Hazard, Kentucky
> SP4 John Gordon, Headquarters Company Medic, Montaque, California
> SP4 Donald Boyer, Bravo Company, Riverside, California
> PFC David Keaton, Bravo Company, Yolyn, West Virginia
> SGT Gerald Cragg, Bravo Company, Chicago, Illinois
> SP4 Gregory Quinn, Bravo Company, Augusta, Maine
> PFC John Bettencourt Jr., Bravo Company, Chelmsford, Massachusetts
> SP4 Paul Cronk Jr., Bravo Company, Ashley Falls, Massachusetts

Darkness, both literal and emotional, was settling in. Flares began drifting down around the 25ᵗʰ Division perimeter. Thoughts of those in the Quonsets nearby would not go away. Nor would thoughts of parents and siblings and wives and girl friends and children whose worst nightmares would become realities in a short time. I walked back into triage, still crowded, and spoke with soldiers on litters and gurneys.

Some appeared to be sleeping but most were awake, pleased to see someone they knew. Actually, pleased to see, period. In attempts to locate wounds the medics had slit their jungle fatigues down both legs from waist to cuff. Some would be going home. Others would return to their respective units in the near future. They all waited to learn their fate, grateful that they were not among those evacuated last.

Between two of the 12ᵗʰ Evac wards I bumped into the Battalion Three (S-3). He had been up and going for at least two days and nights without rest or sleep. He looked worse than I felt. He placed a hand on my shoulder and I placed one on his. We stood facing one another for a few seconds, silent with eyes closed. I thought he might be praying, as I surely was. After those few seconds, I gave his slumped shoulders a light pat with both my hands, and we went our separate ways. Night covered the land and many who resided there. Some days are dark!

My assistant was waiting patiently in the jeep, as he had for past several hours. This had been his first encounter with events like that day and the previous night had brought. I told him to take the jeep on back to the chapel, about a mile away. I was going to walk.

Things sort of leveled out during the next 45 minutes on the dusty, dark Cu Chi road leading from the 12th Evacuation Hospital to the Second Battalion area. Some words from the Book of Proverbs in the Old Testament kept running through my mind. I began silently repeating them over and over, for myself and for those who would mourn 15 more soldiers: *Trust in the Lord with all your heart and lean not on your own understanding. In all your ways acknowledge Him and He will direct your paths.*

"Believe that, and get through this," I said to myself. Then another thought popped up, one I shared with Major Loffert later: "There are times when you think there is no way to go on from your present state. It is then that you have to reach deep and pull on a reserve that you didn't know was there. But when you do pull on that reserve, you discover it is enough."

I arrived at the chapel to find my assistant waiting. "Want to get some chow?" he asked, "Headquarters is serving late. By the way, when did you last eat?"

"When was it? Early this morning, I guess. Lead the way, I'd like to see what is on the menu this time of night." It was breakfast at night. Fresh eggs, all you can eat, excellent yeast rolls, crisp bacon. Even the mess sergeant recognized a needed boost in morale. Sleep even came, though interrupted by dreams of November 15-16, 1967.

CHAPTER 17

War Is What
They Say It Is

His hand froze to the sword.

—2 Samuel 23:10

Journal entry, 29 May 1967—"Badly wounded, he called out to God, Jesus, Mary... and mother."

He had a perpetually good-natured streak about him. I called it happy-go-lucky. But something more serious than usual seemed to be on his mind that evening as we both had a sandwich in the little building known as our Officer's Club. During my first month and a half with the 2/27 I had spoken with Lieutenant Hewell Grant several times. Like most of the lieutenants in the battalion, he was a platoon leader.

During our talks I learned that his father was president of a theological school, one that I was familiar with and had at one time considered applying to for post-graduate training. His father's name was well known to me also, so Lieutenant Grant and I had some common ground from the start. Maybe because of his father, he had high respect for my chosen profession.

But what he wanted to tell me in the O-club that monsoon-soaked night had nothing to do with his father or the institution of higher learning he led. Rather, it had to do with a dream that came on the heels of something that had happened during a firefight.

"Friar," he said, "something more weird than I've ever before encountered happened last week." (A few of the younger officers, who were knowledgeable of Robin Hood and his band, had begun calling me Friar Tuck). "A few nights ago I emptied my 12-Guage into a VC, hitting him five times with 00 buckshot. Later, I was lying on the ground trying to get a little sleep and dozed off for a few minutes. And I had a dream. I dreamed that I was lying in bed with my wife. Three guys appeared in our bedroom and began making jokes. They were pointing and laughing at us. I quietly picked up my shotgun and shot them all dead. Here is the weird part, Chap. I was glad! They crumpled to the floor like the VC had fallen to the ground earlier in the evening. I reloaded the gun and went to sleep."

He wasn't looking for a response from me, which was good, because I surely did not have one, except one that we mutually agreed on: "War does some odd things to people."

I never made sweeps through rice fields with my "congregation" without thinking of the farmers who were at work in the same place. The tiny women and children, wearing hats that were the size and shape of the wood bowl that my mother once used to mix dough for delicious homemade biscuits, were busily placing rice plants in the ankle-deep water, one sprig at a time. Often we would pass within ten feet of their squatting forms, but they would never look up. Not a word was said, not by the workers and not by the soldiers walking across their property.

I often wondered what those people were thinking as they viewed endless lines of green-clad soldiers, with fierce looking weapons walking through their fields. There must have been some questions: Will this war ever come to an end? Will the outcome of this war benefit us at all? Hurt us? What is this war even about?

The latter of their potential questions came to mind as a result of a conversation with a long-time American missionary. He spoke their language and seemed to know the hearts of the Vietnamese, especially the poor, the peasants. He told me that very few of the country people had ever been to a place larger than their own small village, and that most knew nothing about politics beyond the fact that their leader was a village chief.

"They have little preference," the missionary said, "as to what kind of political ideology is in control. They just want to farm their one or two hectares of land, harvest their rice, sell a little, barter a little, send their children to the village school and live their lives away from the noise and danger."

Those words took on special meaning late one evening when the two companies I was accompanying set up for the night in a farm village near Bao Trai. I befriended a little boy who was, I'm sure, hoping to sample some food that had been convoyed out to us. I gave him a paper plate of roast beef and mashed potatoes. He took it to a small house with a thatch roof about 50 feet away.

In ten minutes he was back with two adults, who I took to be his parents. They spoke in an excited manner, displaying wide grins as they did, and began pointing to the black cross that was sewn on the left collar of my fatigue shirt. Of course their words meant nothing to me, but their demeanor told me they were not angry about something.

Sergeant Taylor saw my predicament and summoned our interpreter, who told me the people were excited about the cross because they knew it to be a Christian symbol.

The family nodded their heads and patted my shoulders as the South Vietnamese soldier explained their excitement. Then he said, "Dai Wei (Captain) these people would like for you to sleep in their house tonight." My hesitation and reluctance were met with more smiles and gestures to follow them.

I took my poncho liner and air mattress into the little two-room cottage and placed it on the floor of what I assumed was the living room. The parents nodded their approval with blackened tooth smiles and went into the other of their two rooms.

On a crude table, two feet above the head of my air mattress was a photograph of two people. In front of the picture was a lighted candle that burned through the night. Each time I looked up, which was often, the figures in the photograph seemed to be looking toward the other room. I finally arrived at a conclusion that the homeowners had positioned it that way.

Before daylight the next morning, when I heard soldiers stirring about, I eased up and out to where the mess sergeant had coffee brewing. Our interpreter was having a cup and I asked him about the picture and the candle. In the same casual manner I might tell someone the meaning of Good Friday, he told me that the exhibit on the table had to do with ancestor worship. The two persons in the photograph may have been the man's grandparents.

"You not know it," he said, "but in night you sleep in family shrine and holy place."

Here were these people, I thought, out here in an isolated village, their possessions consisting of a water buffalo, a two-wheel cart, a plow with one handle, about a dozen chickens and a tiny sliver of land. They were existing, which was, according to the missionary friend I had spoken with, what they wanted to do. Exist.

The Americans, including the Dai Wei with a miniature cross on his collar, would move on in a couple of days, leaving behind cans of pound cake, chocolate bars and left-over food from the field kitchen.

Who would be the next visitors? Who would sleep in the shrine? Maybe Viet Cong tax collectors? The family would have to change allegiance, even if feigned. The Wolfhounds, and no doubt all units with similar missions, had experienced it before in other villages. It was called winning the hearts and minds of the inhabitants. But it was not at all uncommon to pacify a village with well-received deeds on a given day of a month, and be fired on from that same village while passing nearby five days later, or even one day.

To make matters even worse, our guys usually could not return fire until clearance was granted by higher ups. More than once I heard company commanders voice frustration: "What kind of deal is this? One of my soldiers gets shot in the leg (arm, hand) and I can't shoot back because the sniper is firing from a hootch that might contain civilians? What I'd like to know is how do I get hold of the Province Chief and get permission to shoot at people who are shooting at me."

Though the ARVN (Army of Republic of Vietnam) soldiers were usually not very sympathetic with the villager's plight, they did sometimes admit that the situation was unbelievably frightening for the people cowered down in their simple homes. To oppose the V C would mean beatings or assassination, they said. So to survive, they were forced to wait in fear until things got better. And if things did get better they would go back to their labors and hope the bad guys wouldn't show up again. Victims, they were, caught in the middle between terrible alternatives.

Those involved in combat assaults, ambush patrols and front line fire fights fought one kind of battle. Loved ones and families back home fought another. As has been the case since the beginning of armed conflict, they were both in war. At least the soldiers had each other and were all in the same situation. They could share fears, hopes and even letters, as was noted earlier, but most of the families were left to go it alone. They did not attend staff meetings, walk to chow with squad mates, dig in for the night with a buddy who was supposed to stay alert two hours and then sleep two hours.

The home front vigils were often lonely and filled with uncertainty. On the rare nights when things were quiet in the field the officers and NCOs would talk at length about how they missed their families.

Of course, unlike those who had been with the military several years and were making it a career, only a small percentage of the young enlisted men had a spouse or children.

Captain Chuck Springer had a son about the age of my middle child and three years younger than my son. Kids frequently came up in our conversations. We both regretted being separated from them, especially our sons, who were in the formative years of their lives. But we were profoundly grateful that our children had mothers who would "fill the gap" while we were away.

Captain Riley Pitts had a son who, I'm confident, grew up to be a great adult, if a father's admiration and love had anything to do with it.

The military leaders had little time or inclination to become nostalgic or speak of "those back home" to others, but when they did it was heart-felt and real. Lieutenant Tom Murphy had a seven-year old son who, like others in that age group, thought of his dad as his hero for two big reasons: First, he was dad. Second, he wore the uniform of a soldier.

I knew First Sergeant Holland for only a short time, but long enough to know he had a family he loved and that he would see them before Christmas. His most memorable words during our first and only meeting were, "Chaplain, I won't be seeing you in chapel because my port call is already in hand. This strange Asian war and I are parting company for a while."

The first sergeant was right. He didn't make it to chapel. But his name was called there and words were spoken about him the very next week. On a day when he should have been aboard a Freedom Bird bound for America he was instead being honored with a memorial service in the chapel he and some of his soldiers had helped build.

I have mentioned these four specifically because the wives and children they loved would never see them alive again. Those sons who may have looked forward to the day when they could ask Daddy about his medals and the war would never get a chance to do either. Nor would they go fishing or camping together.

Twenty-five years later it was my high honor to fill in a few of the blanks for Tom Murphy's son, who was by then in his thirties. And 33 years later my wife and I were pleased to have Phil Springer, Chuck's son, as a guest in our home. He had a lot of questions, a few to which I had answers. We talked many hours that day and night, as well as at some Wolfhound reunions and at The Wall in Washington DC. Much to my regret, I never had The privilege of meeting any of Riley Pitts' family or First Sergeant Holland's either.

Official letters to next of kin had a tendency to leave family members with questions. Those "we regret to inform you" notifications sounded pretty cold to parents, children and other loved ones, when they really needed some reassuring words, something their broken hearts could grasp. Most company commanders took the time to say things that gave assurance, sometimes in hand-written letters.

Though it was extremely difficult, best friends sometimes wrote mothers and siblings to let them know what a great guy their son or brother was. Some of those letters I was asked to read before they were delivered to the mail clerk. I was always impressed that never one time did they dwell on gory details, but on what positive elements they could mention, including that death was instantaneous for their soldier.

In my letters, which I was careful to send only after confirming that official notification had been made, I told only what I knew first hand. Parents were pleased to learn that their son had attended chapel, visited the orphanage, assisted in distributing clothing to needy children, helped decorate a Christmas tree or donated to a fund that helped another soldier go on emergency leave. That seemed to make their devastating loss a little more bearable. It was not uncommon to receive letters in response to mine, some to express gratitude and some requesting more information.

The latter type from Gloria Murphy reached me on April 19, exactly two weeks after I had written to express sympathy over the loss of her husband Tom. From other letters she had gotten two stories about how Tom had died. I wrote back immediately, telling her that he had been killed by what is known as friendly fire. His platoon had been in contact with an enemy element. Air support from our Air Force came in. The pilot came in low and with close support on the wood line nearest Tom and his platoon.

On a second run he evidently mistook our soldiers for the enemy. On that run he came in low again and dropped some armament known as Daisy Cutters. It was then that Tom, Rosenberry and Cline were hit. The plane, so I was told by those who were close enough to tell, came out of that dive and was starting another run to drop a 500 pound bomb. Before he could do so, radio contact was established between ground troops and the pilot. He pulled out of his run just seconds before releasing the bomb. That, I told her, was how it happened. I reached the area a few minutes later and began performing some very trying chaplain duties.

During my second tour I came to know Edwin Hickson quite well. Private Hickson was an assistant crew chief on a single engine fixed-wing aircraft. He had once attained the rank of Specialist Fourth Class, but a bout with drugs had led to a loss of rank. He was reduced to E-2 from E-4, which didn't seem to bother him much. His knowledge of the aircraft, known as a Beaver, remained, irrespective of rank. He was trusted to work on his plane and even taxi it from place to place. He could do it with skill and precision. It was in the Beaver he worked on, cranked and taxied that he met his death.

I wrote his father a letter of condolence, assuring him that Edwin was well liked and had attended the Wings of Freedom Chapel several times. In my letter I told the father how a few days before his death, Edwin had asked some really intelligent spiritual questions, including how to become a Christian. I told him we had talked about the First and Greatest Commandment, as Jesus had called it: "You shall love the Lord you God with all your heart, with all your soul, and with all your mind. This is the first and greatest command." He had been intensely interested in those words. After a lengthy discussion he asked for a New Testament and I gave him one. He smiled and nodded his head in agreement as he underlined *Matthew* 22:37-38 and *John* 3:16, among others that I pointed out to him.

Not many days later his father wrote back, expressing gratitude for my letter and a need to learn more about the particulars of his son's death. If I could share anything he would be eternally grateful, he wrote. I responded the same day: "Edwin, I'm sure you know, was a great young man, personable, handsome, strong of body. Because he told me he had shared some of his deep fears and addictions with you, you also know that he had fought some hard battles with sinister forces in the past.

"I honestly don't know where soldiers get drugs over here. Maybe the chaplain is not supposed to know. But those who want them can find them, and from what I have heard, they are cheap. He had shared some of his battles and victories with me, the latest about a week before his untimely mishap. The part about victories was what pleased me. There had been enough losses.

"One day I heard sirens on and near the airstrip, which is no more than 200 yards from the little chapel, where much of my time is spent when I'm not visiting soldiers at other sites. I ran to the flight line and discovered a Beaver had crashed and burned almost directly in front of the control tower.

"Of course you know now that Edwin was in the cockpit. Mechanics working on another Beaver and an Otter told me that Edwin had cranked his aircraft and was going to taxi it from a hanger to a spot on the apron, something the non-pilots did all the time. But this time, instead of parking the plane in its normal spot he continued to the end of the runway and turned it toward the other end. The control tower operators were frantically calling out: 'Identify yourself! What is your intention?'

"It was later discovered that the plane's radio was not turned on. He revved it up, released the brake, and somewhat crookedly began rolling down the runway. At less than enough speed to get airborne, the little plane climbed, almost vertically, to an altitude about twice the control tower's height. It stalled and crashed almost exactly in the center of the runway. There was a fire, which the fire trucks were battling when I got there a couple of minutes after the crash.

"Your son was dressed in OD boxer shorts and a T-shirt. Of course he had not donned a flight helmet. It is small consolation, I know, but Edwin died on impact. Those closest to the crash site were convinced he could have felt no pain. That word was important to me and it surely must be even more important to you. I was with the firefighters when they extracted his lifeless body. Three days later, as I reported earlier, a memorial service was conducted in his memory. The chapel was filled to capacity."

About 10 days later I received one of the shortest letters that ever crossed my desk. In response to my letter he wrote only one line: "Thank you, chaplain. War is just a terrible thing, isn't it?"

As a postscript to his words, I pinned a final note: "Yes, Mr. Hickson, it is."

The war for some does not end when the shooting stops, the treaty is signed or the enlistment is up. "You can't go home again," in its original context refers to another subject altogether, but it also describes many young people who had a difficult time coming back from war. Things were so different. The people had changed. The mission was no longer evident. After so many months of living on the edge, being around those who did not "understand," was difficult for them to deal with.

I really did not fully realize, or even believe, a certain situation could exist until I saw it played out. My first tour had barely begun when I met SP4 Coston, who was on his way home and out of the army. His enlistment would be up two months after returning to the states, and he would probably get an early out, which he did.

Coston had two scars on his left arm and one big scar on his right thigh. One of his wounds had been inflicted in September, 1966 and the other just before Christmas the same year. Two purple hearts. Neither was serious enough to come under the million-dollar wound category. When I met him he was off the line and clearing. He wanted to get into college, hopefully meet the girl of his dreams, settle down with a good part-time job while going to school, make plans for the future and forget that there was such a thing as the U S Army. When he came by to check out he asked if I would offer a prayer for his future, which we did together. Other duties and other soldiers soon caused memories of him to fade.

Sometime during the month of August the S-1 asked me if I'd like to give some words of welcome to a bunch of replacements. They were en route from the Replacement Detachment and were due to arrive any minute. I told him that I'd be pleased to say a few words to the new guys, most of whom would be dealing with uncertainty and fear. They had, after all, just left Camp Alpha, where outgoing soldiers would have shouted discouraging words to them.

The truck brought them right to battalion headquarters. I asked the personnel sergeant to send them to the chapel, where they could sit down and relax a few minutes before going to their assignments. They were all about to become Second Wolfhounds. I spoke with them about five minutes, encouraged them to call on me anytime they wished and led them in singing a verse of "America, The Beautiful." When they left the chapel one soldier lingered, turned to me and said, "Chaplain, you remember me?" I did remember. It was Coston. Back again was the soldier who, a few months before, could not wait to get out of here.

"Specialist Coston," I said, "what are you doing back here? As I recall you were a genuine short timer when you left and were going to get an early out."

"Yes sir, that was me. Couldn't wait to get rid of that uniform and begin making a great name for myself out in the world. Maybe find me a great girl friend."

"You obviously decided to re-up. Did you re-up for your old unit or did that just happen with a luck of the draw?

"I told the reenlistment office I wanted to go back to Vietnam and join my old unit with the 2/27. They informed me that with two Purple Hearts I could go to a place of my choice and mentioned Germany. But I missed the guys here and told them the place of my choice was 'Nam. Send me back there. If necessary I'll sign waivers," he said with a note of triumph.

"What happened," I asked Specialist Coston, "that made you want to come back?"

"It just was not what I expected. I stayed angry half the time. Couldn't concentrate on my college classes. People there were acting like Vietnam and the soldiers over here didn't even exist. There was one club, I guess it was a fraternity, that demonstrated against the war. I got in a shouting match with them before deciding to just ignore the whole bunch.

"One day I wore a miniature Purple Heart ribbon on my civilian shirt and those crazies made fun of it. All my professors except one could hardly get to what they were supposed to be teaching for bad-mouthing the army and everything about it. Guys I had gone to high school with were belly-aching and moaning about cafeteria food, gas being high and their parents not sending them enough money. One day my math class let out because the air-conditioner wasn't keeping the room cool enough, and I thought of the guys over here who stay sweat-soaked all day long. One day in freshman speech, my assignment was to make a five-minute informative speech on any subject. I chose what I knew best—the M-60 machine team in combat. I talked about each team member's job and how every man depended on the other. I described the noise, the fear, the cries for a medic when someone was injured. I talked about how it was to live in a hole at night, and pray that we'd get a resupply of ammunition before the bad guys probed our perimeter again. I told them about claymores, how to set them effectively and how Charlie sometimes crawled up in the dead of night and turned them so they would fire back at us instead of out at the people who wanted to kill us.

"I finished my speech in four minutes and 45 seconds. And every member of the class, except two older guys, veterans of the Korean War, laughed. The professor, that worthless wacko, looked at me like I had just crawled out of a hollow log. After that I just said the heck with it. I went to the recruiter and began the re-up procedure. Maybe someday I'll be able to fit in again. I sure hope so, because you can't stay here all your life. Well, I guess you can if you die young."

That soldier back for his second tour in one of the infantry company's most dangerous jobs left me shaking my head in silence. We shook hands and I walked with him toward his old company's day room. On the way we met some guys who remembered him. "Hey, dude," one said, "want to get some good old army chow?" He was back where people accepted and understood him.

Then I remember what Lieutenant Grant and I had agreed on about six months before: "This war does some odd things to some good people." Then it occurred to me that another phrase should be added: "….on both sides of that big ocean."

CHAPTER 18

Return And Reunion

Let him go home, or he may die in battle.

—Deuteronomy 20:5b

Journal entry, 9 July 1967—"Baptized Specialist Smalls. Good and bad exist together."

Probably no one knows who first used the words, but I first heard them from Captain Humphrey, the battalion artillery liaison officer.

At his farewell ceremony in a little grassy area between the TOC and 2/27 headquarters building, he gave his brief "going away" speech. It began these words: "Well guys, I do want you to know that I leave here with mixed emotions—joy and happiness!" Most left Vietnam with the same sentiments. The camaraderie experienced the past twelve months would be sorely missed, but not as much as family and home had been missed.

Both of those mostly identical emotions were on my mind when Chaplain Keith Sink called from Division with a welcome announcement: "Your replacement has been identified and is in country."

For a minute or two his message left me both pleased and saddened, but mostly pleased. "You are not the indispensable man," I told myself. "These soldiers will make it just fine."

Certainly, that was true. Still, for a brief time my own questions bombarded me: "Who would respond to the Farr and Harmon families if they wrote back with questions after receiving my sympathy letters about their sons? Who would assist the surviving Combat Trackers in dealing with the losses they had suffered on that fateful day/night of 15/16 November? Would anyone feel compelled to stay in touch with and encourage Specialist Garcia, who became a double amputee on 18 November?

"Don't worry," I told myself, "others will handle things better than you did."

Knowing that if history repeated itself (and it always did), the 2/27 would not be in base camp for very long, I worked most of the night to plan memorial services for 20 soldiers. Fifteen had been evacuated just hours before, on that dark day of 16 November. Four others had given their lives on 12 November and one on 11 November. In pre-military chaplain days I had once conducted two funerals on the same day. That was bad enough. During the earlier days of 1967, ten Wolfhounds had been remembered in one service, but never twice that number in one day.

I decided to have four separate memorial services in the chapel, beginning with the four Combat Tracker Team members, who were the first KIAs just two days before in the Hobo Woods. Fellow team members served as honor guards. I requested that they bring one of their dogs to the service, in remembrance of Ace, the faithful German shepherd that had been killed with his handlers.

Prince sat quietly on his haunches in the middle of four honor guards during the half-hour service. Just outside the front entrance of the chapel four rifles, with helmets atop them, were arranged vertically and in a perfectly straight row. One of the helmets had a leash draped over it. Soldiers filed somberly by the rifles, stopped at each, and saluted. When Prince was led by the memorial display he seemed to hesitate an extra second or two in front of the helmet with the leash. It could have been my imagination. But had he stopped to look at and sniff Ace's leash, it would have been fitting. Those were extremely smart animals.

Soon after the 0830 service concluded, Bravo Company and others assembled to remember their six friends who had died on the CA (Combat Assault) in the Hobo. Average age: 21. Making it even rougher, Bravo was still dealing with the loss of their highly respected CO, who had been killed just six days earlier. At 1030 most of Charlie Company filed into the screen-sided chapel that had become as much a part of us as the TOC, mail room and mess halls. Five more were honored at that time, including the medic who was killed while giving aid to Ace's handler. It had not been a month since those guys had lost Captain Pitts, their CO. *And now, five more,* they were thinking, while dealing with their own mortality. You could see it on their faces, and sense it as they saluted five helmets outside the chapel's front entrance.

The last service began at 1130 on that dreadful Saturday morning. It was for five who had been killed on 11 and 12 November. The day's total: 20. The company commanders or company executive officers were invited to speak some words of eulogy and remembrance at services for their respective units, and they usually did. The 2/27 CO spoke at the fourth and last service of the day, as he always did if the service was for a company commander or someone from the battalion staff. I was never comfortable with a generic type ceremony and always tried to add a personal touch about each of those who were being remembered. Fellow soldiers and close friends knew things that, when shared correctly, made the deceased soldier seem less a statistic and more a person.

The last 20 names had not yet been added to the Memorial Wall on the day their memorial services were held, but the brass plates had been ordered. As at every such service, soldiers brushed their hands lightly across the names as they departed. When my replacement arrived five days later my assistant and I were at work gluing the latest names to the Wall. That made 93.

There would be one more on my watch. The new chaplain was a bit flabbergasted with those long rows of brass plates. "How long to get this many?" he asked.

"Less than a year!" I answered.

He looked at it again and said, "Man!"

Five days before Thanksgiving the Second Wolfhounds were alerted for another operation in an area that was familiar to them. That news led to a late-night staff meeting. Reports on the prospects for that one reminded me of what I had heard in my first such meeting eleven and a half months earlier.

That one was with LTC Sheldon. Following him was LTC Peter, who was commander for six months. Conducting the mid-November briefing was LTC Walter Adams, who told us that the battalion would be kicking off an operation in the notorious Iron Triangle the next day. "In just a few hours from now," he informed us.

During the afternoon and early evening, he and his senior staff officers had been at Division Headquarters going over tactical plans for the operation. The next step was to fine-tune it down to company level. That was what the late night meeting was about. Operation Atlanta was set to begin at 0900 (9:00 AM) the next day. At the conclusion of the staff briefing, the company commanders, two of them quite new, left in a run. There were a lot of details to finalize before 0900. Sleep time would be limited.

Trojan Six also had a lot to do before the night was over, but he asked me to remain a few minutes. "Chap, I have a request to make of you," he said. "How much longer do you have to go on this tour?" he asked.

"I guess about 12-13 more days," I answered. "Personnel thinks my port call will be the first or second of December." The S-1, who was standing with us, confirmed it.

"I knew you were getting short," Trojan Six said. "And I'm not ordering it, but I would like you to consider not going to the field any more. Just relax a little, meet and get your replacement oriented and spend some time clearing. That's about all I wanted to say, that, and to express my gratitude for your tireless efforts among the soldiers of this battalion.

"You have truly been a 'real friend to the grunts.' Much appreciated, Chaplain. Please know that I very much appreciate what you have done here."

The S-1 walked back to the Holy Hootch with me. "Did you pick up on the Colonel's words?" I asked him. "How do you interpret what he said?"

"I tell you what I think it is. What I all but *know* it is," he responded. "He is trying to protect you. He has talked with the S-3 and me about it. In these last few days he'd like you to be in potentially safer places. Keep you out of the line of fire and off helicopters. That's the way I see it."

"Huh!" I said in response. "But if the battalion stays out for long I'll really feel a need to get the new chaplain out and introduce him around. So we'll see how it works out."

Sunday again. If things continued on schedule, this would be my next to last one. With all four line companies in the field, attendance was light on that third Sunday in "Turkey" month. I had become so accustomed to hitching rides to troop areas on Sunday afternoon that not doing so that day was strange and difficult, almost like I was not performing my duties properly, even though I was covering the Ambush Academy and ministering to numerous soldiers at Row Bravo. There was plenty to do, but time began to drag.

Then came Thanksgiving Day, and a special 1030 service at the Wolfhound Chapel. While enjoying a tremendous meal at the Headquarters Company mess hall, I saw Keith Sink heading my way with a big grin on his face.

"What is going on with you?" I asked. "You look like a Division Chaplain who is aching to lose another game of pinochle to a lowly Battalion Chaplain."

"Well, maybe later. But right now I want to give you another reason to be even more thankful on Thanksgiving. Your replacement, Chaplain Herbert Thornton, is on the way to Cu Chi on the afternoon convoy."

"That is good news," I said. "Since he is en route, I don't suppose you can speak with him, but if by chance you do, tell him to surround himself with sandbags and try his best not to get ambushed." Keith laughed and said he'd attempt to send him a telegram.

At 1500 I caught a chopper bound for the Iron Triangle with a load of chow. I wanted to share an evening thanksgiving meal with troops in the field. After three days of straight Cs, they would love it. Bravo and Charlie were dug in close to one another, so I had a joint field service with them about 1630.

A large number of men assembled. Probably too many in a bunch where incoming mortar rounds were a possibility. It was the same for Alpha and Delta Companies, and had another big joint service with those two after their Turkey and Dressing meal. Just before sunset I grabbed a ride on a chopper that was taking a soldier with a non-combat injury back to Cu Chi.

It had been a good Thanksgiving Day, very unlike the previous Thursday. Besides that, I was now officially a single digit midget. "Seven days and a wakeup," as short timers liked to put it.

My assistant and the Wolfhound Watcher were waiting near the landing pad. "My replacement should be in," I told him. "Let's go by the Division Chaplain's office and see if we can meet him."

He was there. He and Keith had just finished an evening meal of turkey sandwiches, leftover cranberry sauce and banana pudding—the real kind with vanilla wafers. They pushed a bowl my way, which I joyfully accepted. Chaplain Thornton was deep in jet lag and badly in need of some sleep. He was going to bunk in the same little hut I had spent some time in almost a year earlier. Experience told me he was undergoing some feelings of ambivalence.

He joined me in the battalion the next day. I began checking him in and me out. The personnel NCO said, "Chaplain, I'm glad you came by. Just learned this minutes ago, your port call is 1 December." Wow, that is one week from today. And did you see the time? Zero one thirty (1:30 AM) on December 1."

"Thanks, Sarge," I joyfully said, "I don't care how early it leaves, I plan to be on it."

Herbert met the Battalion Commander on Saturday. While they conversed a few minutes I cleared the mailroom and supply. Colonel Adams sort of wrinkled his nose and gave me a "you-don't-have-to-do-that" look when I informed him that I'd be taking Chaplain Thornton to the field the next day—Sunday. But he realized the new chaplain would get a better feel for things that way, so he shook our hands again and wished us well. He asked if I planned to stay in the Iron Triangle overnight, and I told him only if I could not get a ride out in the early evening.

Sunday was a busy day as usual, especially when the companies were out. I began acquainting the new chaplain with things he'd need to know most. I asked him if he'd like to speak at any of the services, beginning with the Ambush Academy at 0830, but he begged off, saying that he'd prefer to observe that day and take it on full force next week. After the 0830 service we rushed back to the Wolfhound Chapel and another small crowd at 0930. Then it was to 12th Evac for a 1030 service and back to the battalion chapel to conduct a memorial service at 1130. SP4 Robert Parker, D Company, of Ponca City, Oklahoma was KIA about two hours after I had concluded a field service with Alpha and Delta on Friday. His was the last name I attached to the Memorial Wall. Number 94!

By the time we got to Sunday dinner at Headquarters Company, Chaplain Thornton was quite overwhelmed with what had gone on since daylight. A little of the pressure was relieved when he learned that the hospital service was not an every week thing.

"In fact," I told him, "you may not be responsible for the hospital worship service even once during your tour." Of course the memorial service was not a regular Sunday event either. We agreed to live with the hope that there would never be another of those on any day of the week, and that not another piaster would be needed to purchase name plates with the names of Second Wolfhounds engraved on them. Reality and history told me it was only a faint hope.

"A couple of Hueys are going to make an ammo run to Battalion Forward about 1430. We should be able to hitch a ride on one of them. What do you say we lay out your field gear to be sure you have all the necessities," I said to Herbert. He agreed and unpacked his duffle on the chapel floor.

"You will, of course, discover what you need most," I continued, "but if you like I'll point out what has worked for me."

"If you would, please," he said.

"Here are the main things: Canteen of water, poncho and poncho liner, mosquito net, web gear and web belt, flashlight with red lens, at least one extra pair of socks, steel pot, flak vest and an army green towel. I usually carry about a dozen New Testaments in my chaplain kit, along with wafers and grape juice for communion. I can't speak for others, but I like to wear a towel around my neck like a scarf. It helps guard against mosquitoes and is great for wiping sweat. Also, I keep a yellow smoke grenade hanging on my web gear. If you should have to let gunships or dustoffs know where the good guys are, the smoke will be welcome. Sometimes I take a package or two of Kool Aid and a few cans of my favorite C-Ration items, such as pound cake and fruit cocktail. Most of the time you can borrow an entrenching tools to use in digging a foxhole, but there have been times when I was truly thankful for that little shovel hanging on my own web belt."

We were at the take-off point by 1415. Three Huey's, one more than expected, were being loaded with ammunition and water. Chaplain Thornton and I jumped on the one with the lightest load. He found a clear spot on the metal deck and I sat on a box of M-79 grenades. We were on our way to join the Wolfhounds in the field, Herbert for his first time and I for my last.

The Iron Triangle, a short hop from Cu Chi, was well known as a refuge for the Viet Cong. The 2/27 never went into that part of their AO (area of operation) without making contact, often heavy. Our guys had learned to hit the ground running up there and dig in quickly. The three Hueys, accompanied by a gunship, landed without taking any fire. My replacement and I jumped out while soldiers were scurrying around to hurriedly off-load the ammunition and other supplies.

I asked one of the soldiers where the Battalion CP (Command Post) was, and we headed the direction he pointed. On the way we passed through an Armor unit that was attached to the 2/27 for that operation. The tanks were dug in so deep only a little more than their turrets were visible above ground. The APCs (armored personnel carriers) were dug in almost as deep.

After a quick call on the battalion XO and Sergeant Major, Chaplain Thornton and I made our way to Delta Company. Because they had lost SP4 Parker just two days earlier, I wanted to see those guys first. After talking with soldiers in Parker's platoon for a few minutes, I set up a combination field/memorial service with Delta. The guys were pleased to know that when they returned to base camp their friend's name would be on the little blue Naugahyde-covered board at back of the chapel.

I handed my New Testament with Psalms to a soldier I had baptized in an irrigation canal a few weeks earlier. He read a verse from Psalm 112: *He will have no fear of evil things. His heart is at ease, trusting in the Lord.* I asked the 20 or so in attendance if they wanted to sing a song. They did, and a squad leader started it on key: "Amazing grace, how sweet the sound...!" As was so often the case, we concluded with The Lord's Prayer. I felt a little nostalgia as the young men stood, gathered their weapons, waved and walked away. Lieutenant Gary Jones knew I was due to depart for the states in four or five days. He stayed a minute to say so long and talk about the wedding vows he and Anne hoped to exchange in my presence "someday."

He took my stateside address (Fort Sill, Oklahoma) with the intention of letting me know where he would be going when his 365 days had ended. We shook hands and he returned to the Vietnam War. Of course I never saw him again and, as an earlier chapter revealed, the wedding never took place. The infamous 1968 Tet Offensive saw to that.

Night was approaching again. I located Bravo and Charlie and introduced Herbert to the company commanders. We quickly set up for a field service fifty meters from where a tracked vehicle was dug in and camouflaged, and near where a chow line was going to be. I hung my tattered chaplain flag on a bush and printed a sign on a piece of C-Ration carton—"Chapel Here—1730 Hours."

Dozens of soldiers, on their way to the chow line, saw the flag and stopped by for what would be my last field service. (There had been, I estimated, approximately 150 previous ones). I based some brief thoughts on the 15th verse of John, chapter 17: *I do not pray that you should take them out of the world, but that you should keep them from the evil.*

Chaplain Thornton and I served the Lord's Supper by asking those in attendance to dip a communion wafer in grape juice I had transported in my combat chaplain kit. Sort of like the senior moment that we hear so much about these days, a "short-timer moment" must have hit me on the last minute of my last field service with the Second Wolfhounds. In preparing to lead the Lord's Prayer as a benediction, the words left me. After leading that familiar prayer hundreds of times, I could not recall how to start it that day in the Iron Triangle. Missing only a couple of beats, I said, "Chaplain Thornton, would you please lead us in the Lord's Prayer?" Which he did: "Our Father, who art in heaven…"
I didn't dare mention why I had suddenly asked him to lead us. Maybe it was because I didn't want him to think he was replacing a chaplain who had become senile at age 35.

The Slick (UH1 Helicopter), loaded with supplies, landed a couple of minutes after the guys completed the words from Matthew 6: "For thine is the kingdom, and the power, and the glory, forever. Amen."

Chaplain Thornton had found a place to dig in with Charlie Company that night. "They will help you feel cared for and secure," I assured him. We walked to the LZ (Landing Zone). The empty food and drink canisters were quickly loaded. After learning the pilot was returning non-stop to Cu Chi, I shook hands with my replacement and jumped aboard. It revved up, lifted a few feet, nosed down, and began gaining altitude.

Because snipers often fired on choppers in that area, the co-pilot signaled that we were going to circle and climb to about 2000 feet before leveling off to fly southwest to our destination. As we turned and climbed in a tight circle I kept my eye on the chaplain below. His brand new jungle fatigues shined bright green in contrast to the faded and muddy ones the grunts were wearing.

I knew the gist of his thinking at that moment, for it had to be the same as mine had been in the Boi Loi Woods almost a year earlier: "How will it be out here tonight? I have, 360 more days of this! Lord, you are going to help me with this, aren't you?"

When the altimeter reached a point between 1800 and 2000 the pilot pointed to indicate that we were heading for the barn. I looked back at the now tiny figure below. He had not moved or taken his eyes off the retreating helicopter. At last he disappeared and I never heard from or about him again. Was his tour as rewarding as mine had been? That question would remain forever unanswered.

The next day I obtained my plane ticket at transportation and took a last tour of the 12th Evacuation Hospital, which by then consisted of 12 large metal buildings, eight of which were wards. I walked slowly through every one of them, thinking about the dozens, hundreds really, who had spent some time there.

More than 400 WIAs out of my battalion of less than 900 came close to a 50 percent casualty rate. Add to that number the

94 whose names were on the Wolfhound Memorial Chapel Wall and the casualty rate approaches 60 percent. *Where were the more serious cases now?* I wondered. In how many military hospitals and VA centers were they housed? How many, some still only 19 or 20, were in wheel chairs? In every ward I uttered a short prayer for those who were there, for those who had been there and for those who were yet to come.

The morgue, I purposely saved for last. But I chose not to enter it on my next to last day in Cu Chi. Instead, I walked slowly around the 60-foot long building, taking at least 15 minutes to traverse those 180 or so feet—only about 60 steps total. Averaging no more than 12 feet a minute, I stopped frequently to listen. In my mind I could hear a trumpet close by sounding Taps. Another, in the distance and barely audible, echoed the nearer one. Somber notes, sounded as a reminder of the death of those who had barely begun to live.

A happy bunch climbed aboard the old troop-carrying truck at 0730 the next morning.

I climbed into the back of the two-and-a-half ton with 25 smiling GIs, but the driver, a 28-year old private E-2, who had once traveled the U S in a big rig, would have none of that. "Chaplain, you get up here in the front and bring us luck," he said.

The guys in the back joined in: "Yeah, Chaplain. You get in the front and make that driver get us to the Freedom Bird on time."

They cheered when I opened the door to jump in and yelled, "Okay driver, head this monster toward the USA!"

The mostly happy GIs in the back had come well stocked. Kids waited by the side of the road at every village and were showered with candy and gum. Some even tossed out their left-over piasters, which they commonly referred to as funny money. The convoy arrived at Long Binh Junction, better known as LBJ, at 1000. Dusty and wind-blown, soldiers dismounted the bone-rattling rough vehicle and began out-processing, which was completed by 2130 (9:30 PM). Then it was time to start griping about what every soldier knows is the Army's favorite way of doing things—Hurry up and Wait.

The homeward-bound 707 was scheduled to depart Bien Hoa at 0130, but when that 90 minutes past midnight time came the place was shrouded in thick fog. Visibility was near zero. The terminal took on the appearance of a flophouse, with tired GIs sleeping on the floor anywhere they could find a place to plop down their duffle bags. The welcome announcement came at 0300 and was greeted with cheers: "Have your papers ready. Prepare to board." At 0400 the plane lifted off Vietnamese soil.

I expected our takeoff to be accompanied by a lot of hilarity. But there was almost no cheering or loud talking. There was no spontaneous applause when landing gear was heard folding underneath. Very few were saying anything at all. Maybe it was that they just could not believe departure was actually a reality.

After a stop in Tokyo to refuel, we set out on a non-stop flight to Travis Air Force Base, near San Francisco. After our second in-flight meal, many of the passengers began strolling up and down the aisles. I was among them.

The cross on my left collar caught the attention of three young men, all of whom approached me in the next few hours. The first one located me and asked, "Chaplain, can I talk with you a minute?" We stood together in an open space near one of the exit doors.

"What's going on?" I asked the long-faced soldier, who told me he was 22.

"I'm scared to go home. I want to go but I don't know if I can face what is going to be there. I left a ring on the finger of a girl I've known since we were in the 11th grade. We graduated from high school together and started college at the same time, though not at the same school. Finances got so tight I dropped out at mid-term of my junior year and volunteered for the draft, and before you know it I'm a ground-pounder with the Big Red One.

"My decision would not lessen her love for me, or our plans to be married, she said. I tried to write her at least twice a week and she wrote me even more often, until about three months ago. I blamed her reduced correspondence on the fact that she was in her last semester of college. And I understood why she wouldn't have as much time to write.

"But then, Chaplain, two weeks ago, about the time I was taken off my rifle squad and given a job in the rear, I got the first letter in three weeks from her. She wanted me to know there would not be a wedding for the two of us, because she is now the wife of another man.

"Two months ago she and a guy she had met in college were married. I was sort of numb at first. More than that, I was big-time numb. And now I'm scared to go back to a place where our plans for the future were made. Chaplain, I don't expect you to do anything about this. No one can. But I sure would appreciate it if you'd pray that I'll find ways to deal with my fear, and that I'll be able to get over the one I still love."

Somewhere over the Pacific at 40,000 feet, we prayed. His war was not over.

Before we landed at Travis, I spoke with the other two. One, age 18, sobbed like a baby while telling me that his mother was dead. Emergency leave was his reason for being on that airplane. "And it ain't just that," he said, "she was killed by a drunk driver, a stupid drunk driver, and I'm afraid my daddy might go after that guy if the law don't do something. And the Lord forgive me for thinking such a thing, but I feel like helping my daddy do it."

"My goodness, son, what a blow this is for you and your family. Hopefully you will find that the law has started the wheels of justice turning by the time you get there. I sure hope you and your dad won't let revenge drive you to some acts that might make things even worse." What else could one say?

The third soldier I met between Tokyo and California had learned the day before he received a port call that his wife of three years would not be there when he arrived home. Their year-old son would be with the soldier's parents and on the dining table would be papers that listed all the reasons she no longer wished to be his wife.

"Bottom line, Chaplain," he said, "she has found someone else." He went on to say that he knew such things happened to people, but never expected that it might happen to him. All I could do was suggest that maybe things would look different once they spoke face to face.

"See if she will go with you to a professional counselor, or maybe to your priest or pastor, if you have one," I suggested. "Talk with her about how that little boy will need both a mom and dad as he gets started in life."

Those soldiers, especially the last one, made me want to fall down in the aisle of that airplane and thank God for my family, a loving wife and three wonderful children waiting at home. They were anticipating my arrival fully as much as I was anticipating arriving. Though not falling prostrate to do it, I breathed a prayer of thanksgiving for that quartet in Okmulgee, Oklahoma and a prayer of intercession for the three saddened and confused GIs I had met on the flight home, as well as for every person on that plane.

Unlike the return to the USA I experienced three years later, things went well. We arrived in Travis Air Force Base terminal at 5:00 o'clock in the morning to the cheers of at least a hundred people. It was 1 December 1967. It would be like a different world in mid-December, 1970.

After 23 months at Fort Sill, Oklahoma, I was on my way to Vietnam again. Being a chaplain to college graduates, who were getting commissions through OCS (Officer Candidate School), had tested my physical abilities to the limit. I had loved it and regretted that it could not continue. But when the Chief of Chaplain's office says "we need you in Southeast Asia again," you pack up and get ready to go. In Vietnam, I would see some of the second lieutenants that had been active in my chapel program at Fort Sill, and would conduct a memorial service for one of them.

Near the end of my second tour, which involved chaplaincy ministry at Marble Mountain, Hue, Phu Bai, Chu Lai, Tri Be, Camp Eagle and Udorn, Thailand, I hitched a ride on a C-123 to the huge U S Airbase at Cam Rahn Bay. After several delays and one night sleeping on the terminal floor, my name came up on the manifest.

A planeload of happy soldiers boarded and found their seats. Their happiness was even more evident about three hours later when, out over the Pacific, the captain made an announcement: "Hey guys, we have a strong tail wind that helps this bird fly at more than 700 miles per hour ground speed. So we aren't going to stop at Guam as planned. We are going non-stop to Seattle. Those who weren't asleep cheered loudly and the big commercial aircraft roared on.

We lifted off Cam Rahn Bay at midnight and landed at Sea-Tac airport, half way around the world, the same midnight.

Everyone was feeling (and looking) pretty grungy as we neared the West Coast. My khaki uniform, which had been carefully maintained for the trip home, looked like it had been in constant use for more than 24 hours, which it had. But nobody cared. Everyone, officers and enlisted alike, looked about the same. Except one.

I had nodded to a young soldier who had passed my seat with a folded uniform in his hands. A few minutes later he walked back up the aisle wearing a pressed uniform that smelled faintly of rice starch. His jump boots were shined to a high gloss. Over this left shirt pocket were several ribbons. On the top row was a Purple Heart with an oak-leaf cluster, signifying a second award, and a Silver Star. Also pinned on his shirt was a Combat Infantry Badge (CIB). Three stripes on each sleeve identified his rank: Sergeant. Maybe he was meeting someone and wanted to look his best, I thought. If so, he was doing a good job of it.

I congratulated him on his ability to find a place and the time to spruce up for our arrival in the United States. I also learned that he was 19—a twice wounded, Silver Star recipient, combat veteran, E-5 sergeant, who graduated from high school a year and a half earlier.

He asked me if I'd pray for his seriously ill grandfather in North Carolina. I gladly did.

A surprise awaited us as we entered the Sea-Tac airport terminal. It was a little past midnight and we expected to see no one except a few sleepy passengers awaiting flights. An artillery captain and I walked out of the tunnel together and faced a hundred or more demonstrators, heaping uncomplimentary epithets on the soldiers ahead of us. Mostly to myself, probably, I said aloud: "What in the world is going on here?"

The captain said, "This is quite a mob, but nothing like the one I encountered in the San Francisco airport three months ago, when I was returning from TDY."

"I knew from reading the Stars and Stripes that there was some unrest in our land," I said to him. "There were some signs of it in Hawaii when I met my wife on R and R back in August, but nothing like this. This is too much for tired and lonely soldiers."

The demonstrators, mostly college-age with a few middle-agers mixed in, seemed to focus on the younger GIs for the most bitter disdain. Standing against the wall about 30 feet farther up the concourse was the Silver Star-wearing soldier from North Carolina. Three bearded young men and a young woman, wrapped in a green army blanket, all wearing peace-symbol emblazoned head bands, were showering him with more trash talk than professional sports teams are accused of heaping on their opponents. "Hey, if it isn't the hero! How many babies did you shoot soldier boy? You got any ears in your pocket? Whazza matter with you, no conscience at all? Did our great Uncle Sam give you that lettuce above your pocket for wiping out a village or more than one village?" On and on they went, while the youngster stood visibly shaken, fists doubled, knuckles white.

The artillery captain walked on toward baggage claim, shaking his head. I stopped between the soldier and his tormentors about 20 feet away, and said, "Look at me, Sergeant Leonard. Don't say anything to the guys doing all the yelling. Pretend they are not there."

"But Chaplain, I can't make any sense of this. All I did was join up and do what I was asked to do. My dad fought with Patton's army across France and Germany. How could I face him ever again if I had run off to Canada or somewhere? I haven't killed any babies or collected any ears. I just don't understand this scene."

"I don't either, believe me, I don't either. But doing what you and other soldiers in this terminal are tempted to do will only make matters worse. It will not be worth it to get arrested and ruin what has been a good tour, one you'll be proud to share with your children and grandchildren some day.

"You're back alive, in time to celebrate nearly every American's favorite holiday in a week. Don't get tossed in jail for something you didn't cause. Most people, starting with those who count most, are proud of you for doing what you were called on to do. I hope you will simply step right on past these guys, don't say a word to them. Don't even look their way. Get your luggage, claim your ticket for the flight home, think about cheering up your sick grandpa and get ready for a Merry Christmas."

He moved on and the demonstrators turned their attention to those behind us.

It took a while to get over Vietnam. Late night noises soon faded into just what they were, simply loud noises, such as back-firing vehicle engines that initially prompted a run to a non-existent bunker or foxhole. Those who cared understood.

I remember those soldiers for their bravery, for their humor, their innovative spirits, their love for one another, their "no-quit" attitudes in the face of death, and for their overall youthful zeal. Most of all though, I will remember them for their faith: Men/boys who fought and prayed. *"Assuredly, I say to you, unless you become as little children, you cannot enter the kingdom of heaven."*—Jesus.

As for getting over Vietnam: Some never did. With time, most got past it and moved on. Sadly, a few never did.

Glossary

AK-47—A Russian-made rifle that was used against Americans in Vietnam

AO—Area of Operation

APC—Armored Personnel Carrier. Troop carrying tracked vehicle

AWOL—Absent Without Leave. Sometimes called "Going over the hill."

BC—Body Count as referring to the enemy

Bird—A colonel (O-6). Sometimes called a "full bird." Also a helicopter

BOQ—Bachelor Officers Quarters

CA—Combat Assault, which usually took place from a helicopter

Charlie—Shortened version of Victor Charlie or Viet Cong or VC

CIB—Combat Infantry Badge

Claymore—A command detonated mine used by American soldiers

CONUS—Continental United States

Cs—C-Rations or field rations that often replaced hot meals

CTT—Combat Tracker Team or Dog Handlers

DEROS—Date scheduled to return to the States

FO—Artillery Forward Observer

FYI—For Your Information

GRO—Graves Registration. Morgue

Hootch—Small house

ID—Infantry Division
KIA—Killed in Action
LAW—Light Antitank Weapon. Similar to a bazooka
LBJ—Long Binh Jail. Military confinement facility in Vietnam
LZ—Landing Zone. Usually a cleared place in the field where helicopters land
MedCap—Medical Civil Action Program.
Med Evac—Medical evacuation. Most med evacs were by helicopter or "dustoffs"
MOS—Military Occupational Speciality
M-16—Principle weapon (rifle) used by American soldiers in Vietnam
NCO—Non-commissioned officer. Sergeant.
NVA—North Vietnamese Army
OCS—Officer Candidate School
O-Club—Officers Club
PZ—Pickup zone.
ROTC—Reserve Officer Training Course
RPG—Rocket Powered Grenade
RTO—Radio/Telephone Operator
SP4—Specialist Fourth Class. Equal in rank to corporal
Slick—A stripped-down helicopter used to transport troops and supplies
TOC—Tactical Operations Center. Where commander was in contact with field units
USAREUR—United States Army in Europe
VC—Viet Cong or Vietnamese Communist. Sometimes called Charlie
WIA—Wounded in Action